The Other Californians

Protecting the Settlers.

The
Other
Californians

PREJUDICE AND DISCRIMINATION
UNDER SPAIN, MEXICO, AND
THE UNITED STATES
TO 1920

Robert F. Heizer & Alan J. Almquist

UNIVERSITY OF CALIFORNIA PRESS
BERKELEY · LOS ANGELES
LONDON

University of California Press
Berkeley and Los Angeles, California
University of California Press, Ltd.
London, England
Copyright © 1971 by
The Regents of the University of California
First Paperback Printing, 1977
ISBN 0–520–03415–5
Library of Congress Catalog Card Number: 76–121186
Printed in the United States of America
Designed by Dave Comstock

1 2 3 4 5 6 7 8 9 0

Contents

Preface to the Paperback Edition

The authors have taken the opportunity presented by the second printing of this book to make a very few changes in the text. We became conscious, after the book was published, of occasionally imposing on the reader our own emotional reactions, and it is these subjective expressions which we have modified or deleted.

A collection of 168 documents in the form of official letters from military personnel, Indian Agents, and unsigned articles in California newspapers dating from 1847 to 1865 dealing with the treatment of California Indians will be published shortly by the Peregrine Press of Santa Barbara. These documents will provide some of the original material which was used in writing *The Other Californians* and may, therefore, be looked on as a companion volume.

Preface

It is the authors' hope to provide in this book a social history of non-Anglo ethnic groups in California's past as illustrated by attitudes of prejudice and acts of discrimination directed against these groups. Historians have been aware that racial prejudice was displayed by California whites, but in general they have treated the subject as though it was an unimportant one, perhaps because race prejudice in the last century was not always considered inhumane in the collective conscience of Americans.

We have drawn our information from many sources, and we have quoted liberally in the belief that the wording of the original accounts illustrate the atmosphere of the times much more objectively and forcefully than anyone could describe it. Long documents have not been incorporated into the text, but have been collected at the end in a separate section.

Prejudice against ethnic or racial minority groups is something which men in all societies have practiced. The social problems of prejudice have never been more attentively considered than at this time. It is not our intention here to single out the state of California for particular emphasis in the belief that intolerance was more prevalent there than elsewhere. California is a state with many and varied ethnic groups represented in its total population—groups who came and lived here for various social and economic reasons and who happened to find themselves residents of what became, in 1850, the political unit named California. Racial discrimination in California is not something new, but goes as far back as the first settlement of the area by Europeans. What we present here is a regional chapter of the history of attitudes and acts of intolerance in the United States toward "others."

Our historical review covers the century and a half from 1770 to about 1920. We have not traced the history of discrimination beyond 1920 because after that time the situation becomes much more complex. Other books treat with the last fifty years of minority group history in California, and we have simply referred the reader to some of these.

We take this opportunity to express our thanks to the following persons who have helped locate information or have aided us in editorial matters: Mrs. Henry Castor, Professor Sherburne F. Cook, and Professor Donald C. Cutter.

All men are by nature free and independent,
and have certain inalienable rights,
among which are those of enjoying and
defending life and liberty; acquiring,
possessing and protecting property;
and pursuing and obtaining safety and happiness.

Article 1, Section 1, California State Constitution (1850)

I. The Indian Under Spain and Mexico, 1769-1846

The discovery, exploration, and colonization of Upper California by the Spanish military and Franciscan missionaries covers the three centuries from 1542, with the first voyage of coastal exploration by Cabrillo, to 1834, the year in which the Franciscan missions, numbering twenty-one, were secularized. From 1821, when Mexico secured independence from Spain, until 1846, when California was seized by United States military forces, the state was under Mexican rule. Our story here will stress the reactions of two culturally distinct peoples, native Indians and Spanish overlords, who, primarily through the religious fervor of the latter, precipitated the beginnings of what would become a long debilitating progression of bitter and increasingly violent relationships. "The mission environment was in large measure conditioned by the desire of the invading race to convert the other to a new way of thinking, a new religion. Economic and political factors were undoubtedly involved, but the driving force was provided by a group of men inspired primarily by religious, not material zeal."[1]

Much of the material contained in this chapter comes from missionaries' accounts, travelers' diaries, and letters, which, even though they tend toward bias, at least offer a partial insight into the actual situation of the times. In the published reports and

1. S. F. Cook, *The Conflict between the California Indian and White Civilization*, 1:8.

narratives of such travelers as Font, Duhaut-Cilly, von Langsdorff, Vancouver, La Perouse, and Beechey are to be found graph-
ic descriptions of the ports and places visited.[2]

Pedro Font was one such early explorer in California. At first
a missionary at San Jose de Pimas, Font, when approached with
the idea, agreed to accompany Juan Bautista de Anza on his second expedition from Horcasitas, Mexico, to Monterey as chap-
lain and recorder of the journey's events. The following excerpts
are from Font's *Complete Diary*, 1775–1776.

> Finally, these people (the Yuma Indians) as a rule are gentle, gay,
> and happy. Like simpletons who have never seen anything, they mar-
> veled as if everything they saw was a wonder to them, and with their
> impertinent curiosity they made themselves troublesome and tiresome
> and even nuisances, for they wearied us by coming to the tents and
> examining everything. . . . Moreover, it seems as if they have hang-
> ing over them the curse which God put upon Nebuchadnezzar, like
> beasts eating the grass of the fields, and living on herbs and grass
> seeds, with a little game from deer, hare, ground squirrels, mice and
> other vermin.

> [Concerning the Cahuilla tribe] . . . in my opinion these are among
> the most unhappy people in all the world. Their habitation is among
> the arid and bleak rocks of these sierras. The clothing of the men is
> nothing at all, and the women wear some tattered capes made of mes-
> cal fibers. Their food consists of tasteless roots, grass seeds and scrub-
> by mescal, of all of which there is very little, and so their dinner is a
> fast. Their arms are a bow and a few bad arrows. In fine, they are so
> savage, wild and dirty, disheveled, ugly, small and timid, that only
> because they have the human form is it possible to believe that they
> belong to mankind. . . . It is to be noted that although many of the
> rebellious Indians were heathen, many also were reduced Christians.
> And it is known that these mountain Indians (Serranos) who are very
> similar to those whom we saw from San Sebastian forward until the
> mountain was crossed are the most degenerate people of all in that
> country. And I would almost dare to say that just as the Sierra de Cal-
> ifornia, because of its unfruitfulness and rockiness, looks like the

2. For a list of such visitors see F. J. Weber, "The California Missions and Their
Visitors."

wastebasket of the world so the Indians who inhabit it are the dross of human kind.[3]

We reproduce in part his further reflections on the Yuma tribe to show how this man, devout and sincere as he felt himself to be, justified the imposition of the guidance of the Catholic church on the heathen:

I might inquire what sin was committed by these Indians and their ancestors that they should grow up in these remote lands of the north with such infelicity and unhappiness, in such nakedness and misery, and above all with such blind ignorance of everything that they do not even know the transitory conveniences of the earth in order to obtain them; nor much less, as it appeared to me from what I was able to learn from them, do they have any knowledge of the existence of God, but live like beasts, without making use of reason or discourse, and being distinguished from beasts only by possessing the bodily or human form, but not from their deeds.

But, considering that the mercy of God is infinite, and that so far as it is His part, he wishes that all men should be saved, and should come to the knowledge of the eternal truths, as says the Apostle St. Paul, *Qui omnes homines vult salvos fieri, et ad aqnitionem veritatis venire* (Ep. I ad Timoth, cap. 2); therefore, I cannot do less than piously surmise, in favor of those poor Indians, that God must have some special providence hidden from our curiosity, to the end that they may be saved, and that not all of them shall be damned. For, as the theologians say, if there should be a man in the forest without knowledge of God and entirely remote from possibility of acquiring the necessary instruction, God would make use of His angels to give him the necessary knowledge for eternal salvation. And that man *in sylvis* whom the theologians assume as a hypothesis, is typified without doubt by some of the Indians whom I saw, and by others who must be farther inland and whom I have not seen. For if God has permitted those people to live for so many hundreds and even thousands of years in such ignorance and blindness that they hardly know themselves, or, as I believe, that they are rational beings, what can we infer, especially in view of a God so merciful that *Misericordia ejus superexaltat judicium?*[4]

3. P. Font, *Diary of the Anza Expedition*, pp. 109, 144–145, 204.
4. *Diary*, pp. 110–112.

Under the title, *A Historical Account of the Indians of California*, Fr. Geronimo Boscana, a Franciscan missionary attached to San Juan Capistrano, wrote (ca. 1825):

> The Indians of California may be compared to a species of monkey, for naught do they express interest, except in imitating the actions of others, and particularly in copying the ways of the "razon" or white men, whom they respect as being much superior to themselves; but in so doing, they are careful to select vice, in preference to virtue. This is the result, undoubtedly, of their corrupt, and natural disposition. . . . The Indian in his grave humble and retired manner, conceals a hypocritical and treacherous disposition. He will deceive the most minute observer, as has been the case with many, or with all, who have endeavored to learn his true character, until time has revealed to them his true qualities. He never looks at any one, while in conversation but has a wandering and malicious gaze. For benefits received, he is never grateful; and instead of looking upon that which is given, he beholds only that which is withheld. His eyes are never uplifted, but like those of the swine, are cast to the earth. Truth is not in him, unless to the injury of another, and he is exceedingly false.[5]

Plight of the Mission Indians

Beechey's visit to the California coast was made at a time when the missions were at the height of their prosperity. In his book, *A Narrative of a Voyage to the Pacific Ocean and Beering's Strait in the Years 1825–1828*, Beechey has given an interesting record of his observations in the ports of San Francisco and Monterey. Beechey describes the conditions in which he found the missions.

> The missions have hitherto been of the highest importance to California, and the government cannot be too careful to promote their welfare, as the prosperity of the country in a great measure is dependent upon them, and must continue to be so until settlers from the mother country can be induced to resort thither. As they are of such consequence, I shall enter somewhat minutely into a description of them. Each establishment is under the management of two priests if

5. A. R. Boscana, "Chinigchinich: A Historical Account of the Origin, Customs, and Traditions of the Indians at the Missionary Establishment of St. Juan Capistrano, Alta California," pp. 335–336.

possible, who in upper California belong to the mendicant order of San Francisco. They have under them a major domo, and several subordinate officers, generally Spaniards, whose principal business is to overlook the labour of the Indians.

The object of the missions is to convert as many of the wild Indians as possible, and to train them up within the walls of the establishment in the exercise of a good life, and of some trade, so that they may in time be able to provide for themselves and become useful members of civilised society. As to the various methods employed for the purpose of bringing proselytes to the mission, there are several reports, of which some were not very creditable to the institution; nevertheless, on the whole I am of the opinion that the priests are innocent, from a conviction that they are ignorant of the means employed by those who are under them. Whatever may be the system, and whether the Indians be really dragged from their homes and families parted by armed parties, as some assert, or not, and forced to exchange their life of freedom and wandering for one of confinement and restraint in the missions, the change according to our ideas of happiness would seem advantageous to them, as they lead a far better life in the missions than in their forests, where they are in a state of nudity, and are frequently obliged to depend solely upon wild acorns for their subsistence.[6]

The main function of the mission was, of course, conversion of local Indian populations to the faith of the Spanish padres.[7] In the course of such conversion it was necessary to bring the native, either by force or enticement, from his village to within the sphere of influence of the mission and the mission padres. Once within the confines of the mission proper the Indian met with his first experience of Spanish culture.[8] Beechey continues:

In a few days a willing Indian becomes proficient in these mysteries, and suffers himself to be baptized, and duly initiated into the church. If, however, as it not infrequently happens, any of the captured Indians show a repugnance to conversion, it is the practice to imprison them for a few days, and then allow them to breathe a little fresh air in a walk round the mission, to observe the happy mode of life of their

6. Pp. 11, 14.
7. H. E. Bolton, "The Mission as a Frontier Institution in the Spanish American Colonies"; C. A. Hutchinson, *Frontier Settlement in Mexican California*, p. 44.
8. Cf. Cook, *Conflict*, vol. 1.

converted country men; after which they are again shut up, and thus continue to be incarcerated until they declare their readiness to renounce the religion of their forefathers.[9]

State of the Missions: Observers' Reports

Not all of the Indians who came to the missions measured up favorably to the standards set by the Spanish priests. As early as 1796 topics of conversation included some of the reasons why the Indian might not be completely satisfied with his new way of life. A few of the governing officials in California even went so far as to attempt reform of the neophytes' condition. Diego de Borica, seventh governor of California, was appointed in 1793, but did not reach the capitol at Monterey until November 9, 1794. After attending to more pressing duties of his position he turned his attention to the deplorable condition of the Indians at the missions, where he found that the neophytes were often treated with cruelty and even brutality by the mission priests.

In a letter to Alberni commanding the San Francisco post, Governor Borica asked that he "make an investigation among the troops who know how the neophytes are treated at the mission (San Francisco) to determine the reasons why there are now some two hundred fugitives." In another letter Borica outlines what he considers to be the state of the missions in 1795–1796, and the bad condition of the neophytes. He lists four factors which he apparently considered to be those most important in contributing to neophyte discontent: (1) loss of liberty; (2) labor; (3) their great filth; (4) bad living quarters.

Much popular opinion was put forth as to what actually were the reasons for Indian discontent in the missions. "That the neophytes were not all completely happy and contented in their new environment was entirely obvious to those who lived with them and watched over them. Indeed the failure of the converts to appreciate the efforts made on their behalf was a continual source of perplexity and sadness to the missionaries."[10] Governor

9. *Narrative*, p. 15.
10. Cook, *Conflict*, 1:67–68.

Borica wrote in 1796 that according to law the mission Indians were to be free after ten years, "but those of New California at the rate they are advancing will not reach the goal in ten centuries"; and Governor José Joaquín Arrillaga, when referring to the mission Indians, said in 1801, "If it comes to civilization, they still have far to go."

Beechey observed that, "In some of the missions much misery prevails, while in others there is a degree of cheerfulness and cleanliness which shows that many of the Indians require only care and proper management to make them as happy as their dull senses will admit of under a life of constraint." He also noted, "The Indians after their conversion are quiet and tractable, but extremely indolent, and given to intoxication, and other vices. Gambling in particular they indulge in to an unlimited extent: they pledge the very clothes on their backs, and not infrequently have been known to play for each other's wives."[11]

These problems also drew comment from other Europeans who chanced to visit the territory as explorers and travelers. Lasuen in 1800 wrote:

> And if they alleged, as proof of cruelty, the number of Indians who have fled . . . I had the satisfaction of replying that they were already coming back and that they assured me that none had gone for fear of work, nor of punishment, but because of fear of the disease, contagious and mortal, which was actually prevalent in the mission at the time; also on account of their natural preference for the wilderness.[12]

Von Langsdorff wrote in 1812:

> Notwithstanding all this, an irresistible desire for freedom sometimes breaks out in individuals. This may probably be referred to the national character. Their attachment to a wandering life, their love of alternate exercise in fishing and hunting and entire indolence, seem in their eyes to overbalance all the advantage they enjoy at the mission, which to us appears very great.[13]

11. *Narrative*, pp. 17 and 28.
12. "Representacion; San Carlos Mission, Nov. 12, 1800."
13. *Langsdorff's Narrative of the Rezanov Voyage to Nueva California in 1806*, p. 171.

Beechey observed further:

> After they (the Indians) became acquainted with the nature of the institution and felt themselves under restraint, many absconded. Even now, notwithstanding the difficulty of escaping, desertions are of frequent occurrence, owing probably, in some cases, to the fear of punishment—in others to the deserters having been originally inveigled into the mission by the converted Indians or neophytes . . . in other cases again to the fickleness of their own disposition.[14]

Abella reported in 1817:

> Let the more intelligent Indians be asked why they run away and they will reply: "The same things happen to us as to every son of Adam. Naturally we want our liberty and want to go hunt for women."[15]

The historian Hittell states, however, that the mission fathers

> not only compelled them to almost incessant labors, but failed to furnish them with sufficient food to sustain them in working condition; and at the same time for the most trivial offenses they hand-cuffed, imprisoned and unmercifully beat them. When the miserable Indians learning too late that their former gentile life even with its precariousness and constant warfare was far preferable to christianization such as it was thus exhibited, attempted to regain their lost freedom by flight, they were hunted down and punished with tenfold rigor. Nor were stripes reserved for the men alone, but women too were stripped and flogged, the only difference being, that the men were lashed publically while the women, as related by La Perouse, were removed to an enclosure at such a distance that their sobs and screams could not be heard. These barbarous cruelties added to the miserably slavish kind of existence which the neophytes were compelled to live at the missions, rendered them in many instances desperate; and, whenever an opportunity occurred, notwithstanding the risks they ran, they took to flight and trusted themselves rather to the mercies of savage gentile tribes, even though their hereditary enemies, than return to the stocks and whipping posts of the missions.[16]

Neophyte Discontent: Indian Accounts

The following items constitute the testimony of Indians

14. *Narrative*, pp. 170–171.
15. "Letter to Sola, January 29, 1817."
16. T. H. Hittell, *History of California*, 1:563–565.

at Mission Dolores (San Francisco) who escaped in 1797 but were caught. On their return each was asked to state why he absconded; here are some of their answers as recorded at the mission:

> He had been flogged for leaving without permission.
>
> The same reason. Also, he ran away because he was hungry.
>
> He had been put in jail for getting drunk.
>
> He had run away previously and had been flogged three times.
>
> He was hungry. He absconded previously and when he returned voluntarily, he was given twenty-five lashes.
>
> He was frightened at seeing how his friends were always being flogged.
>
> When he wept over the death of his wife and children, he was ordered whipped five times by Father Antonio Danti.
>
> He was put in the stocks while sick.
>
> His wife and son had run away to their country, and at the mission he was beaten a great deal.
>
> Because of a blow with a club.
>
> His mother, two brothers, and three nephews died, all of hunger, and he ran away so that he would not also die.
>
> His wife sinned with a rancher, and the priest beat him for not taking care of her.
>
> They made him work all day without giving him or his family anything to eat. Then, when he went out one day to find food, Father Danti flogged him.
>
> After going one day to the presidio to find food, when he returned Father Danti refused him his ration, saying to go to the hills and eat hay.
>
> When his son was sick, they would give the boy no food, and he died of hunger.
>
> Twice when he went out to hunt food or to fish, Father Danti had him whipped.[17]

On certain occasions the remarks and comments of the Indians themselves were recorded, and the following are a few examples of how the Indians felt about the situation which confronted them.

> [A certain Indian of San Antonio ran away] "because he wanted to live away from the mission. He did not get a bit of land to farm and

17. Cook, *Conflict*, 1:70–71.

also he could not stand the oppression under which they live, and the many floggings they are given." (1831)

[Some Indians came to San Carlos saying that many were running away from San Francisco Solano] "because the Indians do not like Father Altimira." (1823)

[Many Indians have run away at the time of mission secularization saying they are now a] "free nation. They cry with one voice: We are free and will not obey or work." (1834)[18]

An actual account of the condition of the neophyte at the mission was given by an Indian, Julio Cesar, and it bears witness to those descriptions given by Hittell.

Julio Cesar, a full blooded Indian, was born in San Luis Rey in the year 1824, Padre Ventura being the missionary father according to the information given to me, but when I entered the service of the mission at the age of 14 years Padre Francisco was in charge. . . . When I first entered the service of the mission, I was employed in singing in the choir, in the masses that were sung. . . . Don José Joaquín Ortega during his administration appropriated for himself most of the property of the mission, although he took none of the lands. It is said that Sr. Ortega stripped the mission, entirely finishing everything, even to the silver, vases, etc. I was not at that time in the mission there when Sr. Marron began his administration, but I know that he found hardly anything; in the house and the storehouses there was nothing. . . . When Don Ortega was established as administrator there, I grew up and worked in the fields as a groom and finally always with him, but when a Mass was given I had to go and sing. For my services I received nothing but my food and clothing. . . . When I was a boy the treatment given the Indians was not good. We were paid nothing, only being given our food, a breech-clout and a blanket and this every year, and many whippings for whatever fault, however light. We were at the mercy of the administrator who used to order the whippings as often and as many as he had a mind to.[19]

Opposition to the mission system on the part of the neophytes took the form of either flight or rebellion. Cook has cal-

18. Quoted from Cook, ibid., p. 69.
19. Julio Cesar. Cosas de Indios de California, reletadas a Thomas Savage en Tres Pinos (San Benito Co.) por Julio Cesar, natural de San Luis Rey, para la Bancroft Library, 1878. Manuscript in Bancroft Library.

culated from mission statistics that an average of 10 percent of mission converts were fugitives.[20] The loss of so many persons, plus the fact that runaways were classed as apostates, was of great concern to the missionaries. The neophyte exodus became so widespread that by 1818 laws were enacted by the Spanish authorities which prohibited the Indians from going about on horseback. The mission padres hoped as well, but to little avail, that by making it difficult for the Indians to possess horses they might in fact stop the raids upon the missions, which were becoming an increasingly difficult problem to handle.

Other Approaches

That all of the Mexican citizens of California were in agreement with the way the missions were handling the Indian problem is doubtful. A growing number of individuals began to voice strong protests against the missions and their treatment of the Indians. One such letter, dated August 27, 1831,[21] remarked that a neophyte of San Diego had committed a robbery and that the prosecutor, Rafael Gomez, asked for a very light sentence and took the occasion to make a bitter attack on the missions, particularly the practice of flogging Indians. Gomez held that the missions were responsible for the tendency toward robbery on the part of the Indians, and undoubtedly he went to extremes in his statements; however, it is noteworthy that, as this case shows, there was a strong reaction at this time on the part of the civil authorities against the mission system. This reaction seems in part to have taken the form of giving relatively light punishment to Indian criminals, both neophytes and gentiles.

If most foreigners to California saw in the Indians an energy potential to be exploited, not all approached them with the same designs and strategy as did the Spanish. Statements by several observers at the Russian colony at Fort Ross show that the Russians took an entirely different approach toward their relationship with the local Indians than the Spanish took. In contrast

20. *Conflict*, 1:57–64.
21. Provincial State Papers, Benicia Military, 72:11. MS Bancroft Library.

to the Spaniards, the Russians were neither missionaries nor colonists, but were, instead, employees of a Russian chartered company, which had come to California for commercial reasons.

Tchitchinoff, who was a youthful employee at Fort Ross between 1818 and 1824, recorded in his memoirs concerning an exploring trip in the mountains behind the fort: "We had orders to go on until we met the Indians and then only proceed with their consent. Consequently we stopped there until we could find an opportunity of conversing with the natives."[22] On the same trip the group saw plenty of game, but were told not to shoot any lest they alarm the natives. This consideration stood to the self-interest of the Russians, who needed the cooperation of the Indians, yet it indicates that it was both policy and practice to treat the Indians as people.

Duflot de Mofras, traveling in California in 1841, noted that the Russians had gathered "tribes of Indians" about them at Fort Ross, whom they treated kindly and remunerated fairly.

The Russian administrator at Fort Ross, Kostromitonov, who knew the Indians well, spoke highly of their capacity to learn necessary skills: "They appear stupid only because of their immoderate laziness and lightheartedness. However, they need only once observe some work that is not too difficult or complicated, in order to copy it immediately."[23]

Expeditions against the Indians

As villages in the vicinity of the missions became emptied and their occupants installed in the mission establishments it became necessary to make expeditions to round up more converts. Such expeditions found increasing resistance, and were often forced to fight. Generally the Spanish guns and horses were able to prevail over pedestrian arrow-shooting natives. We cite

22. Z. Tchitchinoff, "Adventures of Zakahar Tchitchinoff, 1802–1878." MS Bancroft Library. P. 284.
23. Quoted from M. J. Kennedy, "Culture Contact and Acculturation of the Southwestern Pomo" (Ph.D. diss., University of California, Berkeley, 1955), p. 67.

here one account of a Mexican expedition of 1837 to the lower
Stanislaus River in the San Joaquin Valley:

> We took the hostile Indians who numbered 200, including the
> Gentile and Christian fugitives, by pretending that our Indian aides
> would buy all their arrows even though it left them without a shirt.
> The purchase was concluded. We invited the Gentile and Christian
> Indians to come and eat *pinole* and dried meat. They all came over to
> our side of the river. Then when they were on our shore we surrounded
> them by the troops, citizens and Indian aides, and took them all pris-
> oners. . . . We separated 100 Christians from the prisoners and at each
> half mile or mile these were forced on their knees in prayer, and were
> made to understand they were going to die.
>
> Each one of them received four arrows, two in front and two in
> each shoulder. Those who were not killed by this process were killed
> with lances. The lieutenant did not want to make these executions be-
> cause he had no courage, but I answered that if I were to put it to my
> father, he would do the same. On the way the 100 Christians were
> killed in the manner already explained. We reached the camp where
> we were going to stop with the 100 gentile prisoners. . . . The Lieu-
> tenant told me to decide what was best to do. I answered him that this
> would be to shoot the prisoners, first Christianizing them—letting
> them know they were going to be shot and asking them if they wanted
> to become Christians. I ordered Nazarro Galindo to take one bottle of
> water and I took another. He began at one end of the line and I at the
> other. We baptized all the Indians and then shot them through the
> shoulder. I doubled the charge for the 30 that remained and they all
> fell.[24]

It is related in George Simpson's *An Overland Journey Round the
World, During the Years 1841 and 1842:*

> In the palmy days of the missions, the practice of sending out soldiers
> to bag fresh subjects for civilization tended to embitter the naturally
> unfriendly feeling of the red man, more particularly as the aborigines
> of the interior were constitutionally more restless and energetic than
> the savages of the coast; and the revolution of 1836 aggravated the
> evil by turning loose into the woods a multitude of converts, whose
> power of doing mischief, besides being increased by knowledge and
> experience, was forced into full play by a sense of the injustice and

24. S. F. Cook, "Expeditions to the Interior of California, 1820–1840," p. 198.

inhumanity of the local government. But the Indians of all descriptions are, from day to day, rendered more audacious by impunity. Too indolent to be always on the alert, the Californians overlook the constant pilferings of cattle and horses, till they are roused beyond the measure even of their patience by some outrage of more than ordinary mark; and then, instead of hunting down the guilty for exemplary punishment, they destroy every native that falls in their way, without distinction of sex or age. The bloodhounds, of course, find chiefly women and children for, in general, the men are better able to escape, [the soldiers] butchering their helpless and inoffensive victims after the blasphemous mockery of baptism. The sanctifying of murder by the desecration of a Christian rite, however incredible it may seem, is a melancholy matter of fact, the performers in the tragedy doubtless believing that, if there be any truth in the maxim that the end justifies the means, surely the salvation of the soul is sufficient warrant for the destruction of the body. I subjoin a more detailed description, on authority of an eye-witness. When the incursions of the savages have appeared to render a crusade necessary, the alcalde of the neighborhood summons from 12 to 20 colonists to serve, either in person or by substitute, on horseback; and one of the foreign residents, when nominated about three years before, preferred the alternative of joining the party himself, in order to see something of the interior. After a ride of three days they reached a village, whose inhabitants for all that the crusaders knew to the contrary, might have been as innocent in the matter as themselves. But, even without any consciousness of guilt, the tramp of the horses was a symptom not to be misunderstood by the savages; and accordingly all that could run, comprising, of course, all that could possibly be criminal, fled for their lives. Of those who remained, nine persons, all females, were tied to trees, christened and shot. With great difficulty and considerable danger, my informant saved one old woman by conducting her to a short distance from the accursed scene; and even then he had to shield the creature's miserable life by drawing a pistol against one of her merciless pursuers. She ultimately escaped, though not without seeing a near relative, a handsome youth who had been captured, slaughtered in cold blood before her eyes, with the outward and visible sign of regeneration still glistening on his brow.[25]

Mission fugitives, considered apostates, were followed down and

25. Pp. 194–195.

captured, either to be returned to the mission or killed on the spot.

In January 1833 the American fur-trapping party under the direction of Joseph Walker was in the San Joaquin Valley and was visited by a party of "Spaniards" in search of a group of Indians which had "eloped from the St. Juan Missionary station [San Jose Mission], and taken with them 300 head of horses." Some of the Americans joined the party, and somewhere in the Sierra foothills found and attacked the camp, only to discover there most of the horses butchered and a

> few old and feeble Indians, with some squaws and children. . . . The disappointment of the Spaniards now exceeded all bounds, and gave our men some evidence of the depravity of the Spanish character. By way of revenge, after they found there was no use in following the Indians into the mountains, the Spaniards fell to massacreing, indiscriminately, those helpless creatures who were found in wigwams with the meat, and cutting off their ears. Some of them were driven into a wigwam, when the door was barricaded, and a large quantity of combustible material thrown on and around the hut, for the purpose of setting fire to it, and burning them all together. This barbarous treatment our men would not permit, and they went and released the prisoners, when the Spaniards fell to work and dispatched them as if they were dogs.[26]

By 1820 the natives of the interior had decided to resist, as Cook says, "not through any political or cultural unification, but through a common response to a uniform style of treatment."[27] Horses taken from mission herds and adoption of simple military tactics (sniping from cover, occasional use of dug trenches) made the Indians a more serious enemy to battle. It has been noted that by the time of secularization the natives had begun to actively take up the offensive in their raids against the white settlements.[28] Documents of the times show raiding and stealing of domestic livestock to be a common occurrence. The situation became so

26. Z. Leonard, *Adventures of Zenas Leonard, Fur Trader and Trapper, 1831–1836*, p. 222.
27. Cook, *Conflict*, 2:32.
28. Cook, *Conflict*, vol. 1.

serious as to warrant a proclamation from Governor Pío Pico in Monterey in which it was stated, "The savages of the north have been committing serious depredations. With sufficient force and the help of all it would be possible to destroy them."[29] It is pretty clear that by the 1840s the Mexicans who were concentrated along the coastal margin were on the defensive, and it is probable that the American annexation prevented the ultimate driving out of the Mexican overlords, who numbered fewer than five hundred.

On occasion Indians were released from the mission and allowed to live in a town whose main population consisted of *gente de razon* ("rational persons," meaning those who spoke Spanish and lived as the Spanish did). In theory such emancipated Indians were equals and had acquired enough education and facility in speaking Spanish to be entitled *gente de razon*. But, it seems, if we may judge from a report written by Father N. Duran addressed to Governor José Figueroa about 1835, that this was not the case. Duran said of the two or three hundred "free" Indians living in the Pueblo of Los Angeles:

> They live far more wretched and oppressed than those in the missions. There is not one who has a garden of his own, or a yoke of oxen, a horse, or a house fit for a rational being. The equality with the white people, which is preached to them, consists in this: that these Indians are subject to a white commissioner, but they are the only ones who do the menial work. . . . For offences which the white people consider small, or as nothing among themselves, those Indians are placed over a cannon and given one hundred lashes on the naked body. . . . All in reality are slaves, or servants of white men, who know well the manner of securing their services by binding them a whole year for an advanced trifle. This abuse the natural fraility of the Indian makes possible, because he does not look beyond the present. If he wants to free himself from future servitude by flight or in any other way, he experiences the full rigor of the law.[30]

29. California Archives, Provincial State Papers, 6:169 (1845?). MS Bancroft Library.

30. Quoted from C. A. Hutchinson, *Frontier Settlement in Mexican California*, pp. 222–223.

After Secularization

The power of the missions was stripped away when the missions were secularized in 1834.[31] The missionaries, angered by secularization, now actively supported the Indians in their complaints against the civil authorities just as the military element had previously done against the missionaries. That the shoe fit on the other foot was shown in one letter dated Monterey, March 7, 1836. This letter concerns the complaints of one Fr. Mercado against J. M. Ramirez, the administrator of San Antonio Mission property, alleging cruel treatment of the Indians. The complaints of Fr. Mercado included: abusive language, extreme floggings (100 lashes), imprisonment for not working when sick. He said that the Indians were universally complaining and were very restive. The defense stated that in order to get any effective work done, the Indians being so lazy, it was necessary to take severe measures. The decision was rendered that Ramirez had not exceeded his authority. In general, the court held, this administrator did not chastise the Indians any more severely than the missionaries had done before him. The Indians undoubtedly were lazy and poor workers. Flogging the Indians for running away was generally practiced by the missionaries previously. The civilian authorities had to contend with liquor, which the missionaries had been able to keep away from the Indians.

The writer of a letter to the alcalde of Los Angeles dated Monterey, April 23, 1836, quotes a letter from the citizens of San Diego, who complain of the bad conditions since secularization, particularly the forays of Indians stealing horses. The outcome of this protest was that the governor was supposed to appoint a commission to control the situation.

A note is heard from another citizen, Sr. Arguello, to the governor in Monterey (August 3, 1839). He states that "the number of Indians who have run away [since secularization of the

31. On secularization, see Hutchinson, *Frontier Settlement*, chaps. 3–7; M. P. Servin, "The Secularization of the California Missions: A Reappraisal"; E. B. Webb, *Indian Life at the Old Missions*, chap. 20.

missions] to take up criminal pursuits is so great that the entire southern district is paralyzed. Repeated complaints [to the authorities] have had no effect. Particularly the cattle hands run away, taking a great many cattle with them."

After 1841 the situation became so confused and the power of the Mexican administration so weak that even nominal control over the military activity of the citizens was lost.

Fr. N. Duran of Santa Barbara, in a letter to Governor Pico dated November 16, 1845, expresses the opinion that as the Indians "get their heads full of ideas of liberty, there is no human power which can repress their scandalous conduct, which consists of drunkenness and the stealing of women and cattle."

Indians and the Ranchos

Soon after the first missions were established in 1769 Mexican colonists (*pobladores*) came to California, established ranches, and thus formed the nucleus for the towns (pueblos) of Los Angeles and San Jose. Since most of the readily accessible Indians were taken into the missions, these early ranchers worked their properties with conscript Indian labor. The hacienda-peon system of Mexico was thus imported to California. By 1840 there were several dozen of these large Mexican ranches to which were attached in some cases many hundreds of Indian serfs. When the Mexican government awarded large land grants to non-Mexicans such as Hugo Reid, B. D. Wilson, John A. Sutter, Theodore Cordua, George C. Yount, Robert Livermore, John Marsh, and John Bidwell, nearly every one of these found it useful to acquire the services of a large resident group of Indians, who labored in return for whatever the estate owner was inclined to give in the way of remuneration—usually very little.

During the post-mission period of Mexican rule (1834–1846) those Indians who were deprived even of the old mission buildings as a place to live either returned to their former way of life in native villages or attached themselves to Mexican or American ranchers (who held Mexican land grants) and worked in return for food and shelter. When Indians attached themselves voluntarily to a rancho, they became part of a system of peonage. But there were not always enough such volunteers, and the record for this period indicates that the ranch owners often bought Indians who had been seized, or made Indian-collecting forays themselves.[32] George Simpson in 1842 describes the Indians under the care of General Vallejo at his ranch near Sonoma:

> During the day, we visited a village of General Vallejo's Indians, about 300 in number, who were the most miserable of the race that I ever saw, excepting always the slaves of the savages of the northwest coast. . . . They are badly clothed, badly lodged, and badly fed. . . . Though not so recognized by the law, yet they are thralls in all but the name, borne to the earth by the toils of civilization superadded to the privations of savage life, they vegetate rather than live. . . . This picture which is a correct likeness not only of General Vallejo's Indians, but of all of the civilized (i.e., former Mission Indians) aborigines of California, is the only remaining monument of the zeal of the Church and the munificence of the State.[33]

Another example concerns the California pioneer J. A. Sutter, proprietor of Sutter's fort and founder of the city of Sacramento. James Clyman wrote at the time of his visit to the fort in 1846:

> The Capt. [Sutter] keeps 600 or 800 Indians in a complete state of Slavery and I had the mortification of seeing them dine I may give a short description 10 or 15 Troughs 3 or 4 feet long ware brought out of the cook room and seated in the Broiling sun all the labourers grate and small ran to the troughs like so many pigs and feed themselves with their hands as long as the troughs contain even a moisture.[34]

Lt. George Derby, while engaged in topographical reconnaissance in California in 1849 for the United States government, visited the ranch of Nicholas Altgeier (a former employee to whom "Captain" Sutter deeded a piece of land on the Feather River in 1842). Derby wrote:

> Almost 100 wretched Indians, playfully termed Christians, live in the vicinity [of Altgeier's house] upon the bank of the Feather River, sub-

32. See Cook, *Conflict*, 2:26–30, for instances.
33. *An Overland Journey Round the World*, pp. 177–178.
34. "James Clyman, American Frontiersman," pp. 173–174.

sisting upon acorns (which, pulverized with roasted grasshoppers, they form into a cake) and salmon, with which delicious fish the river abounds. The more intelligent and docile of these creatures are taken and brought up on the farm, where in time they become excellent *vaqueros*, a herdsmen, and where they are content to remain, receiving in return for their services such food and clothing as it may suit the interest or inclination of the owner to bestow upon them.[35]

The observations of the anonymous author of *Notes on California and the Placers*, published in 1850, refers to Indians

who have been *subdued* to labor at the different rancheros. For the good behavior of the latter, the rancheros are responsible. No doubt all these respectable proprietors are *Wilmot proviso* men, and eschew slavery, but their mode of recruiting the number of their laborers is something more exceptionable, than if they obtained their supplies from the far-famed slave-market at Washington. The process is, to raise a posse and drive in as many of the untamed natives as are requisite, and to compel them to assist in working the land. A pittance of food, boiled wheat or something of the kind, is fed to them in troughs, and this is the only compensation which is allowed for their services. Their condition is worse than that of the Peons of Yucatan, and other parts of Mexico, and yet there are no slaves in California!

Summary

The Indians were important to the Spanish missionaries between 1769 and 1834 as a source of heathen to convert and instruct in the Catholic religion. Many of the missionaries were ignorant and brutal men; others were kind and sensitive men who felt sympathy for the Indians who were forced to endure the rather spartan way of life in these mission outposts on Spain's northwestern frontier. The Spanish government, which was headed by the king in Spain, was interested in the missions primarily because they helped to establish and hold at small cost the large and potentially valuable area of Alta California and thus formed a buffer against possible Russian encroachment from the north or the establishment of the British in what would other-

35. *The Topographical Reports of Lt. Geo. H. Derby*, pp. 15–16.

wise be claimed but unoccupied Spanish territory. One would imagine that after Mexico secured independence from Spain in 1821 the new Mexican republic would consider California worth developing, but there was not much interest in the area and few events occurred except secularization of the twenty-one missions in 1834. The Mexican government was fully aware that California could not be held against any determined attempt to seize it, but did little to bolster its defenses. Through all of this the Indian was ignored, except as a source of labor to be exploited. This is not surprising, for all colonial powers in the seventeenth and eighteenth centuries held a similar attitude about the native peoples who happened to live in territories under their control.

The upshot of the Spanish mission system which operated from 1769 to 1834 and of the period of Mexican control ending in 1846[36] was a heavy decrease in the numbers of California Indians from an original population of about 300,000 to about 100,-000. The surviving Indians got very little for this heavy price. Between 1769 and 1834, 53,600 Indians were converted. Fifteen thousand neophytes were released from the missions in 1834.[37] A very few of these could read, and most of them were acquainted with the Spanish material culture only to the extent that it was represented in these rather austere frontier outposts. Over 100,-000 Indians lived in the state in 1834, most of them following their traditional hunting-and-gathering way of life in villages. Little was done to instruct the mission Indian into the way of life of the Spanish-Mexicans,[38] and nothing prepared them or the "wild" Indians in the nonmissionized areas for the advent in 1848 of the flood of gold miners who overran the Sierra Nevadas

36. C. A. Hutchinson, "The Mexican Government and the Mission Indians of Upper California, 1821–1835."

37. J. N. Bowman, "The Resident Neophytes (Existentes) of the California Missions."

38. The theory of the mission system was that it would provide a literate and self-sufficient population of Catholicized natives. On the desire of the missionaries to civilize the Indians, and for reasons why the mission system failed to accomplish this, see Hutchinson, *Frontier Settlement in Mexican California*, pp. 109, 130–131, 146, 225, 231, 306–307.

and the settlers who took up land in the valleys. The Sierras were too far from the missions on the coast as an area in which to hunt for converts, and the heavy Indian population here was wholly unprepared for the gold rush. The Indians were, so to speak, caught in the rear, and they suffered casualties from disease and homicide so severely between 1848 and 1870 that the native population was reduced to about 58,000. The American settlement appears to have had a far greater demographic impact than the Spanish-Mexican one. The widely held view of Americans that elimination of Indians in new territories was necessary seems to have been effectively put into practice.[39]

39. S. F. Cook, "The Destruction of the California Indian."

II. The Indian and the White Californian, 1850s to 1870s

The bulk of American immigration into California following upon the Mexican War and the discovery of gold was strongly race conscious. It was plagued by what Josiah Royce called "a diseased local exaggeration of our common national feelings towards foreigners ... [and] a hearty American contempt for things and institutions and people that were stubbornly foreign. [Additional characteristics were] a general sense of irresponsibility which they seldom recognize at all, charging to the foreigners themselves whatever trouble was due to our brutal ill-treatment of them."[1]

A good many of the explorers and writers at this time added fuel to the fire by repeating stories of the inferior qualities of California minority groups, especially the Indian.

An overland traveler during this period had something better to say about the California Indians he came across during his travels. Alonzo Delano wrote in 1849:

> For intelligence, they are far behind the Indians east of the Rocky Mountains, but although they are affectionate and kind to each other, as is the custom among all civilized tribes, their women are held to be inferior to males, and are reduced to unmitigated slavery. The men are idle vagabonds, and spend most of their time lounging, occasionally shooting birds and small game, or spearing fish, and, as it seemed to me, more for amusement than from any desire to be useful to their

1. *California, a Study of American Character*, pp. 275–276.

families. While thus engaged the women were almost constantly occupied. . . . The Indians of California are more swarthy in complexion
and of smaller stature than those east of the Rocky Mountains; and
although they may be placed in situations where they will fight
bravely, they are less bold, and more cowardly in the main, than those
on the Great Plains west of the Missouri; while they are more gentile
in their natures, and become willing slaves to those who will feed and
clothe them, if they are not overworked. They have more of the Asiatic
cast of countenance than the eastern tribes, and are easily controlled
if properly managed. Strict justice, and a uniform but firm and gentle
behavior, will conciliate them, and gain their goodwill and respect.[2]

Possibly a more fair though less literary account of the actual
conditions of the Indians in California at this time was given
by George C. Yount. Yount, a Napa Valley pioneer before the
gold rush, was a man who apparently appreciated the plight of
the Indian and realized, for the most part, the sociological factors
involved:

In their wanderings for a place of encampment, the party first encountered that species of Red Men peculiar to California and the
Sierra Nevada range. From their mode of living on roots and reptiles,
insects and vermine they have been called Diggers. In fact they almost
burrow in the Earth like the mole and are almost as blind to everything
comely. At the time our trappers supposed they had now found the
lowest dregs of humanity. But . . . they were in error. They were des-
tined to find a race even lower than these. . . . It is not eight years since
the above named valley [Napa] swarmed with not less than eight
thousand human beings, of whom there are now left as many hundreds. They have been hunted down by the murderous white man.
Ardent spirits have been afforded them by the same all exterminating
foe; diseases of the filthiest and most fatal kind have been contracted
and disseminated from the same source, the same intruders have
usurped the land, scattered and exterminated their game and fish,
corrupted their habits, as well as infected the persons of their females,
which has rendered them feeble, torpid and indolent. Hence they
murder their off-spring at birth, to rid themselves of the care and toil
of nursing and raising them into life. If they do not murder them the
little innocents come into life diseased and are born only to suffer
and to die.[3]

2. *Across the Plains and among the Diggings*, p. 130.
3. *George C. Yount and His Chronicles of the West*, pp. 154–155.

From the diary of J. Goldsborough Bruff, who came to California in late 1849, we read the following conversation, which he overheard spoken by the carpenters employed in building a house on the Sacramento River. The diary is dated November 17, 1850, and reference is to the Civil Code written and adopted by the first session of the California legislature. We think the passage worth citing here since it constitutes a contemporary record of the attitude of newly arrived California white laborers toward Indians.

"Have any of you seen the laws about Indians?" asked some one above. "No!" responded several, simultaneously. —"Well," resumed the interrogator, "I have; —it's hung up at Neele's ranch, where any one can go and read it for himself." It says, first: enacted, that if an Indian steals a horse, or a steer, he shall be whipped, with not less than 25, nor more than 39 lashes.—And if a white man does the same, he shall be imprisoned for several months, and fined $1,000. —"Now, gentlemen, what sort of a law is that?" —"A d——d Digger to get off with 39 lashes, and a white man to be fined and imprisoned!" "I say *that* law won't work!" —"Who made these laws?" —"Why, I'll tell you; —a set of d——d Yankees, New Yorkers, Pennsylvanians, etc." —"Sich laws wont do here, no how you can fix it!" —"My uncle, —Jno: W.——, of Louisville, Ky. is a great lawyer; he was twice in Congress; and when I was a boy, he made me read law, in his office; and I aint forgot what I read, neither: There's no sich d——d laws to be found in the laws of the United States!" To this learned harangue, —questions and answers; a fellow, in a gruff voice replied, "Well, stranger, if I catch an Indian stealing from me, I'll shoot him, by G—d!" A third person approved of the sentiment, and swore that he would shoot them in spite of any of their d——d yankee laws; and he'd like to see any d——d officer try to arrest him for it, by G—d!" This discussion and commentary upon the laws, lasted about two hours; when they came to the conclusion, that any other but Lynch Law, was a d——d humbug.[4]

The California Indians occupied their minority position largely in default of other minorities. There were Mexicans, but at first they were not selected for the full treatment; there were

4. *Gold Rush: The Journals, Drawings and Other Papers of J. Goldsborough Bruff*, p. 457.

practically no Negroes; and it was to be several years before enough Chinese arrived to make them sufficiently numerous to be a worthwhile target for prejudicial attention. The views held by writers quoted above were held also by many of the members of the constitutional convention of 1849 and the newly formed state legislature of 1850, and it was under this persuasion that most of the legislation enacted into law for this period was created. In this light this chapter will deal with the history and background of legislation passed from the time California became a state, on September 9, 1850, until the more pressing problems of oriental immigration began to dominate the political scene in the 1870s.

"Wars" of Extermination

A disregard for Indian rights of any sort was officially affirmed by Governor Peter H. Burnett of California in his annual message of January 1851 when he said:

> That a war of extermination will continue to be waged between the two races until the Indian race becomes extinct, must be expected; while we cannot anticipate this result with but painful regret, the inevitable destiny of the race is beyond the power and wisdom of man to avert.

Governor John Bigler apparently could not restrain himself from making certain philosophical observations concerning the larger question of what was at the heart of such conflict. He wrote:

> I assure you, sir, that I deplore the unsettled question of affairs in the North; but the settlement of new countries, and the progress of civilization have always been attended with perils. The career of civilization under the auspices of the American people, has heretofore been interrupted by no dangers, and daunted by no perils. Its progress has been an ovation—steady, august, and resistless.[5]

In the same year, 1852, Governor Bigler wrote to General E. Hitchcock, who was commanding the United States forces in

5. California, *Senate Journal*, 3d sess., 1852, p. 714.

California. His letter, which is printed in the documents section, p. 207, shows clearly how little humanitarian regard he had for the California Indians.

Attacks on Indian villages by volunteer military companies or regular army units, and casual killings, were common until about 1870. The justification for these attacks varied with each incident. At times it was purely a sporting event, at others it was to chastise local Indians for stealing cows and horses, and on some occasions it was to inflict what was felt to be well-deserved punishment for an Indian killing of a white settler or miner. Dispossessed natives often became so hungry that they risked stealing livestock rather than die of starvation, and most of the instances of Indians killing whites were in retaliation for some outrage committed earlier by whites. But for every white man killed, a hundred Indians paid the penalty with their lives.[6]

The Clear Lake massacre of 1850 actually involved two separate attacks on Indian villages by United States troops serving under Captain N. Lyon. On Indian Island in Clear Lake the troops attacked the village, and the number killed, Captain Lyon states in a letter, "I confidently report at not less than sixty and do not doubt extended to a hundred and upwards." The body of troops then proceeded down the Russian River to a village on a brush-covered island formed by a slough. Captain Lyon reports, "Their position being entirely surrounded they were attacked under most embarrassing circumstances, but as they could not escape, the Island soon became a perfect slaughter pen, as they continued to fight with great resolution and vigor until every jungle was

6. The demographic and social effects of the American period from 1848 to 1870 has been treated in detail by S. F. Cook in *The Conflict between the California Indian and White Civilization*, vol. 3, in which he produces figures of Indian deaths from homicide, starvation, or disease in this twenty-two-year period amounting to 48,000 persons. The mean annual decrease in Indian numbers during this period was 3.0 percent per year. Cook's monograph is amply documented, and for the record of this period the reader is referred to his work. See also O. C. Coy, *The Humboldt Bay Region, 1850–1875*, pp. 137–196; T. H. Hittell, *History of California*, 3:884–936.

routed. Their number killed I confidently report at not less than seventy-five."[7]

Another Indian massacre, which is less well known but which was more destructive of life than the one at Humboldt Bay in 1860, occurred at Hayfork on the South Fork of the Trinity River in 1852. It was amply reported in the newspapers of the day[8] and is recorded in some pioneer accounts.[9] Some Indians killed a white man named Anderson near Weaverville. They were followed and attacked, and 150 persons were killed. Three survivors (a woman and two children) "were taken prisoners."

A letter of R. McKee, Indian agent and former Indian treaty commissioner, to L. Lea, United States commissioner of Indian affairs, of April 5, 1852 reads:

> Since my regular despatch per this steamer was mailed, I have received from the temporary agent in Shasta and Scott's valleys very unpleasant news, revealing the murder almost in cold blood of some thirty or forty Indians at the ferry to upper crossing of the Klamath, and at Indian Flat, two miles above, on or about the 12th ultimo. Some time before, a young Indian . . . had, it appears, been shot by a man named Irvin R. Tompkins. He (the man shot) was connected with the Indians at the ferry, some of whom made complaints about his death, and gave some miners in the neighborhood the idea that they (the Indians) contemplated revenge. Instead of going to the agent, who, with his interpreter, could have settled the matter amicably in a few minutes, the miners went down to "Happy Camp," expressed their fears, raised a party, returned, surrounded the rancheria at the ferry, and shot down all the men there, with several women; they then proceeded two miles farther up to the other village, and in like manner surrounded it, and killed the inmates. . . . In all the frontier settlements [of California] there are many men from Missouri, Oregon, Texas &c., who value the life of an Indian just as they do that of a *cayota*, or a wolf, and embrace every occasion to shoot down.[10]

7. U.S., National Archives, RG 98, Letters received, 10th Military District 1850, No. 329a. Letter from Capt. N. Lyon, Anderson's Ranch, May 22, 1850.

8. *Alta California*, April 5, 25, 1852; *Sacramento Union*, May 3, 1852; *Shasta Courier*, April 25, 1852; May 1, 1852.

9. F. A. Buck, *A Yankee Trader in the Gold Rush*, p. 100; J. Carr, *Pioneer Days in California*, pp. 195–197.

10. U.S., *Senate Executive Document* no. 57, 32d Cong., 2d sess., 1853, pp. 11–12.

McKee, attentive to his charge, had requested troops to settle difficulties which had arisen between whites and Indians in northwestern California.

Another incident reported in 1852 shows that little concern was felt for Indians even when they were attacked on federally controlled (reservation) land. In July, O. M. Wozencraft, United States Indian agent, informed Governor Bigler of the facts of the murder of a number of Indians on the Fresno reservation by a band of whites, and asked the Governor "to join with me in maintaining the supremacy of the law, as the only sure means of preventing the recurrence of similar outrages and preventing war." The governor did not respond to the letter, and Wozencraft reports to the superintendent of Indian affairs, E. F. Beale, that he then went to San Francisco

> with a view of having warrants issued for the accused parties, and thus bring them to trial before the federal court, but I am sorry to say that I have been disappointed. The United States district attorney, after giving the subject that attention which its importance demanded informs me that he was not aware of the existence of any law which would apply in this case, the federal court having no jurisdiction in cases where life was taken. The gentleman who commanded the [Indian killing] party in this unfortunate affair was soon after elected county judge; consequently I did not think it worth while to prosecute him in his own county.[11]

In some places the removal of Indians was encouraged by paying bounty hunters for Indian scalps, as illustrated by the following note from the *Marysville Weekly Express* for April 16, 1859, which reprints it from the *Red Bluff Beacon*:

> A new plan has been adopted by our neighbors opposite this place to chastise the Indians for their many depredations during the past winter. Some men are hired to hunt them, who are recompensed by receiving so much for each scalp, or some other satisfactory evidence that they have been killed. The money has been made up by subscription.

One of the most lethal acts committed against Indians in northwestern California was the massacre of about 50 Indians

11. Ibid.

living in a village on Indian Island in Humboldt Bay on February
26, 1860. Attacks made the same day at three other nearby villages brought the total number of Indians killed to 188. An
"official" account of the affair was written by Major G. J. Raines,
U.S.A., in command of Fort Humboldt.[12] Major Raines report
reads:

> I have just been to Indian Island, the home of a band of friendly In-
> dians between Eureka and Uniontown, where I beheld a scene of
> atrocity and horror unparalleled not only in our own Country, but
> even in history, for it was done by men, self acting and without ne-
> cessity, color of law, or authority—the murder of little innocent babes
> and women, from the breast to maturity, barbarously and I can't say
> brutally—for it is worse—perpetrated by men who act in defiance of
> and probably in revenge upon the Governor of the State for not send-
> ing them arms and having them mustered in as a Volunteer Company
> for the murder of Indians by wholesale, goaded also by Legislative acts
> of inquiry into such matters. At any rate such is the opinion of the
> better class of community as related to me this Sunday morning. I was
> informed that these men, Volunteers, calling themselves such, from
> Eel River, had employed the earlier part of the day in murdering all
> the women and children of the above Island and I repaired to the place,
> but the villains—some 5 in number had gone—and midst the bitter
> grief of parents and fathers—many of whom had returned—I beheld a
> spectacle of horror, of unexampled description—babes, with brains
> oozing out of their skulls, cut and hacked with axes, and squaws ex-
> hibiting the most frightful wounds in death which imagination can
> paint—and this done . . . without cause, otherwise, as far as I can learn,
> as I have not heard of any of them losing life or cattle by the Indians.
> Certainly not these Indians, for they lived on an Island and nobody
> accuses them.[13]

12. Letter to Assistant Adjutant General, March 10, 1860. Old Files Division,
Adjutant General's Office, File No. 75C, 1860.

13. Major Raines then describes the murdered Indians, as he found them in each
lodge, the number killed being as follows: first lodge, two women, three children;
second lodge, one man, five women, two children; third lodge, two women; fourth
lodge, three women, five children; fifth lodge, four women, one child; sixth lodge,
one woman. In addition to these Major Raines says that eighteen women and an
unknown number of children had been carried away by the Indians for burial
before his arrival.

In his letter to the assistant adjutant general, March 10, 1860, Major Raines writes further, "About 188 Indians, mostly women and children have been murdered, Viz., 55 at Indian Island; 58 at South Beach; 40 on South Fork Eel River and 35 at Eagle Prairie."[14]

When W. H. Brewer, a member of the Geological Survey of California, was in Tehama County in 1862 he wrote:

> These Indians are peaceable and nearly harmless when in no larger numbers than they are here, notwithstanding the unnumbered wrongs they have endured from the mining population of whites. As I hear of these wrongs, of individual cases, related from time to time, I do not know which feeling is the stronger awakened, that of commiseration for the poor Indians, or of indignation against the barbarous whites. There are now "Indian troubles" at various places in the upper part of the state—white men are murdered, etc., troops are out—and as yet I have not heard a single intelligent white man express any opinion but that the whites were vastly more to blame than the Indians.[15]

A more "official" statement than that of Brewer is contained in a letter from Col. Francis L. Lippitt writing from Fort Humboldt on March 5, 1862, to Major R. C. Drum:

> You can readily imagine that in this state of things no Indian can show his head anywhere without being shot down like a wild beast. The women and children, even, are considered good game, not only in the mountains but here all around us, where families who have brought up Indian children (whose parents have been massacred) have to exercise constant watchfulness to prevent their being murdered. The horrible massacre some time since on Indian Island, in this harbor, of some 150 peaceable and friendly Indians, mostly squaws and children, you have no doubt heard of. . . . Secondly, the State volunteers' campaign of last year, which was a mere series of Indian hunts, whose only object was to slaughter, of course. The last act in that bloody drama, the fight at

14. The Humboldt Bay massacre of 1860 is described and commented on in the *San Francisco Bulletin*, February 28, 1860; March 2, 13, 28, 30, 1860; May 24, 1860; June 1, 9, 1860; the *San Francisco Herald*, April 26, 1860; the *Sacramento Union*, May 14, 1860; the *Humboldt Times*, March 3, 1860. See also Coy, *Humboldt Bay Region*, pp. 157–159; Hittell, *History*, 3:920–922.

15. *Up and Down California in 1860–1864*, p. 300.

the head of Redwood Creek, did not much tend to prepare the Indians for subjection.... The Indians to be sent here will require a very strong guard, not so much to keep them from escaping as to protect them from the Indian-killing whites that are but too numerous about.[16]

"Sowing the Wind and Reaping the Whirlwind"

Newspaper accounts of the 1850s described an ever widening circle of violence which surrounded Indian-white relationships. In the *Humboldt Times*, in 1855 and 1856, there appeared the following items concerning the Indians who inhabited the land along the Klamath river:

January 20, 1855—Citizens of Orleans Bar had a meeting and decided to kill on sight all Indians having guns after January 9, and to burn rancherias where guns were found after that date. On the 9th some whites went to Red Caps to destroy the ranch and were fired on by the Indians and three killed. Indians of this vicinity it is thought are able to muster 3,500 warriors, armed with guns and six-shooters. Indians of Trinidad, Mad and New Rivers have left for the mountains. Whites are asking for troops and Colonel Henley.

January 27, 1855—The War [of December 1854–January 1855] if it can be called, was brought on by the whites and under the most aggravated circumstances. The facts are, as we are informed, that about the 10th of December, a ruffian in attempting to commit an outrage upon the person of an Indian woman, who was accompanied by an Indian boy, the woman clung to the boy and the white man drew his revolver and shot the boy down, who later died from the wound. . . . The man, after bullying around for some time, left for parts unknown. The Indians, thinking to get revenge, killed an ox that had formerly belonged to this man, but learning that he had sold it, they offered to pay the present owner the value of the steer, which was refused. The Indians became frightened and by their conduct filled the minds of the miners with suspicion. The miners tried to disarm the Indians without paying the value of the guns, and upon the Indians refusing to surrender them, the miners burned the Indian Ranches, with their winters supply of provisions, which they defended by killing the whites engaged in so doing. Blood has been spilt. A peace must be conquered, to save the Indians who surrendered their arms. They should be removed to some reservation. Every man who sells a gun to an Indian should be convicted and swing.

16. *War of the Rebellion Records*, series 1, vol. 50, pt. 1, 1897, pp. 907–908.

February 3, 1855—At the beginning of hostilities, Captain Judah went with 26 men to the Klamath. There the *Weitspeck* and other Indians surrendered their arms. But the miners gathered together and wanted to immediately start a general massacre of all Indians—friendly or otherwise—they could find and hunt down. Captain Judah has succeeded in temporarily keeping the whites in check, but needs reinforcement to handle the whites. The friendly Indians are giving him every assistance. If the miners are allowed to continue the hostilities, mining, etc. on the Klamath will be ruined for several years.

May 26, 1855—Indian difficulties again threatened. Indians at the mouth of the Salmon have taken to the mountains. Bad white men have told Indians that the Indian agent wants to get them all in a crowd on a reservation where he can kill them. The immediate cause of their going was the recent unprovoked and cowardly murder of two prominent Indians at the mouth of the Salmon, whose fidelity to whites has never been questioned. Certain whites are trying to stir up another outbreak.

August 11, 1855—On the 27th the Indians killed ten men and wounded two others on the Klamath near Scott's Bar. They killed three at work at Buckeye Bar, four packers at Peckham's ranch and between there and Buckeye they killed five more and wounded two. Two of the murderers were hung on the 31st at Yreka and the negroes who furnished them with guns were lynched.

October 4, 1856—The Bald Mt. Diggers killed 5 head of cattle belonging to the white farmers. The latter banded together and surprised an Indian ranch east of Hempfield's Ranch on the divide towards Redwood Creek and killed at least 10 of the 40 or 50 Indians there.

Another incident involving Indians was the burning of the house of Colonel Stevenson at Tehama in the middle of May, 1859. It was believed that the fire was set by Indians, this information coming from an Indian boy, apparently a chattel of Colonel Stevenson. A sympathetic, or at least objective, newspaper reporter wrote the following story published in a San Francisco newspaper on May 18, 1859,[17] and entitled "Sowing the Wind and Reaping the Whirlwind":

17. Name of newspaper not known. Quotation taken from clipping in the authors' possession.

The terrible calamity that a few days since, befell the families of Mr. Stevenson and Mr. Kronk, in Tehama, and by which no less than seven lives were lost, caused a thrill of horror to run through the public pulse; and especially so when it was announced, with seeming truth, that the Indians were the instigators of the fire. If it had this effect here at this distance, it must have produced a still more potent one in the immediate neighborhood of the sad catastrophe, and among those who were acquainted with the sufferers and their family relatives, hence we do not wonder that they signed petitions asking the Governor to order a campaign against the aborigines there, and offered to enroll themselves in the service of the State to do a good share of the necessary fighting.

There is no proof, that we have seen, that the Indians caused the fire at Col. Stevenson's house, save the boy's own word, and that should not be taken, for it is not improbable that the boy himself had fancied some indignity towards his person, and sought revenge in this mode, in accordance with the historical feelings of his race.

But, even if the grown Indians did advise him to this course or if they had with their own hands at the dead hour of the night, placed the torch to the domicile, what else could be expected? Have not the people of Tehama hunted them like deer over the plains, through the ravines, across the mountains, and among the chapparal and brushwood—everywhere—with the sole purpose of shooting them down without a why or wherefore, whenever they could draw a bead upon them? Have not the people of Tehama, within the past six weeks, sent out—in defiance of law, of humanity, of Christianity, of justice, of the common feelings of civilized man—two expeditions of twelve to twenty men each, to murder—aye, that's the word—to murder these Indians wherever and whenever they could be found? And for this diabolical purpose did they not hunt them into and through the mountains, and gorges, and woods, day after day and night after night, and did they not shoot them down as they did a dog, whenever they could set eyes upon them. Certainly we so understand the facts to be, from their own local papers, and the statement has never been publicly denied!

Is it any wonder, then that the Indians would retaliate? They would be far nobler than civilized beings if they did not. They, if these charges are true, are but paying back in kind fiendish wrongs—foul murders—committed on themselves by men who claim to be civilized, who have not the excuse that the barbarian savage has for these heartless or wanton acts of aggression. True, they made innocent women and children suffer, but can reasonable men suppose that they, when thus goaded on to frenzy, will wait to consider the distinction between the guilty and the innocent? The white men of the Tehama . . . have treated the Indians far worse than ever the Indians treated them, and if . . . they did not expect the red men to retaliate, . . . then they are ignorant of human nature and of the current history of the land.

Now that they have raised this storm about their ears—now that they are in fear of their lives—the legitimate results of their own wanton acts—they cry aloud on the people of this state to protect them from the vengeance of these whom they, in their hour of triumph showed no mercy. . . . If their lives are in actual danger, and if it is shown that they are not able to protect themselves from the men they have hunted for months, the State should, for the sake of the women and children, go to their rescue; but we have not pity for the white men of Tehama who treated the Indians as their papers said they did, or who stood by and permitted others to do it.

If a few of them were to be treated in the same way, the State would not lose much by the operation, and the lesson might serve as a warning to others. If the Tehamaites had observed the golden rule, "Do unto others as you would they should do unto you," they would not now be trembling in their boots for fear of the Indians. But the guilty fear and fly from their own shadow! Let this be a warning to them to behave themselves hereafter; and if they will promise to conduct themselves like the average white men to the Indians, they may perforce remain among them, the Governor ought to succor them if they are in need of aid—but he should not move a peg until they pledge themselves *to do right in the future.*

The sequel to this event was reported in the *San Francisco Bulletin* on May 31, 1859, in a brief story entitled "The Lynching of the Indian Boy in Tehama County."

A few days ago the Indian boy who set fire to the house of Col. Stevenson, was taken from the custody of Sheriff Dunn, by a number of citizens and hanged. The Sheriff had taken him to the Court House and left him in a room adjoining the Court room, and while absent for a few moments, the boy was taken by the mob. . . . The boy was but twelve or fifteen years of age. The *Tehama Gazette* says that he was only ten years old. What good will the hanging of this stripling accomplish? Will it deter other Indian boys from committing a similar act? If so, the act is defensible. If not, what then? That the boy deserved hanging, if he was capable of appreciating the magnitude of his crime, is very true; but why not have let him be hung in a legal manner? There was no danger of his escaping.

A newspaper account of April 12, 1859, reports in detail on "The Indian War in the North." It is presented in its entirety in the documents section, p. 210, to illustrate the opinion of the day that such acts were justifiable because they reduced the risks of settling in areas where Indians remained.[18]

To Exterminate or to Protect?

In one of the volumes of the Pacific Railroad Reports,[19] Whipple, Ewbank, and Turner wrote the following evaluation in 1853 of the plight of the Indian, now overwhelmed by the American tide which had extended itself to the Pacific shore:

> The aborigines are, upon every side, hemmed in by descendants of a foreign race. Year by year their fertile valleys are appropriated by others; their hunting-grounds invaded, and they themselves driven to narrower and more barren districts. The time is now arrived when we must decide whether they are to be exterminated; if not, the powerful arm of the law must be extended over them, to secure their right to the soil they occupy; to protect them from aggression; to afford facilities and aid in acquiring the arts of civilization, and the knowledge and humanizing influences of Christianity.

The repudiation by Congress of the treaties of 1851–1852 made with the California Indians (see chapter 3), and the failure of both the state and federal governments to provide for the protection of the California Indians, show that little ear was given to such advice. An eloquent plea to help the Indians, which did not lead, however, to any improvement in the welfare of the Indians, was voiced in 1860 in the Majority Report of the Special Joint Committee [of the state legislature] on the Mendocino War:

> The march of civilization deprives the Indian of his hunting grounds and other means of subsistence that nature has so bountifully provided

18. A full official report on these and subsequent campaigns in 1859 is in W. C. Kibbe, *Report of the Expedition against the Indians in the Northern Part of the State.* Chas. T. Botts, State Printer, 1860. 10pp.

19. 1856, vol. 3, pt. 3, p. 7.

for him. He naturally looks at this as an encroachment of his rights, and, either from motives of revenge, or what is more likely in California, from the imperious and pressing demands of hunger, kills the stock of the settler as a means of subsistence, and in consequence thereof, a war is waged against the Indian, with its incidents of cruelty, inhuman revenge, rapine, and murder, which we are sorry, from the evidence before us, to be compelled by some few of our citizens. . . . There is no longer a wilderness west of us that can be assigned to them, and our interest, as well as our duty and the promptings of humanity, dictate to us the necessity of making some disposition of the Indian tribes within our borders that will ameliorate their sad condition, and also secure the frontier citizen from their depredations. . . . We are unwilling to attempt to dignify, by the term "war," a slaughter of beings, who at least possess the human form, and who make no resistance, and make no attacks, either on the person or residence of the citizen.[20]

The Minority Report took the opposite position in finding the Indians of Mendocino County a treacherous, bloodthirsty, settler-murdering and stock-killing people. Stating the opinion that the detachment of the Sixth U.S. Infantry consisting of one lieutenant and twenty-three men on duty in Round Valley had done nothing useful, the report says that "the conclusion is irresistible that the detachment there stationed is nothing more than a substantial definition of the word *nuisance*." The Sixth Infantry detachment apparently hindered the freedom of action of Indian-killing irregulars, and the report states that the resident settlers "now have an organization of their own for mutual protection, and neither the howlings of the pseudo-philanthropists, nor the malignant denunciations of the slanderous press, will deter them from exercising the rights of self-defense." The Minority Report recommended that the federal government

should first cede to the State of California the entire jurisdiction over Indians and Indian affairs within our borders, and make such donations of land and other property and appropriations of money as would be adequate to make proper provision for the necessities of a proper management.

20. California, Legislature, *Majority and Minority Reports of the Special Joint Committee on the Mendocino War*, pp. 1–2, 6.

Such a recommendation sounds as though the intent was to make it possible to care for the Indians properly and humanely, but what immediately follows shows what the author had in mind:

> The State should, then, adopt a general system of peonage or apprenticeship, for the proper disposition and distribution of the Indians by families among responsible citizens. General laws should be passed regulating the relations between the master and the servant, and providing for the punishment of any meddlesome interference on the part of third parties. In this manner the whites might be provided with profitable and convenient servants, and the Indians with the best of protection and all the necessaries of life in permanent and comfortable homes. By the adoption of such a policy, most of the Indians now on the reservations and those termed domesticated, residing among the whites, might be speedily provided for. It would be necessary to sustain the reserves [i.e., reservations] for a few years longer, in order that the wild tribes might be gathered in upon them, and kept until disposed of as apprentices. This course I am apprehensive would be denounced by those who affect to believe in the doctrine of universal equality; but a long acquaintance with the nature, character, and habits, of the California tribes, suggest to me that the policy toward the Indians . . . would be the most ameliorative of the sad condition of that ill-fated race.[21]

This recommendation, if implemented by legislative action, would have changed the then legal indenture of Indians, authorized under the Act of 1850 and amended in 1855 (see pp. 212, 216), to a compulsory indenture system which would have constituted a general system of Indian slavery.

Appended to the report on the Mendocino War (in which several hundred Indians were killed by volunteer military companies formed of local settlers) are a number of depositions which provide an abundance of detailed information on Indian conditions and reservation matters in Mendocino County. George Rees, overseer of Nome Cult Farm (operated by the federal government in Round Valley to grow food for the Round Valley reservation Indians) stated, "I do not think that it is necessary that an armed force should be sent here for the protection of the

21. Ibid., pp. 9–12.

property of the citizens; I think there is already a sufficient force [i.e., in the Sixth Infantry detachment] here; I think that the force here is needed to protect the reserve from the depredations of certain white men in the valley." The depositions make it quite clear that the white settlers, engaged mainly in raising stock, had through their activities caused a great diminution in the wild food available to Indians. Occasional horse, sheep, or cattle killings by hungry Indians did occur, and these "depredations" were usually punished by an expedition to "chastise" Indians, the result usually being the killing of a number and the taking of women and children as "prisoners of war," to be sold as "apprentices." Indian depredations, therefore, offered the excuse for securing women and children and thus made possible what was essentially a system of slavery.[22] The following remarks, taken from the testimony referred to illustrate this: "I do not consider the Yuca [Yuki] Indians in this vicinity hostile by any means; I do not allude to the killing of stock; I mean hostility to white men." "I think that the treatment received by the Indians from some of the white settlers has tended to exasperate them and caused them to destroy stock in a spirit of revenge." "The game is scarce, having been killed by the [white] hunters; the prevailing motive for [the Indians] killing stock is to get something to eat, although they kill some for spite; to spite some settlers who have been out killing them." "Unless some provision is made to feed these Indians they will kill stock, and consequently the whites will punish them."

"An Act for the Government and Protection of Indians"

Leaving for a time the bloodier events of the day, it is important to note that a particularly influential piece of legislation affecting the lives of the California Indians was chapter 133 of the *Statutes of California*, enacted into law on April 22, 1850, and entitled An Act for the Government and Protection of Indians. This act was the first of a series which provided for the indenture or apprenticeship of Indians of all ages to any white

22. See *Report of the Commissioner of Indian Affairs for 1861*, p. 149.

citizen for long periods of time. Indenturing of Indians from 1850 to 1863 was a common practice. We do not know how common it was because most of the records of this activity have not been preserved. Indenturing was a legal means of securing the person of an Indian, but another common practice was to avoid the legal method and purchase Indians, mostly children, outright.

This act, and its sequel passed on April 18, 1860,[23] opened the door, however, to the white slave dealers who did a thriving business providing "apprentices" to farmers and miners, who in turn legitimized these indentures by obtaining the local justice court's permission as provided through these laws. An editorial in the *Humboldt Times* on February 23, 1861, commented:

> This law works beautifully. A few days ago V. E. Geiger, formerly Indian Agent, had some eighty Indians apprenticed to him and proposes to emigrate to Washoe [i.e., to the Comstock mining district at Virginia City] with them as soon as he can cross the mountains. We hear of many others who are having them bound in numbers to suit. What a pity the provisions of this law are not extended to greasers, Kanakas, and Asiatics. It would be so convenient, you know, to carry on a farm or mine when all the hard and dirty work is performed by apprentices.

Kidnapping and Slavery

In 1853 the district attorney of Contra Costa County reported in a letter to the superintendent of Indian affairs in California, E. F. Beale, the following:

> Ramon Briones, Mesa, Quiera, and Beryessa of Napa County, are in the habit of kidnapping Indians in the mountains near Clear Lake, and in their capture several have been murdered in cold blood. There have been Indians to the number of one hundred and thirty-six thus captured and brought into this county, and held here in servitude adverse to their will. These Indians are now said to be in the possession of Briones, Mesa, and Beryessa, and sundry other persons who have *purchased* them in this county. It is also a notorious fact that these Indians are treated inhumanly, being neither fed nor clothed; and from such treatment many have already died, and disease is now threat-

23. *Statutes of California*, 1860, chap. 231.

ening destruction of the remainder. All the Indians I allude to were brought here forcibly and against their will. From my observation, that class of population who have these Indians treat them more like brutes than human beings. There is also a regular organized company of persons who capture and sell these Indians, and several have lately been so disposed of to William and Ramon Castro. There is now pending a suit against the persons above named for kidnapping these Indians, but the statutes of this State afford no adequate protection against cruel treatment of Indians.[24]

On October 14, 1854, Colonel Henley transmitted to his superiors in Washington a letter written by two special agents, McDaniel and McQueen, appointed by him to determine the facts in the matter of kidnapping Indian children. The letter reads in part:

[In Beryessa Valley on Putah Creek] we found something like one hundred and fifty Indians whose condition is that of slavery. We made enquiry in regard to the kidnapping referred to in your letter of instructions and found the Beriessa family in possession of a numerous gang of Indians at work on their ranch of different tribes, all of whom had been driven in from the [Sacramento] valley and [Coast Range] mountains of Stone Creek by violence and they (the Beriessa family) and certain Sonora Mexicans living with them are constantly in the practice of selling the young Indians both male and female to whomsoever will purchase them, and we have ascertained to whom they have sold several of them.[25]

On May 5, 1855, the *Humboldt Times*, published in Eureka, reported:

Colonel Henley has been endeavoring to discover persons engaged in the nefarious trade of stealing Indians. A large number of children have been brought down and sold in the agricultural counties. They bring from $50 to $250 each. Such conduct has the effect of making Indians very shy of coming into the Reservations, as they think that it is a trick to deprive them of their children.

Five years later the same newspaper (December 22, 1860) commented again on the practices of kidnapping and selling of

24. U.S., *Senate Exec. Doc.* no. 57, 32d Cong., 2d sess., 1853, p. 10.
25. U.S. National Archives, O.I.A., RG 75. Letters Received from California 1854, H–703.

Indian children, and noted that they were bringing from thirty to fifty dollars apiece from settlers who used them as servants.

In 1856 E. A. Stevenson, agent for the Nome Lackee reservation on the west side of the upper Sacramento Valley, stated in his report:

> Of the Indians residing in this neighborhood, a large number are on the ranches or farms of private individuals, who are using them as working hands, and who seem to have adopted the principle that the Indians belong to them as much as an African slave does to his master, and that they have the right to control them entirely. Many of these Indians have left their places and come to the reservation, and have been followed and demanded by the persons claiming them as private property. This system of slavery is, in my opinion, far more objectionable than that which exists in any other country, as the Indians claim to be the rightful owners of the soil. I cannot therefore too strongly recommend that some course be adopted by which it may be promptly broken up.[26]

Several letters from army personnel stationed in California in the 1860s describe the kidnapping of Indian children. From Lieutenant Edward Dillon, at Fort Bragg, to Captain C. S. Lovell, commanding the Sixth Infantry, U.S. Army, at Fort Humboldt, on May 31, 1861:

> I have the honor to report that there are several parties of citizens now engaged in stealing or taking by force Indian children from the district in which I have been ordered to operation against the Indians. I am reliably informed that as many as forty or fifty Indian children have been taken through Long Valley within the last few months and sold both in and out of the country. The parties, I am told, at least some of them, make no secret of it, but boldly assert that they will continue to do so and that the law cannot reach them. It is pretended, I believe, that the children are purchased from their parents but all who know these Indians can fully appreciate the value of this assertion. It is needless to say that this brutal trade is calculated to produce retaliatory depredations on the part of the Indians and exasperate them to a high degree.[27]

26. U.S., *House Document* no. 1, 34th Cong., 3d sess., 1856, p. 802.
27. *War of the Rebellion Records*, series 1, vol. 50, pt. 1, 1897, pp. 494–495.

Col. Francis J. Lippitt in a letter to Major R. C. Drum on Indian affairs in the Humboldt military district, dated Fort Humboldt, January 12, 1862, wrote as follows regarding the kidnapping of Indian children:

> Individuals and parties are, moreover, constantly engaged in kidnapping Indian children, frequently attacking the rancherias, and killing the parents for no other purpose. This is said to be a very lucrative business, the kidnapped children bringing good prices, in some instances Mr. Hanson tells me, hundreds of dollars apiece.[28]

Another report of 1861, written by Capt. T. E. Ketcham, Third Infantry, California Volunteers, commanding Fort Baker, states that Indians were sold for $37.50 apiece and that one of the traders made $15,000 in the last season's business.[29] At the price stated, this man would have disposed of 400 Indians. Even troops, it seems, were involved in the business. Note the following from D. C. Buell, assistant adjutant-general and acting inspector-general at Fort Gaston, to Capt. C. S. Lovell at Fort Humboldt, on July 13, 1861:

> The volunteers from Lieutenant Martin's camp brought away with them three Indian children, whom they captured during their recent operations against the Indians, and whom, I learn, they design to retain in their services. I deem it proper to bring this matter to your notice, because I imagine it will meet with the disapprobation of the department commander, to whom I shall feel it my duty to report it, as well as other like cases which have occurred in some of the detachments now in the field.[30]

An editorial in the *San Francisco Bulletin* of December 6, 1861, in the form of an extended and sympathetic review of the Indian problem, observed:

> It is notorious that there are parties in the northern counties of this State, whose sole occupation has been to steal young children and squaws from the poor Diggers, who inhabit the mountains, and dis-

28. Ibid., p. 803.
29. Ibid., p. 982.
30. Ibid., p. 535.

pose of them at handsome prices to the settlers, who being, in the majority of cases, unmarried but at housekeeping, willingly pay fifty or sixty dollars for a young Digger to cook and wait upon them, or a hundred dollars for a likely young girl. Recent developments in this vicinity are apparent proof of this.

Kidnapping as Cause of "Indian Wars"

California newspapers,[31] officials in the office of Indian Affairs,[32] and other observers[33] cited the organized bands of Indian kidnappers who operated independently, or followed troops on Indian campaigns and collected women and children after an attack on a village, as one of the main causes of the "Indian wars" which were common in the late 1850s and early 1860s.

A letter from one G. H. Woodman of Mendocino appeared in September 1860 in the San Francisco newspapers appealing for help to reduce the Indian murders of whites and killing of stock. In view of his subsequent activities, one may ask if he did not make this request for assistance in the hope of causing an "Indian war" from which he could directly profit by collecting the orphaned children left after their parents were killed. A commentary in the *San Francisco Bulletin*, February 3, 1860, takes a position sympathetic to the Indians, which was unusual at the time:

> G. H. Woodman, of Mendocino, states in a letter to the *San Francisco Herald*, that the Indians there commenced killing stock on September 20, and have killed four hundred head, and have murdered three white men and adds: "If we do not have assistance—immediately, we shall be compelled to move our families and stock out of this valley."
>
> Well, if their whole stock shall be killed and their families driven out of their homes, they will have none but themselves to blame; and it would be but partial justice and punishment to them for the inhuman

31. For example, *Sacramento Union*, July 19, 1862.
32. For example, letter from G. M. Hanson, Yuba City, July 23, 1861, in U.S. National Archives, O.I.A., RG 75, Letters Received from California, 1861, H–275; *Report of the Commissioner of Indian Affairs for 1861*, p. 56, reporting on Nome Lackee Reservation.
33. For example, Brewer, *Up and Down California*, p. 493; Cook, *Conflict*, 3:52–63.

murders they have committed upon the Indians there. They themselves have been the foulest murderers, or have permitted the murder of unoffending Indians, without raising a word of objection; yet they now whine and call upon others for assistance, because a few of their cattle have been killed, and their own necks are in danger. Men who have behaved as they have towards the Indians deserve no protection. The country would suffer no loss by their absence in this vicinity. Murderers are hanged—there, there is no law to punish them, and the Indians have to defend themselves, and are justifiable in their retaliation.

Occasionally some attempt was made to discourage the kidnapping and sale of Indians, by arresting white men with children in their possession, but such cases were infrequent, and usually led to nothing. For example, the same G. H. Woodman referred to above was arrested on or about March 6, 1863, according to the *Mendocino Herald* of that date, for kidnapping and offering for sale thirteen Indian children. On March 27, 1863, it was reported in the *San Francisco Bulletin* that he was in possession of the children with the consent of the parents. Woodman was tried (and acquitted), in the opinion of one newspaper because he had been "framed."[34]

In another case which we can generally follow in the newspapers of the times, three men, Laurie Johnson, James Wood, and James Freak, were arrested at the instigation of the superintendent of Indian affairs for Northern California, George M. Hanson, near Colusa in October, 1861, and charged with kidnapping and having in their possession five Indian children seized near Spruce Camp, Eel River, Humboldt County.[35] The children, three to four years of age, had originally been in a group of thirteen, four having been sold a few days earlier to local ranchers for from fifty-five to eighty dollars each. The three men were brought to court in Marysville, Yuba County, and it was argued by their counsel, J. A. McQuaid, that Yuba County had no jurisdiction in the case. Judge Bliss ruled that they were not legally held in Yuba

34. *Sacramento Union*, March 26, 1863.
35. *Sacramento Union*, October 18, 1861.

THE OTHER CALIFORNIANS

County, whereupon the deputy sheriff of Yuba County proceeded to rearrest them. Judge Bliss then held the men on bail of five hundred dollars to appear before a magistrate in Humboldt County. The *Marysville Appeal* of October 19, 1861, notes that the three men "have left town," and the same newspaper on October 24 notes that the "nine little Indians . . . have all been provided with comfortable homes, most of them in Marysville." We have not found any record of the appearance before a Humboldt County magistrate of Johnson, Wood, and Freak, probably for the reason that the affair ended when they "left town."

In December 1861, G. M. Hanson wrote to his superiors in Washington about the instance just outlined:

> In the month of October last I apprehended three kidnappers, about 14 miles from the city of Marysville, who had 9 Indian children, from 3 to 10 years of age, which they had taken from Eel river, in Humboldt County. One of the three was discharged on a writ of *habeas corpus*, upon the testimony of the other two, who stated that "he was not interested in the matter of taking the children"; after his discharge the two made an effort to get clear by introducing the third one as a witness, who testified that "it was an act of charity on the part of the two to hunt up the children and then provide homes for them, because their parents had been killed, and the children would have perished with hunger." My counsel inquired how he knew their parents had been killed? Because, he said, "I killed some of them myself."[36]

Main Provisions of Indenture Act

The indenture act of 1850 "for the Government and Protection of Indians" in effect outlined many rights and responsibilities of persons classified as Indians in the state of California as well as punishment to both white and Indian for failure to comply with the provisions of the act. It gave jurisdiction of certain Indian matters to local justices of the peace and appeal to the county courts. The act also established legal means by which whites might take custody of Indian children or hire Indian adults. It may be noted that the penalty exacted from any white man "who

36. *Report of the Commissioner of Indian Affairs for 1862.* Document 63, Letter from Superintendent George Hanson, p. 315. Washington, GPO, 1863.

46

shall neglect to clothe and suitably feed such minor Indians, or shall inhumanly treat him or her, *on conviction thereof* [emphasis added], shall be subject to a fine of not less than ten dollars." It is, of course, difficult to imagine any conviction of a white man in view of the fact that section 6 of the same act provided that "complaints may be made before a Justice of the Peace by white persons or Indians; but in no case shall a white man be convicted of any offense upon the testimony of an Indian, or Indians. In all cases it shall be discretionary with the court or jury." On April 28, 1855, section 6 of the Act for the Government and Protection of Indians was amended to read: "Complaints may be made before a Justice of the Peace, by white men or Indians, and in all cases arising under this Act, Indians shall be competent witnesses, their credibility being left with the jury."[37]

In 1851 an act entitled An Act to Regulate the Proceedings in Civil Cases in the Court of Justice of this State had specified more precisely the qualifications of witnesses.[38] Section 394 of this act defined the persons who could *not* be witnesses (including those who were of unsound mind and children who were under ten years of age); included in the prohibition were Indians, or persons having one-fourth or more Indian blood in an action in which a white person was a party, and Negroes, or persons having one-half or more Negro blood in an action to which a white person was also a party.[39] But in 1863 new enactments by the legislature stated that "Indians or persons having one-half or more Indian blood, or Mongolian, or Chinese, shall not be permitted to give evidence in favor or against any white person."[40] As it stood, then, in 1863, and until 1872, Indians could be the most compe-

37. *Cal. Stats.*, 1855, chap. 144, p. 179.

38. *Cal. Stats.*, 1851, chap. 5, title 11, p. 114.

39. As a historical footnote to the provisions in the act we have been citing, we note that "one-eighth part or more Negro blood" was enough to disqualify a potential witness (*Cal. Stats.*, 1850, chap. 99, sec. 13, p. 230). Section 4, dealing with the competency of Negro witnesses, was untimately removed by omission of the entire section with an amendment to an act passed in 1863 (*Cal. Stats.*, 1863, chap. 70, p. 69).

40. *Cal. Stats.*, chap. 70.

tent of witnesses as long as they did not testify in proceedings in which white men were involved. In 1872 section 3 of *California Statutes*, 1863, was repealed by omission.[41]

The remainder of the act of 1850 dealt with obligations and punishments of Indians, and it is interesting reading. For this reason the complete act is printed in the documents section, p. 212.

Vagrancy and Slavery

Vagrancy among Indians was doubtless considered somewhat of an evil in the early 1850s, but from the standpoint of the white Californians a noticeable scarcity of available cheap labor was certainly a much greater evil.

Section 20 of the act provided that any Indian not engaged in a profession or task who "shall be found loitering and strolling about, or frequenting public places where liquors are sold, begging or leading an immoral or profligate course of life, shall be liable to be arrested on the complaint of any resident citizen of the county." The justice hearing the case would determine if the accused Indian was a vagrant and would authorize an officer of the court to hire out the convicted Indian within twenty-four hours to the best bidder for a period not exceeding four months for the highest price which could be had at a public auction.[42] A provision in section 20 enabled the Indian to remain free if he could provide a bond determined by the justice. No doubt it would be interesting to compare the amount of bond required of the Indian and the amount bid for his services. Section 20 was indirectly, but effectively, repealed in the Penal Code of California in sections 487 (1870) and 647 (1872), which exempt California Indians from the crime of vagrancy.

The *Napa Reporter* for December 20, 1858, ran the following item under the headline "Selling Diggers at Auction."

41. See *Code of Civil Procedure Annotated*, sec. 1880, chap. 2, *Witnesses*, p. 405.
42. This is strikingly similar to the Mississippi law of 1865 which stated that any black not lawfully employed by January 1866 would be arrested as a vagrant, and if he failed to pay the fine of fifty dollars, he could be hired out to the person who paid the fine.

It is said that when a Digger Indian gets drunk in Fresno county, and is fined for it, and happened not to be able to pay the amount (which must generally be the case) he is put up to auction and sold to the highest bidder—we presume to pay his fine. One was recently sold for $1.25. If this article were marketable, somebody might make a fortune by selling drunken Diggers in Napa City; they are plenty enough, but the Digger market is dull.

In 1860 the Los Angeles City Council approved an ordinance which read:

When the city has no work in which to employ the chain gang, the Recorder shall, by means of notices conspicuously posted, notify the public that such a number of prisoners will be auctioned off to the highest bidder for private service, and in that manner they shall be disposed of for a sum which shall not be less than the amount of their fine for double the time they were to serve at hard labor.

Pitt quotes a letter of August 30, 1852, from Charles Brinley, overseer of Abel Stearns's Rancho Alamitos, in which he asks Stearns to "deputize someone to attend the auction that usually takes place at the [Los Angeles] prison on Monday's and buy me five or six Indians."[43]

The slavery thus countenanced involved Indians almost exclusively, and their fines ranged from one to three dollars per person for a week's work.[44] J. Ross Browne at about this time wrote satirically about this ordinance and the Indians' condition in Los Angeles: "The inhabitants of Los Angeles are a moral and intelligent people, and many of them disapprove of the custom [of auctioning off prisoners] on principle, and hope that it will be abolished as soon as the Indians are all killed off."[45]

Another voice was heard in 1852 objecting to this practice: B. D. Wilson, in his official report on Indian conditions, which was written in 1852 and published in 1868.[46] Wilson concluded

43. L. Pitt, The Decline of the Californios: A Social History of the Spanish-speaking Californians, 1846–1890, p. 113.

44. J. D. Forbes, The Indian in America's Past, p. 95; J. M. Guinn, "The Passing of the Old Pueblo," p. 117.

45. The Indians of California, pp. 3–4, 54.

46. J. W. Caughey, The Indians of Southern California in 1852: The B. D. Wilson

that the legislation concerning Indians was a case of "*All* punishment. *No* reform."

Approved on April 30, 1855, was an act entitled An Act to Punish Vagrants, Vagabonds and Dangerous and Suspicious Persons.[47] Section 1 excluded from the provisions of this act the "Digger Indians," but section 2 included "all persons who are commonly known as 'Greasers' or the issue of Spanish and Indian blood who may come within the provisions of the first section of this act and who go armed and are not peaceable and quiet persons." Section 4 prescribed the use of the ball and chain "of sufficient weight and strength to prevent escape" for those persons convicted of vagrancy who worked off their sentences in hard labor outside of the "carcel" (Spanish term for jail).

Whatever misuse of the prevailing laws at the time prompted adoption of section 487 of the new Penal Code of 1870 we can only surmise. By this act, however, a vagrant was redefined as "Every person (except a California Indian) without visible means of living." And with this, one more inequity in the law was closed over.

Amendments to the Act in 1860

An Act for the Government and Protection of Indians, approved by the state legislature on April 18, 1860, amended two sections of the 1850 legislation.[48] The most important part was section 3, which was expanded considerably, and notable clauses of the original act were omitted. Jurisdiction over the custody of Indian minors was transferred from local justices of the peace to county and district judges. The clause requiring the presence of the parents or friends of the Indian minor to be indentured was deleted. The only requirement now was that the white petitioner

---

Report and a Selection of Contemporary Comment; R. F. Heizer, *The Indians of Los Angeles County: Hugo Reid's Letters of 1852, p. 3;* W. H. Oswalt, *This Land Was Theirs,* pp. 180–181; B. D. Wilson, *The Indians of Southern California in 1852.*

47. *Cal. Stats.,* 1855, chap. 175.
48. *Cal. Stats.,* 1860, chap. 231.

have custody of the child with the *consent* of the parents. Written consent by the parents was not required; a sworn statement of the person having possession of the Indian minor was sufficient. And the term "articles of indenture" was substituted for the term "certificate of custody" as the legal mechanism binding an Indian into the custody of a white. It is worth noting that while the person having to care for the indentured Indian was still required to clothe "and suitably provide the necessaries of life," the new act now provided for extensions of the duration of indentures.

The new age of majority for the Indian minors was changed for males from eighteen to twenty-five years of age, and for females from fifteen to twenty-one years of age; but for persons indentured between the ages of fourteen and under twenty years of age, the males could be apprenticed until they reached thirty years of age, and the females until they reached twenty-five years of age. The period of indenture was not in actuality so sharply defined, however, since there are the instances in Humboldt County (see table, Data on Seventy Humboldt County Indentures, p. 54) where Joe and Ella, a married couple, each twenty-three years of age, were bound over in January 1861 for a period of ten years, and of Bob and Ellen, each twenty years old, were indentured in November 1861 for ten years. Curiosity alone makes us wonder why children under fourteen years of age at the time of their indenture reached the age determined by statute to be the age of majority for males five years sooner, and for females four years sooner than those indentured minors who were older than fourteen years of age. The amended section 3, as well as section 7, is printed in the documents, p. 216.

Indentures at Eureka, 1860–1863

In the old courthouse in the justice of the peace records at Eureka, Humboldt County, is one bundle of 114 Indian Indentures, involving 181 persons, mostly children. The earliest document is dated August 5, 1860, and the latest November 1863. A typical indenture reads as follows:

This indenture made and entered into 14th day of August A.D. 1860 between A. J. Heustis as county judge of Humboldt County, for and on behalf of a certain Indian boy called and known by the name of Smoky of the first part, Austin Willey of said county of the second part witnesseth:

That whereas the said Austin Willey has in his possession and under his control a certain Indian boy named Smoky. And whereas the said Austin Willey avers that he, with the assistance of James H. Fruit, obtained said Indian of his parents, in Mattole Valley, of this county, by and with their consent. And whereas the said Austin Willey does now apply to me, as the county judge of this county, to bind and apprentice the said boy Smoky to him according to law, to learn the art of household and domestic duties about his premises, and in these respects to hold the relation of an apprentice, until he shall arrive at lawful majority, the age of 25 years, or for the term of seventeen years next following this indenture, the boy being now considered eight years of age. And whereas it appears to me that the second party in this agreement had obtained this boy in a lawful manner, without fraud or oppression, and that the boy Smoky therefore comes justly under the first provision of law, providing for apprenticeship approved April the 18th, A.D. 1860.

Now therefore, I, A. J. Heustis, County Judge as aforesaid, in consideration of the premises, and acting for and on behalf of the said Indian boy Smoky, do by these presents bind and apprentice, as above stated; the said boy Smoky to Austin Willey, for, and during the term of seventeen years, next following this indenture, entitling him according to law, to have the care, custody, control and earnings of said boy during said period, and all other advantages and responsibilities growing out of this indenture and apprenticeship, that the law contemplates.

And the said Austin Willey, the second party in this agreement, doth hereby agree, obligate and bind himself, that he will truly and faithfully discharge all the obligations on his part, growing out of the indenture according to law. That he will suitably clothe and provide the necessities of life for the said boy during his term of indenture. That he will in all respects treat him in a humane manner. That he will not take him out of this state, nor will he transfer him to any party not known in the agreement, without the consent of legal authority endorsed therein; and that in all respects he will carry out every provision of the law that contemplates the safety, protection and well-being of said boy. In witness whereof the parties of this indenture here unto set their hands and seals the date first above written.

Sworn to and subscribed before me on this 14th day of August A.D. 1860.

A. J. HEUSTIS, *County Judge*
of Humboldt County

We summarize the data available to us from 70 of the 114 Humboldt County indentures and add the possibly sentimental observation that the listing here of the names of these unfortunates is their only opportunity to voice, however belatedly and from the cold legal records, their protest against their inhuman treatment by some of California's pioneers.

Ages of 110 persons indentured range from two to fifty, with a concentration of 49 persons between the ages of seven and twelve. Seven are listed as "taken in war" or "prisoners of war"—this notation refers to children five, seven, nine, ten, and twelve years of age. Four children of ages eight, nine, ten, and eleven are listed as "bought" or "given." Ten married couples were indentured, some of them with children. Three individuals seem almost too young to have been so treated—Perry, indentured in September 1860 at the age of three; George, indentured in January 1861 at the age of four; and Kitty (November 1861), also four years of age.

These individuals who were committed to a period of involuntary servitude which can only be termed slavery are, like their masters, long since dead. But that they may not have died anonymously we record here their names and ages and duration of service as ordered by either the justice of the peace or the judge. One hopes that these persons were released with the repeal of section 3 of the 1850 act, though this cannot be taken for granted in view of the fact that in November 1863 one Carrie, age seven, was indentured to Sara H. Bowles some five months after the repeal in April 1863 of the indenture law contained in section 3. Whether the little girl Sara Bowles indentured at age seven lived to gain her freedom in 1877 we will probably never know. And we will not

DATA ON SEVENTY HUMBOLDT COUNTY INDENTURES

Date of indenture	Name, sex, age of person(s) indentured	Indentured to	Period of indenture (years)	Indentured to age
1860				
August	Rolly, F, 12	A. P. Guthree		21
	Jane, F, 9	L. Louis Shaw		25
	Biddy, F, 6	"		25
	Sarah, F, 5	John J. Roberts	16	
	Smoky, M, 8	Austin Willey	17	
September	Mary, F, 7	Mrs. Jane Sweasey	14	
	Nelly, F, 7	Henry Axton	14	
	Dick, M, 12	N. Singley		25
	Rolly, F, 12	"		21
	Charley, M, 10	"		25
	Sherlotte, F, 8	"		21
	Mary, F, 6	"		21
	Perry, M, 3	"		21
October	Indian Henry, M, 20	Albert Swain	10	
	Squaw Nellie, F, 25	"	10	
	Oconsy, F, 15	Wm. Roberts	10	
	Lewis, M, 18	"	10	
	George, M, 8[a]	Leon Chevret		
	Mary, F, 20	Mrs. Margaret Duff	5	
	Jack, M, 17	Wm. Roberts	13	
November	Topsey, F, 7	A. S. Rollins	14	
December	Peter Adams, M, 10	Barry Adams	15	
	Nelly, F, 9	C. J. Ryan	12	
1861				
January	Toney, F, 6[b]	Charles Rider	15	
	Charley, M, 14	Peter Hauck	11	
	Rose (wife), F, 15	"	6	
	Joe, M, 23	Lyman Fish	10	
	Ella (wife), F, 23	"		
	Dave, M, 6	Wm. Eaton Phillips		25
	Lucy, F, 8	Pierre H. Ryan		21
	Kate, F, 6	Wm. McDonald	15	
	Ginney, F, 27	G. Danskin		
	Jim (son), M, 11	"		
	Sarah (daughter), F, 9	"		
	Anna, F, —	"		
	Bob, M, 21	Leon Chevret		
	Mary (wife), F, 22	"		

[a] "Bought 18 months previously by L. C. from C. Clarke of Mattole for $30.00."
[b] "Given by wife of Coonskin."

Date of indenture	Name, sex, age of person(s) indentured	Indentured to	Period of indenture (years)	Indentured to age
	Kitty (daughter), F, 4	Leon Chevret		
	Mad River Billy, M, 18	"		
	Lucy (wife), F, 16	"		
	John, M, 25	J. C. Preston		
	Jane (wife), F, 20	"		
	George (cousin), M, 4	"		
	Julia, F, 7	C. Kinsey		21
	Dick, M, 17	David Jenkins		
	Dan, M, 14	"		
	Jack, M, 26	T. J. Titlow		
	Malinda (wife), F, 27	"		
	Frank (son), M, 3	"		
	Jane (Jack's mother) F, 40	"		
	Charley, M, 25	"		
	Emma (wife), F, 23	"		
	Blue Coat Mowwena, M, 50	Henry F. James	10	
	Bill (son), M, 24	"	10	
	Fanny (wife of Bill), F, 19	"	6	
	Bony (son), M, 19	"	11	
	Teeny (daughter), F, 11	"	11	
	Sorenose Jack, M, 25	Ruben Duncan		
	Mary Kitty, F, 15	John Whaley		
	Sam, M, 13	A. M. Preston		
	Jasper, M, 15	"		
	Mary, F, 12[c]	A. J. Jacoby	9	
	Tom, M, 11	Rufus Phillips	14	
	Nelly, F, 15	Wm. C. Martin	6	
February	Rachael, F, 9[d]	Isaac Hobbs		25
	Dick, M, 18	Wm. Eaton Phillips		
	Kitty (wife), F, 25	"		
	Tom, M, 19	Wm. Nixon		
	Mary (wife), F, 16	"		
	Charley, M, 21	John C. Bull		
	William, M, 15	John A. Biddings	15	
	Tom, M, 11[e]	R. Blum		
March	Charley, M, 11	J. P. Davis		25
	Sylvia, F, 14	A. J. Huestis		25
April	Jasper, M, 15	J. A. Kneeland	15	
May	Little John, M, 24	Rufus F. Herrick	10	
	Blanch (wife), F, 22	"	10	

[c] "Taken from father at Big Bar in May, 1854 and bound under law of 1850."
[d] "Bought from her parents."
[e] "Bought of his mother at Coaski several years since."

Date of indenture	Name, sex, age of person(s) indentured	Indentured to	Period of indenture (years)	Indentured to age
	Peter (son), M, 2	Rufus F. Herrick	23	
July	Bob, M, 13	H. S. Daniels	12	
	Jake, M, 7	Daniel Ready		25
	Sam Houston, M, 5[f]	J. Clark	20	
	Djalma, M, 7	?		
August	Moses, M, 14	J. D. Tewkesbury	18	
	Belsabub, M, 12	"	13	
	Sarah, F, 10	"	15	
	Minne Ha Ha, F, 12[f]	A. G. Turner	9	
	Aaron, M, 8	J. D. Tewkesbury	17	
September	Phyllis, F, 7	Lucian Wright	14	
	Molly, F, 9[f]	?		
October	Nellie Lincoln, F, ca. 17	James H. Fruit	8	
	George Washington Donally, M, 12	Peter Donally	13	
November	Milly, F, 10[f]	Norman Dupern	11	
	Oneta, F, 8	Francis Connor	12	
	Malinda, F, 8	Mrs. E. Abels		
	Bob, M, 20	Jacob Keiffer	10	
	Ellen (wife), F, 20	"		
	Charles, M, 7[f]	Wm. B. Hagans	18	
	Kate, F, 10[g]	"	11	
	Coeness, M, 13	John Moore		25
	Kitty, F, 14	"		21
1862				
January	Franke, M, 25	Wm. Ellery	10	
	David, M, 23	"	10	
March	Hank Smith, M, 7[f]	?		
April	Peter, M, 11	A. A. Hadley		25
	Patrick, M, 8	"		25
May	Charles, M, 8	F. Cassans		17
	Lincoln, M, 5	"		20
June	"Blackhawk," M, 9[f]	W. I. Reed	16	
	Peter, M, 4	Anthony Bowles	21	
July	Fred, M, 7	Robert Gowanlock	18	
August	Peter, M, 5	J. D. Myers	20	
September	Twilight, F, 7[f]	S. F. Hopkins	14	
1863				
November	Carrie, F, 7	Sara H. Bowles		21

[f] "Prisoner of war."
[g] "Purchase from parents."

56

be engaging in undue sentimentalism if we think of the problem faced by Charley and his wife Rose, indentured at ages fourteen and fifteen to Peter Hauck, when Charley was released at age twenty-five and his wife Rose at age twenty-one. We will hope that Mr. Hauck allowed the couple to leave together.

And what of Peter, son of Little John and Blanch, all three of whom were indentured to Rufus F. Herrick in March 1861? Did Peter stay on as "apprentice" to Mr. Hauck for thirteen years after his father and mother had served their period of indenture?

We can conclude only one thing from this survey of the indenture act of 1850 and its subsequent alterations until its repeal in 1863; namely, that this was a legalized form of slavery of California Indians. No other possible construction can be made of the facts.

The extraordinary proprietary rights over the persons of Indians which whites might claim to hold is illustrated by the following account taken from the *Sacramento Union*, August 19, 1865, and headed "Outrage in Mendocino County," some two years *after* the repeal of the Act for the Government and Protection of Indians.

A Correspondent of the Union, writing from Ukiah City, Mendocino County, August 13th, relates the following case of outrage:

Allow me to inform you of a most inhumane outrage that took place here last Wednesday morning. A young man living here in town hired an Indian to go with him after a load of barley. When about one-fourth of a mile on their way, they met one Bob Hildreth, who claimed the Indian as his property and asked the Indian where in h——l he was going. The Indian answering, after barley, he told him to get out of the wagon d——d quick; that he would show him the way to come home. He made the Indian cross his hands behind, when he fastened them with his rope, swearing he would drag him to death. Then, mounting his horse and taking two half hitches around the logger head of his saddle, he put spurs to his horse, throwing the Indian eight or ten feet, with a hard fall—the Indian screaming and begging for his life. The horse, after going some few jumps, became frightened and threw Hildreth off. The rope being tied would not come loose, the horse running zigzag across the road and crossing two ditches before he was caught. The Indian was terribly mangled, his arms being twisted off in his shoulders. So much for slavery in California. Jarboe, the great Indian hunter of Humboldt, who is now dead, claimed to have had those Indians bound to him by one of the most cursed of all laws that were ever passed in this State. Hildreth, buying the property of Mrs. Jarboe, now claims these Indians as part of the estate. She setting the Indians free to go where they please, they will not stay with Hildreth, nor has he any right to them. The Legislature has done much blowing concerning the Indians in this county, but every Act hits them harder. They are held here as slaves were held in the South; those owning them use them as they please, beat them with clubs and shoot them down like dogs and no one to say, "Why do you do so?" James Shores, an Indian slaveholder here, shot one the other day, because he would not stand and be whipped, inflicting a severe wound, but not killing him. Hildreth is bound over in the sum of one thousand dollars for his appearance, but I have my doubts of finding a jury that will convict a man for killing an Indian up here.

Repeal, 1863

Section 3 of the 1850 act concerning right of custody and control of Indian children during their minority was amended by statute on April 18, 1860, giving the power to indenture Indians for "apprenticeship" (however, see the language of the indenture document of the Indian boy, Smoky, p. 52) to county or district judges. Both the original section 3 of the 1850 act and the amended section 3 of 1860 were repealed by statute on April 27, 1863.[49] California, after thirteen years of the most thinly disguised legalization of Indian slavery, and at the midpoint of the Civil War being fought so far from the Pacific shore, and four months after Lincoln's Emancipation Proclamation (whose effective date was January 1, 1863) finally made amends for this barbarity, which was, until the day of manumission of the hundreds of Indians held in bondage, referred to as an act "for the Government and Protection of Indians." That historic document can be viewed as a local version of the Emancipation Proclamation.

49. Fourteenth Session, State Legislature, 1863, p. 743.

Other Restrictive Statutes

On Weapons and Alcohol

Several statutes were enacted in the early 1850s to regulate the acquisition of weapons and intoxicating liquors by Indians. Prohibition under severe penalty of the sale or gift of firearms to an Indian was a precautionary measure that doubtless seemed essential at the time. But it was double-edged to the Indian, to whom hunting was both an occupation and a necessity and to whom game, after the white had reduced and scattered it by the use of firearms, was now beyond easy reach of the bow and arrow.[50]

In 1854 an act was passed which prohibited the transfer of firearms or ammunition to Indians of either sex and made the offense a misdemeanor punishable by a fine from $25 to $500 and/or a jail sentence from one to six months.[51] The gravity of this offense as well as the one concerning the sale of intoxicating liquor to any Indian was again made clear in 1872.[52] In 1913, however, section 398 of the Penal Code was repealed.[53] By this time, with an Indian population reduced to approximately 17,000, the fearful threat of a massive retaliation by armed and intoxicated California Indians was receding from the minds of the California whites. By this time discrimination against the "noble Red man"

---

50. The most thorough study yet made of social, health, labor, and dietary conditions of California Indians in the period 1848–1870 is by S. F. Cook, in *Conflict between the California Indian and White Civilization*, vol. 3. Since few official records, except those of military campaigns against Indians, were kept during these two decades, the main source of information is travelers' accounts and local newspapers. Until 1870 any Indian seen outside a town, off the land of a rancher or miner who was the native's employer and protector, or outside the bounds of a reservation, was likely to be shot down. In town Indians often subsisted on garbage (*San Francisco Bulletin*, February 10, 1858; March 12, 1858; March 12, 1860). Indian women often turned to prostitution (Cook, *Conflict*, 3:83–85; *Nevada Journal*, November 12, 1858).

51. *Cal. Stats.*, 1854, chap. 12.

52. Penal Code, 1872, sec. 398; sec. 397; see also *Cal. Stats.*, 1850, p. 408, sec. 15; 1855, p. 179, sec. 2.

53. *Cal. Stats.*, 1913, chap. 56, p. 57.

was no longer fashionable, and attention had now turned toward the invading "yellow hordes."

On Voting

Indian suffrage was one of the major questions raised during the constitutional convention of 1849, and we will have more to say in chapter 4 concerning this. Article II, section 1, of the first California constitution entitled "every white male citizen of the United States, and every white male citizen of Mexico, who shall have elected to become a citizen of the United States, under the treaty of peace exchanged and ratified at Querétaro, on the 30th day of May, 1848," to vote, provided they were twenty-one years of age and satisfied the residence requirement. At the end of the section there appears the following: "Provided that nothing herein contained, shall be construed to prevent the Legislature, by a two thirds concurrent vote, from admitting to the right of suffrage, Indians, or the descendants of Indians, in such special cases as such a proportion of the Legislative body may deem just and proper."

The first legislature, however, immediately placed itself on record as restricting the vote to *white* citizens. One interesting aspect of the laws restricting minority group suffrage should be noted and can be found in the attempts by the members of the state legislature to define by percentage of "blood" exactly who would fit into the categories which they had constructed in order to determine whether a person was eligible to cast his vote.

In 1850 An Act to Regulate Elections specified those in the population who were entitled to vote.

> Every white male citizen of the United States and every white male citizen of Mexico who shall have elected to become a citizen of the United States under the treaty of Peace exchanged and ratified at Querétaro on the 30th day of May, 1848, of the age of twenty-one years, who shall have been a resident of the state six months next preceding the election and the county or district in which he claims his vote thirty days shall be entitled to vote at all elections which are now or hereafter may be authorized by law.[54]

54. *Cal. Stats.*, chap. 38.

In 1851 another law was enacted calling for a poll tax of three dollars to be collected from each male inhabitant over the age of twenty-one years. Section 5 of this act, however, stated:

> The following persons and property shall be exempt from taxation. The polls of all Indians except those who may be lawfully entitled to vote.[55]

There is no evidence that Indians, whether they paid taxes or did not pay taxes, did vote. Possibly the Indians meant were the "mestizos" (Mexican-California Indians) of Southern California, some of whom were prominent persons of position and wealth. In 1924 Congress conferred citizenship upon all previously noncitizen Indians born within the United States, and in most states this was sufficient to authorize Indians to vote. In California this was taken care of by the Constitution of 1879, in article II, paragraph 1, which stated that every native citizen of the United States shall be entitled to vote at all elections.

On Juries

In addition to the obvious disadvantages of being denied the right to vote, other subtle inequities were to be found in the statute books. Notable examples are chapter 119, passed April 20, 1850: "No other qualifications shall be requisite to render a person a competent juror than that he should be a qualified elector of the County"; and chapter 142: "The qualifications of a juror shall be the same as those prescribed by law for a grand juror."

If a white citizen was ever indicted by an all-white grand jury for wrongdoings against an Indian, not only would the Indian be unable to testify in his own behalf, but his case could only be heard before an all-white trial jury. Such was the plight of the Indian until he was given the right to vote.

On Attending School

The right of the Indian to attend school was never contested by the white majority. With whom he could attend was quite an-

55. *Cal. Stats.*, 1851, chap. 6, pp. 153–164.

other matter. The solution to this problem must have occupied a good deal of the time of the state legislators if we reflect on the bulk of enactments concerning this question over the years.

Statutes passed in 1863 and 1864 provided that "Negroes, Mongolians and Indians" could not be admitted into the public schools, but also provided that

> upon the application of the parents or guardians of 10 or more such colored children, made in writing to the trustees of any district, said trustees shall establish a separate school for the education of Negroes, Mongolians and Indians and use the public funds for the support of the same.[56]

In 1866 the law was relaxed. Chapter 342, in section 56, gave to any board of education the power to admit by majority vote into any public school

> half-breed Indian children and Indian children who live with white families or under the guardianship of white persons.

Section 57 stated that

> children of African or Mongolian descent and Indian children not living under the care of white persons shall not be admitted into public schools except as provided in this act.

And such provisions were listed in section 58:

> When there shall be in any district any number of children other than white children whose education can be provided for in no other way, the trustees, by a majority vote, may permit such children to attend schools for white children provided that a majority of the parents of the children attending such schools make no objections.[57]

Chapter 342 was amended in 1869–70 to omit all of the previous exceptions granting Indian children the possibility of attending school with their white neighbors.[58] The statute was an obvious attempt to return to the more stringent conditions that

56. *Cal. Stats.*, 1864, chap. 209, sec. 68, p. 213. See also *Cal. Stats.*, April 6, 1863, An Act to Provide for the Maintenance and Supervision of Common Schools.

57. *Cal. Stats.*, March 24, 1866, chap. 342, sections 56–58, p. 398.

58. *Cal. Stats.*, 1869–70, chap. 556.

prevailed during the earlier years of the decade. The measure failed to win substantial public support, for again in the legislative session of 1873–74 an amendment was passed which added:

> The education of children of African descent and Indian children must be provided for in separate schools (section 1669). . . . If the directors or trustees fail to provide such separate schools, then such children must be admitted into the schools for white children.[59]

The School Act could still be found on the statute books long after the California Indian had ceased to constitute a significant statistic in the California population.

In 1880 the barriers of race were removed in part. Section 1669[60] was repealed,[61] and section 1662 of the new Political Code was enacted to read:

> Every school unless otherwise provided by law must be open to the admission of all children between six and twenty-one years of age residing in the district; and the Board of Trustees . . . shall have the power to exclude children of filthy or vicious habits or children suffering from contagious or infectious disease.[62]

In 1902, however, the barriers were again put in place, this time owing in part to the heavy immigration of Orientals into California. Section 1662 of the Political Code was amended[63] to include the old provisions found in section 1669, repealed in 1880. Though the liability for children of African descent was omitted, Chinese children were particularly named along with the children of Indian or Mongolian parentage. Section 2 of this act repealed all other acts and parts of acts in conflict with the provisions of this new statute, and section 3 provided for the immediate effect of the act.

Again in 1909 the same basic provisions found in the act of 1902 were included in chapter 594:

59. *Amend. Stats.*, 1873–74, sec. 26, p. 97.
60. *Amend. Stats.*, 1873–74.
61. *Amend. Stats.*, 1880, p. 47.
62. Ibid., p. 38.
63. *Cal. Stats.*, 1902, chap. 77, p. 86.

The governing body of the school district shall have the power to exclude children suffering from contagious or infectious diseases, and also to establish separate schools for Indian children and for children of Chinese or Mongolian descent. When such separate schools are established, Indian, Mongolian, or Chinese children must not be admitted into any other school.[64]

In 1921 the legislature's revision of section 1662 of the Political Code removed the prohibition against Indians attending public school.[65]

64. *Cal. Stats.*, 1909, chap. 594, sec. 3, p. 904.

65. The processes and extent of American Indian integration into white American society lies beyond the range of our present study. The interested reader may begin by consulting the following works: W. T. Hagan, *American Indians*; R. Linton, ed., *Acculturation in Seven American Indian Tribes*; D'A. McNickle, *They Came Here First*; W. H. Oswalt, *This Land Was Theirs*; J. Provinse, "The American Indian in Transition"; G. E. Simpson and J. M. Yinger, eds., *American Indians and American Indian Life*; M. P. Snodgrass, comp., *Economic Development of American Indians and Eskimos, 1930–1967: A Bibliography*; S. Steiner, *The New Indians*. The California Indians' situation today, and the extent of their participation in and degree of integration with the dominant white culture is treated by the Department of Industrial Relations, *American Indians in California*; J. D. Forbes, *Native Americans of California and Nevada*; W. W. Robinson, *The Indians of Los Angeles: A Story of the Liquidation of a People*; State Advisory Commission on Indian Affairs.

III. The Indian and the Lands of His Fathers

The Spaniards made no treaties with California Indians. They did not need to, for the land was theirs to use by right of discovery, and the "Indian problem" was easily solved by establishing missions, twenty-one in all, into which the Indians were drawn so that their souls could be saved and their labors could be devoted to productive ends that served the Spanish crown. Indian title to mission lands was reserved for the natives, but use and occupancy were the privilege of the crown.[1]

When the missions were secularized in 1834, the mission lands and cattle were distributed among the former Indian neophytes. Under Mexican rule (1821–1846) large land grants were made by the government, and it was understood, but not expressed, that the grantee secured the services of the native peoples living on the land.

The Russian American Company established a supply post on the north central coast of California in 1812. The Russians were not interested in colonizing California nor in securing any large land holdings. Their official policy is stated in the regulations of the company, entitled "Matters Related to People Inhabiting the Coasts of America Where the Company Has Its Colonies."[2]

1. Z. Engelhardt, *The Missions and Missionaries of California*, 4:22–23.
2. ARTICLE 57. Since the main object of the Company is hunting of land and marine animals, and since therefore there is no need for the Company to extend its sway into the interior of the lands on whose shores it carries on its hunting, the Company should make no efforts at conquest of the peoples inhabiting those shores.

When Fort Ross was established, the Russians met with local native inhabitants and paid them three blankets, three pairs of trousers, glass beads, two axes, and three pickaxes for the property. The fort was abandoned in 1841, and there is no record of any serious difficulties between the local natives and the Russians during the latter's twenty-nine-year sojourn.

When Mexico after its independence became sovereign over the area of California, the legal relationship with the Indians of that state was not altered a great deal. However, when Mexico lost California to the United States after the disastrous Mexican War, the new immigrant white population knew little about the previous Spanish-founded agreements with the Indians and apparently cared less. The Indian was looked on as a potential troublemaker who would have to be removed from his land to places where the white man had no interest.

John A. Sutter, who had established his fort at Sacramento in 1841, was engaged in 1848 with his partner, James W. Marshall, in building a sawmill at Coloma, and in the process made the discovery (on January 24, 1848) which set off the great California gold rush. Realizing how difficult it would be to preserve the land on which the new sawmill stood, and that the gold in the streams was of great value, Sutter and Marshall attempted to secure some kind of legal title to the land during the interim period between the cessation of Mexican law in 1846 and the institution (to come in 1850) of California civil law. They attempted to do this through an agreement with local Indian chiefs to lease their territory. Sutter had been appointed sub-Indian agent under

---

Therefore, if the Company should find it to their advantage, and for the safety of their trade, to establish factories in certain localities of the American coast, they must do so with the consent of the natives, and use only such means as would help retain their good will, avoiding everything that may arouse their suspicion about encroachment on the independence.

ARTICLE 28. The Company is forbidden from demanding from these peoples any kind of tribute, tax, fur-tribute, etc. Also in peace time, the Company are not to take any captives as long as they are given hostages from these peoples according to the existing custom. These hostages must be kept in decent conditions, and the authorities must see to it that they are not offended in any way.

the United States military occupation of California and attempted to use this position in the effort to legitimize the lease. The lease was forwarded to Col. R. B. Mason, military governor of California, in Monterey.

Governor Mason rejected the claims by stating that the government of the United States did not recognize the right of the Indians to lease, rent, or sell their lands, and that the area of the many tribes was bound to be regarded as public domain the moment the Treaty of Peace was settled with Mexico. Sutter and Marshall drew up the lease, which they represented as being "of great benefit to the Indians," but it is obvious that their humanitarian feelings came to light only after gold was discovered on the Indians' land. Whether one calls the document a lease, an agreement, or a treaty, it is clear that it was motivated solely from self-seeking interests of Marshall and Sutter. The texts of Sutter's letter to Governor Mason and of the lease are reprinted in the documents section, pp. 218 and 219.

Treaty-making, 1851–1852

Long before California had become a state in the Union the federal Constitution assigned control over Indian affairs to Congress through the clause empowering that body to regulate commerce with the Indian tribes. Congress delegated the management of Indian affairs to the War Department when that department was created in 1789. In 1793 Congress made invalid any title to Indian lands not acquired by treaty under the Constitution, thus formally placing Indian relations in the hands of the president in connection with the treaty-working power. By means of numerous treaties the federal government continued a policy begun in colonial times of removing the Indians from the advancing frontier and of gradually extinguishing their title to the public domain through treaties.[3] Usually the basis of the Indian cession

3. G. E. Lindquist, "Indian Treaty Making"; J. C. Malin, *Indian Policy and Westward Expansion*; W. H. Oswalt, *This Land Was Theirs*, pp. 500 ff.; R. H. Pearce, *The Savages of America: A Study of the Indians and the Idea of Civilization*; C. Royce, *Indian Land Cessions in the United States*.

was the exchange of the occupied territory for lands further west, a policy which could no longer be followed when the Pacific coast was reached.

Within two years after James W. Marshall's discovery of gold, troubles between Indians and whites had grown so serious in some parts of the state that by presidential act of 1850 three commissioners were sent out from Washington, D.C., to learn, if possible, what would satisfy the natives and to make treaties with them. Redick McKee, Col. George Q. Barbour, and Dr. O. M. Wozencraft, the commissioners, began in the southern part of California and worked north, negotiating treaties with tribes gathered at army posts and ranches. From March 19, 1851, to January 7, 1852, they met 402 chiefs or headmen of tribes and made eighteen treaties in all. The Indians surrendered their general claims of occupancy covering the major part of the state, in return for specific reservations aggregating about 8,500,000 acres[4] and certain quantities of livestock, clothing, and farming implements.

We may suppose that President Millard Fillmore and the three treaty commissioners were motivated by the highest ideals, and had no intention of doing other than effecting a series of Indian treaties which would be equitable in providing Indians, who had possessory rights, fair compensation for their land and a guarantee of support by the federal government. But, implicit in any Indian treaty that the United States government ever entered into was the assumption that this was a concession by the master group to the subordinate one. "Manifest destiny" never needed a better rationale than that of treating with Indians. Wozencraft, one of the three commissioners, earlier had been a delegate to the California constitutional convention at Monterey in 1849, and we quote in chapter 4 some of his remarks about Negroes and Indians. One can only conclude that the treaty-making of 1851–1852 was something other than an honest and sincere attempt on the part of the federal government, through its

4. R. W. Kenny, *History and Proposed Settlement of Indian Claims in California.*

three commissioners, to help the Indians whose lands had been overrun.

Treaty Pattern

The first two treaties set the pattern for those that followed; large defined tracts of land within the state were assigned the Indians for their sole occupancy and use "forever." The Indians, in turn, agreed to recognize the United States as sole sovereign of all land occupied by them ceded by Mexico, placed themselves under the protection of the United States, and agreed to keep the peace. Measures to improve the condition of the Indians by providing school teachers, farmers, blacksmiths, and farm animals and implements were promised. In most instances subsistence, largely in the form of beef cattle, was granted the Indians, to be delivered to them during 1851–1852 while they were removing to and getting settled on the reservations. The text of a typical treaty, made in 1851, is reprinted in the documents section, p. 221.

The commissioners did not always gain the full cooperation of the Indians whom they searched out in order to negotiate these treaties. The following account of treaties made by the Indian commissioners in the San Joaquin region, giving names of tribes, was published in the *Daily Alta California*, May 10, 1851:

> The *Pit-cach-es*, *Cas-soes*, *Toom-nas*, *Tal-lin-ches*, and *Paske-sas* are subject to chief Tom-quit. The *Wa-cha-hets*, *I-tech-es*, *Cho-e-nim-nis*, *Cho-ki-me-nas*, *No-to-no-tos* and *We-mal-ches* are under a Grand Chief called Pas-qual. There are parts of 2 or 3 tribes which would not come in to treat. Some of these, it is understood, are fractions of the *Chow-chil-hes*. The commissioners finding it impossible to treat with them, Major Savage with 3 companies moved against them, came up with them with only a river between, and had a skirmish, killing 2 or 3 of them.

We do not know how often Indian groups which failed or refused the invitation to come to treat were retaliated against in this manner. Such actions, however, probably became known and had the effect of making it appear wiser for invited groups to attend the treaty-making sessions than to boycott them.

The Legislature and the Treaties

The California legislature's reaction to the federal treaties was one of strong objection. The senate and assembly in 1851 each appointed a committee to look into the matter of the treaties. The members reappraised the land the commissioners had considered practically worthless. The assembly committee was eloquent in its report.[5] The committee reported to the effect that if these reservation areas were actually set aside, the "enterprising population" (which had preempted the Indian lands in the first place and had shown no mercy toward the native occupants) would be "deprived of all their improvements, discoveries, and hard-earned acquisitions."

> The committee to whom was referred the subject of Indian reservations, have had the subject under consideration and beg to leave to submit the following report:
>
> Your committee have learned, with unfeigned regret, that many and extensive reservations of land have been made in various sections of this State for the exclusive occupation and use of the Indian tribes within its limits. These reservations, as your committee are satisfactorily informed, embrace within their limits, in a large majority of instances, extensive tracts of the most desirable mineral and agricultural lands in California. Many of them include large, permanent, and populous settlements of enterprising American citizens who had located upon and acquired rights and interests in the soil long anterior to the conclusion of these treaties with the Indians. These rights and interests have been acquired by the pioneer miner and agriculturist in good faith, upon the implied assurance that the same privileges and immunities would be extended to the toil-worn emigrant in California that has been extended to the first settlers of other new countries within the limits of our Government. Immense labor, exposure, and suffering has been incurred in making discoveries, developing the resources, and making available the immense tracts of mineral lands included in many of the reservations. Rich and inexhaustible veins of gold-bearing quartz, for the purpose of the successful and lucrative working of which many thousands of dollars have been expended in purchasing quartz machinery, have, in the wisdom of the Indian agents,

5. California, *Assembly Journal*, 1852, pp. 202–205.

been considered eligible locations for the untutored tribes of the wilderness, and have accordingly been set apart for that purpose, and the energetic and zealous miner has been rudely ordered by those agents to abandon their claims and go beyond the limits of the reservations. Comfortable family residences have been built on many of them and large tracts of lands put in a high state of cultivation; all of which, by the provisions of the several treaties made with the Indians, will have to be abandoned without the remotest hope of anything like adequate compensation.

These reservations have been made in most of the counties in the State, from the forty-second parallel of north latitude to the southern boundary; and a large majority, if not all of them embrace some of the best mineral and agricultural lands within its limits. Your committee are of opinion that, in the aggregate, these reservations include a population of not less than 20,000 American citizens, and they are also of opinion that the aggregate value of those reservations is not less than $100,000,000.

Your committee have had no means of ascertaining the precise extent of each reservation, but they are satisfied that they are generally from 20 to 30 miles square in extent.

The foregoing are the facts with regard to the Indian reservations as your committee have learned them from sources of the most undoubted character.

After gleaning the facts your committee have considered attentively what would be the probable effects of these wholesale Indian donations upon the prosperity of our fellow citizens who are embraced in them, their effects upon the general interests of the people of the whole State, and also as affecting the welfare of the Indians who were intended to be benefited by them.

As regards the farmers and operative miners who have been embraced within the limits of the reservations the direct effects would be of the most deplorable character. Their acquisitions have been made through immense sacrifices, exposure, and suffering. Dangers and difficulties have been sternly and resolutely met, and the most formidable obstacles encountered. This fact is attested by the careworn faces and emaciated forms to be seen in the deep, dark recesses of every mountain. There is not a mountain stream in California on which is not to be found some sad momento attesting the blasted hopes and wounded expectation of the pioneer miners. They have upheaved the bowels of the earth, diverted the streams from their natural channels, and sent them rushing through the tunneled mountain. Should those reservations be confirmed through the recommendation of the Indian agents, a large class of this enterprising population would be totally deprived of all their improvements, discoveries, and hard-earned acquisitions. They would be forced to shoulder their picks and shovels and seek new fields for the exercise of their enterprise and valor in the unexplored recesses of the mountains. The only plea for the necessity of which is to make room for the introduction and settlement of a few tribes of ignorant barbarians.

The confirmation of these reservations would, in the opinion of your committee, have a most deleterious effect upon the general prosperity of the whole State. The taxable property which would be swept from the State would be immense, which would bring on a corresponding increase of taxation upon other portions of the State. It would make a desert, so far as the interests of the citizens of this State is concerned, of a very large portion of the most desirable mineral and agricultural lands within its borders. California contains but a comparatively small proportion of agricultural lands, and it is greatly to the interests of all classes of her citizens to have as few restrictions and monopolies engrafted upon them as possible. If they are unencumbered they will in a few years be settled and cultivated and will yield ample supplies of all the necessaries and luxuries of life for our population who now obtain their supplies from commerce. But if they are set apart for the exclusive occupation and use of the Indians, the loss to the State and National Governments could not be less than a hundred millions of dollars—at a fair computation of the mineral and agricultural lands.

Viewing these reservations simply as affecting the interests of happiness of the Indians, they are, in the opinion of your committee, most unfortunate selections. The character and habits of the Indian and white populations are totally different. They are by nature unsuited for the society of each other. There is a feeling of hostility existing between them, which is the growth of centuries. The Indian is naturally prone to steal and otherwise depredate upon the white population, and the white man in retaliation takes the life of the Indian; and thus there is produced a continual state of hostility between them. All experience has demonstrated the fact that close contiguity to the white man is not the place for the Indian. This fact is clearly evinced by the history of that unfortunate race from the foundation of our Government to the present time. To avert the danger of a too close proximity, the National Government has for many years adopted the policy of removing the Indians beyond the limits of civilization.

The danger to the Indians attending the adoption of the policy of the Indian agents in this State would be that they would be thrown into immediate contact with a far more powerful and formidable race of people than themselves, and their frequent depredations upon the white settlements would cause certain retaliation, which would result in their complete extermination. Moreover, those reservations are not at all adapted to the wants and necessities of the Indian tribes of this country. For ages they have been in the habit of wandering with unrestricted freedom along the margin of the various streams and over the hunting grounds in this country and subsisting upon the profuse contributions of a beneficent Providence. But now how changed the scene. The march of mind and the energy of civilization has driven the red man from his wigwam and his hunting grounds, and the farmer has leveled many of his acorn trees to the earth. He no longer finds the boundless and unrestricted privileges to which he has been accustomed.

Your committee are therefore of opinion that, considering the character and habits of the Indians—their dispositions and propensities—that instead of being thrown into positions of close contiguity with the white population, they should be removed to regions abounding in game and fish, and which presents all the natural facilities for obtaining their subsistence, to which, from time immemorial, they have been familiarly accustomed.

In conclusion, your committee deem it not inappropriate to state that they have been satisfactorily informed that persons in the employ of the Indian agents have invested considerable capital in mining claims included within the reservations. Claims have been sold to these men by the miners at extremely reduced prices, under the impression that they would be forced to abandon them in a short time. In this way frauds to a great extent have been practiced upon the unsuspecting miner, as your committee have been credibly informed. In the Scott's Valley reservations, in the northern part of this State, preemption claims have been taken up on said reservation by the very men who accompanied the commissioner to that place, and numerous mining claims have been purchased within the limits of that reservation by men who accompanied the agent to that section of the country.

They would state further that the several agents, instead of giving out the contracts for supplying the Indians with beef and other articles in the usual way, by publishing for the lowest bidder, they have given out those contracts to persons who have been, and are now, furnishing supplies to the Indians at immense profits, and to the injury of the National Government many thousands of dollars.

All of which your committee respectfully submit for the consideration of this house, and recommend the adoption of the following resolutions:

Resolved, That our Senators in Congress be instructed and our Representatives requested to use all proper means to prevent Congress confirming the Indian reservations which have been made in this State, but respectfully to insist that the same policy be adopted with regard to the Indian tribes in California which has been adopted in other new States.

Resolved, That our Senators in Congress be instructed and our Representatives requested to urge upon Congress the great evils that would inevitably result to the people of California, the National Government, and the Indian tribes by the confirmation of those reservations.

Resolved, That our Senators in Congress be instructed and our Representatives requested to urge upon the proper authorities at Washington the importance of instituting a rigid inquiry into the official conduct of the several Indian agents for California, as, in the opinion of the legislature, high-handed and unprecedented frauds have been perpetrated by them against the General Government and the citizens of California.

Resolved, That the governor be, and he is hereby, requested to transmit a copy of each of the foregoing resolutions to the President of the United States and to each of our Senators and Representatives in Congress.

THOMAS H. COATS, *Chairman*
S. A. MERRITT
JAMES W. COFFROTH
W. P. JONES

The Majority Report of the Special Committee of the California Assembly, as we have seen, objected strongly to the treaties and proposed that the California senators in Congress "be instructed to oppose the confirmation of any and all treaties with Indians of the State of California" as well as proposing that the Indians be removed "beyond the limits of the State in which they are found with all practicable dispatch."

The Minority Report of the Special Committee of the California Senate, written by J. J. Warner,[6] reads in part:

6. California, *Senate Journal*, 3d sess., 1852, pp. 602–604.

To remove the Indians from this State, I consider as impracticable: there is no place within the territory of the United States in which to locate them. We cannot suppose that the General Government will remove them to Oregon, to Utah, New Mexico, or to the Indian territory east of the Rocky Mountains. And where else will you locate them? On the desert and sterile regions east of the Sierra Nevada, that they may die of starvation? or if, perchance, a few survive, that they may become the Arabs of America? Better, far better, drive them at once into the ocean, or bury them in the land of their birth.

We might stop here, and recommend our government to permit the Indians to remain in their present habits and locations, were it not for that spirit of occupation and appropriation so irresistible to our race. But the public land must be surveyed, must be cut into sections and quarter sections, and if not donated to the State, or settlers, they must be left free for occupancy, by pre-emption, right or sale; and, if not sooner then comes the difficulty. The settler selects the site of an Indian village—he soon wants the land which they occupy—he cuts down the oak, or the pine from which he gathers the nut—he dams the streams and cuts off his periodical supply of fish. The Indian looks on the white man as the aggressor, and stimulated by passion; goaded on by suffering and hunger; he retaliates. War with all its horrors succeeds, and the few who escape death, are removed a few miles into the interior, there to reproduce themselves to suffer in succeeding years a repetition of the same wrongs.

The policy to which, to me, appears more worthy of a nation whose empire extends from sea to sea, and whose area has, within three-fourths of a century, expanded from 521,660 to 3,221,595 square miles, if not one should seek to raise the character of the Indian, to civilize, refine and enlighten, should at least be one that could tolerate their existence, and even allow them a resting and abiding place, on the clay from which they formed. That sufficient portions of land, in different parts of the State, should be appropriated for the cultivation and residence of all such Indians as might need a home; here they would be ennobled, and escape that certain destruction which awaits them on every other side. Here philanthropy and charity, hand in hand, might find a field in which to labor. From them, the farmer, grazier and owner of vineyards, might derive their accustomed and needed laborers. Will it be said that the land is not broad enough for them and us? or that while our doors are open to the stranger from the uttermost parts of the earth, we have not spare room for the residence of the once sole inhabitants of our magnificent empire? Shall future

75

generations seek in vain for one remaining descendant of the sons of the forest? Has the love of gold blotted from our minds all feelings of compassion or justice?

Fate of the Treaties

The California treaties were sent to the United States Senate on June 1, 1852, with the president's recommendation that they be confirmed. The president could scarcely have done otherwise, even though he was by that time fully aware of the sentiments of the California senators and the California legislature. The president had, after all, appointed the treaty commissioners and had given them their instructions, and was hardly in a position to take it upon himself to publicly reject their work. On July 7, 1852, the United States Senate rejected the treaties secretly, and for fifty years they remained classified and were forgotten by all but the Indians until they were made public on January 18, 1905.

What is now clear is that these commissioners tried to make treaties with Indians in various parts of the state, and that they were more assiduous in looking up Indians in the Sierra Nevada region where the gold-mining activity was being carried on. The desert tribes of southeastern California were not visited, probably because their lands were considered useless. No Indians east of the Sierras were visited. As the three commissioners moved about separately they inquired locally about Indians, and from time to time made a camp, sent out requests that "chiefs, captains and headmen" of the local tribes appear on a certain day. When the Indians were assembled they were informed of the provisions of the treaty and asked to sign—in nearly every case each to make his "mark" with an X. The eighteen treaties contain the signatures or marks of 139 representatives of what were called—and probably the commissioners believed them to be—tribes. Using our present knowledge of California Indians, we can identify 67 of the group names as those of tribes or subtribes (tribelets). Forty-five of the names are those of villages. Fourteen names are duplicates, usually in the form of variant spellings of names of villages or tribelets written down without the commissioners apparently being aware of that fact. Two supposed tribes are only personal names of the native signers. Eleven names are not now identifiable —they may be villages, tribelets, or personal names. Of the 52 major tribal groups in California, only 14 are represented, and these either by one or two tribelets out of dozens, or at times by a single village of a tribelet. If it is assumed that the Indians were fully aware that they were ceding their land and were acting with the full knowledge of their village—or tribelet—mates, and if we plot the actual extent of territory held by each of the tribelets or villages whose representatives signed the treaties, we learn that between 6 and 7 percent of the land area of California was involved. A simple map of California is provided here showing the reservation areas specified in the eighteen treaties and the lands ceded by the Indians in return for government aid and a reservation refuge. It would be difficult to find an example of treaty-making in which so few persons without any power to act were assumed to have released control of so much land that did not belong to them.

Senator John B. Weller of California expressed what was generally held to be the reasons why the United States Senate rejected the treaties:

> We who represent the state of California were compelled, from a sense of duty, to vote for the rejection of the treaties, because we knew it would be utterly impossible for the general government to retain these Indians in the undisturbed possession of these reservations. Why, there were as many as six reservations made in a single county in the state of California, and that one of the best mining counties in the state. They knew that these reservations included mineral lands, and that, just so soon as it became profitable to dig upon the reservations than elsewhere, the white man would go there, and that the whole army of the United States could not expel the intruders.
>
> It was, therefore, under this stern necessity that we were compelled to reject the treaties; and now after the Indians have complied with them—after they have done everything in their power to execute them in good faith, by coming down out of their old homes and occupying the reservations, I only ask that an appropriation of $100,000 should be made for their temporary relief—for their support under the circumstances in which they have been placed by the rejection of

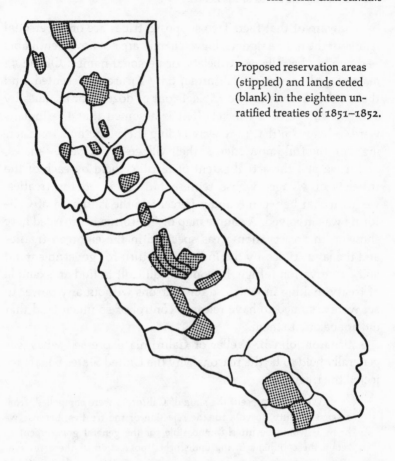

Proposed reservation areas (stippled) and lands ceded (blank) in the eighteen un-ratified treaties of 1851–1852.

the treaties by this branch of the government. . . . It will be hard indeed to explain to these Indians how it came that the formal treaties made with your accredited agents have been violated.[7]

Apparently Washington realized that something had to be done to alleviate the desperate situation of Indians in California. In a letter dated September 4, 1852, to Edward Beale, now super-intendent of Indian affairs for California and replacing the three Indian agents (McKee, Wozencraft, and Barbour), the commis-

7. *Congressional Globe*, 32d Cong., 1st sess., p. 2173.

sioner of Indian affairs stated that one of the items approved by Congress on August 30, 1852, for the Indian Service in California was an appropriation of $100,000

> for the preservation of peace with those Indians who have been dis-possessed of their lands in California, until permanent arrangements can be made for their future settlement. . . . Of the appropriation of $100,000 made for the preservation of peace among the Indian Tribes of California, the treaties having been rejected by the Senate, it has been determined to apply $25,000 to the purchase of suitable presents for those Indians who have been dispossessed of their lands, and for transportation of the same. This purchase will be made by or under the direction of Pearson B. Reading, esq. of whose experience, and knowledge of what is most suitable for the Indians of California, the department desires to avail itself; and it will be made in time for the goods to be shipped to your address, by the steamer of the 20th: instant.[8]

Article XI of the Treaty of Guadalupe Hidalgo bound the United States to observe that "special care shall . . . be taken not to place its Indian occupants under the necessity of seeking new homes" when removal of Indians was carried out or settlement was made by citizens of the United States. The federal government could legitimately claim that it was acting correctly in 1851 in terms of this article of the treaty between the United States and Mexico when it made the eighteen treaties with the California Indians. But in 1853, Edward F. Beale, superintendent of Indian affairs in California, in his report to the commissioner of Indian affairs provided ample documentation to support his assessment of the condition of the California Indians "who are reduced to despair—their country, and all support, taken away from them; no resting place, where they can be safe, death on one hand from starvation, and on the other by killing and hanging."

Some Later Treaties

After the major attempt of the government to make treaties with the Indians in the early 1850s had failed, the government

8. U.S., Congress, *Senate Document* 4, pp. 29–30 (1853).

still maintained a policy as mediator between the various groups of Indians when disputes arose between them. In 1867 a treaty was signed between the Mohave and Chemehuevis with the help of federal arbitration, which established peace between the tribes and, going a step further, outlined the boundaries of the area in which the tribes lived. In other words, by a treaty of peace between two Indian tribes the federal government actually declared and recognized the right of occupation of certain territories to specific groups of Indians.

A copy of a treaty between the Mohave and Chemehuevis tribes of Indians, signed March 21, 1867, is on file in the War Department with the annual report of the commander of the Department of California for 1867. It is reprinted in the documents section, p. 224.

The treaty made with the Klamath and Modoc Indians in October 1864 was not observed by either the Indians or the government, and the misunderstandings which resulted ultimately led to the Modoc War of 1872–1873, in which the Modoc Indians, under Captain Jack, gave an excellent account of themselves against regular army troops.[9] In March 1873 an attempt was made at arranging a peace, and Captain Jack indicated that he was tired of fighting and wished to lead his people to another area where they could live in peace. In this attempt at mediation Captain Jack said:

> I wish to live like the white men. Let everything be wiped out, washed out, and let there be no more blood. . . . I have got but a few men, and don't see how I can give them up. Will they [the whites] give up their people who murdered my people while they were asleep? I never asked for the people who murdered my people. I only talked that way. I can see how I could give up my horse to be hanged, but I cannot see how I could give up my men to be hanged. I could give up my horse to be hanged and wouldn't cry about it; but if I gave up my men I would have to cry about it. I want them all to have good hearts now. I have

9. J. M. Allen, *We-ne-ma*; W. H. Boyle, *Personal Observations on the Conduct of the Modoc War*; C. T. Brady, *Northwestern Fights and Fighters*; W. S. Brown, *California Northeast, the Bloody Ground*; D. P. Payne, *Captain Jack, Modoc Renegade*.

thrown away everything. There must be no more bad talk. I will not. I have spoken forever. I want soldiers all to go home. I have given up now, and want no more fuss. I have said yes, and thrown away my country. I want soldiers to go away, so I will not be afraid.[10]

Captain Jack's intentions were judged not to be trusted since he objected to giving up some of his men who had killed some whites, and the war continued. After further killing on both sides the Modocs were defeated, six of the Indian leaders were hanged at Fort Klamath in October 1873, and the defeated tribe was split up, part being sent to Indian territory and located on the Quapaw reservation and the balance to the Klamath reservation in Oregon.[11]

Indians on Reservations

After the treaty rejection the government had induced many of the California tribes to move to temporary reservations, but many were at once driven off by white miners and settlers. Reprisals by the evicted Indians then made the situation worse than before. Congress was forced to act and did so by authorizing establishment of reservations. On April 13, 1853, Jefferson Davis, secretary of war, whose department had charge of Indian affairs, notified the commander, Headquarters Department of the Pacific at Benicia:

> By an act [Indian Appropriation Act of March 3, 1853] passed at the last session of Congress, the President is authorized to make five military reservations from the public domain, of not exceeding 25,000 acres in the state of California or in the territories of Utah and New Mexico bordering on said state, with the view of removing the California Indians thereto for subsistence and protection.[12]

The first such reservation was established at Tejon in late 1853 and the second in September 1854 at Nome Lackee, twenty miles west of the town of Tehama. T. J. Henley, successor to E. F. Beale as superintendent of Indian affairs in California, in 1854 urged

10. H. H. Bancroft, *California inter pocula*, pp. 523–524.
11. Ibid., pp. 446–560.
12. U.S., Congress, *House Executive Document 76*, 34th Cong., 3d sess., 1857, p. 79.

the establishment of three additional reservations, one of which would be outside the state and east of the Sierra Nevadas and to which all California Indians would ultimately be removed in order to "rid the state of this class of population." With two of the three authorized California reservations in operation, Congress in March 1855 authorized the creation of two more reserves, making five in all. The Mendocino, Fresno, and Klamath reservations were formed in 1856 and 1857. Some of these had a short life, and by 1867 there were only four authorized reservations— Hoopa Valley, Round Valley, Smith River, and Tule River.[13]

In spite of a declaration by authorities that residence of Indians on the reserve was to be optional and that military assistance did not extend to collecting Indians and keeping them on the reservation against their will, soldiers were sent to gather the Indians from the eastern half of the Sacramento Valley and take them across the river to Nome Lackee. The story of the brutality of this military expedition is partially described by Anne H. Currie when she discusses the Bidwell Rancheria.[14] The "Bidwell Indians" of the Sacramento Valley under the protection of General Bidwell were the only group who were not forced on the "death march," as later generations would refer to this episode.

Other problems plagued the Indians on the newly formed reservations. General John E. Wool, in a letter to Senator John B. Weller, dated Benicia, California, October 5, 1856, states that the Nome Lackee reserve had not been surveyed and therefore, it appeared to him, "the military would have no right to expel a white man from the reserve, nor to interfere with him even if he should take from the reserve one or more squaws, or one or more Indian children."[15]

13. For a review of federal Indian policy and reservation history, see E. E. Dale, *The Indians of the Southwest: A Century of Development under the United States*, chaps. 4 and 6; W. H. Ellison, "The Federal Indian Policy in California, 1846–1860"; A. W. Hoopes, *Indian Affairs and Their Administration with Special Reference to the Far West, 1849–1860*.

14. "Bidwell Rancheria."

15. U.S., Congress, *House Document 76, Indian Affairs on the Pacific*, 34th Cong., 3d sess., 1857, p. 144.

Food and Fraud

Besides the fact that the Indians could not feel safely protected on a government reservation against the attacks of white
men, they quickly learned that they were not going to get the aid
that had been promised to them. In 1874, the Honorable J. K.
Luttrell asserted in Congress that of the fifteen annual appropriations which had been made for a certain tribe the Indians had
never received a dollar of them, the Indian agents having appropriated the money to themselves.[16] The following indicates the
informal methods by which Indian relief appropriations were being distributed by government agents in the lower San Joaquin
Valley.[17]

> *Memorandum of Conversation of Superintendent Beale with Agent*
> *O. M. Wozencraft, San Francisco, September 14, 1852*
>
> Question 1. With whom were your contracts for beef made?
> Answer. The first with Mr. S. Norris.
> Question 2. By whom were they issued to the Indians?
> Answer. By the traders appointed by myself.
> Question 3. What proof had you that they were issued to the Indians?
> Answer. No other proof than the word of the traders themselves.
> Question 4. How were the weights estimated?
> Answer. By asking any persons who might be on the ground to say
>   what they thought the average weight of the drove to be.
> Question 5. Have you any further proof than the mere word of the
>   traders, that the Indians ever received the beef without paying
>   for it?
> Answer. None; I have not any. I generally saw the beef which was
>   issued during the negotiation of the treaties. It was not weighed.
> Question 6. Have you not given drafts on the government for cattle
>   which are not yet delivered?
> Answer. Yes.
> Question 7. Have you not ordered beef to the amount of fifteen hun-
>   dred head to be delivered between the Fresno and Four Creeks,
>   without ever having been in the Four Creeks region?
> Answer. I have never been to the Four Creeks region, but have or-
>   dered the beef.

16. S. Powers, *Tribes of California*, p. 247.
17. U.S., *Senate Exec. Doc.* no. 57, 32d Cong., 2d sess., 1853, pp. 2–3.

Question 8. How many Indians do you suppose the Four Creeks country to contain?

Answer. I do not know.

Question 9. If you did not know, how could you determine the amount of cattle necessary for their subsistence?

Answer. From what was promised them by the treaties.

Question 10. How do you know that the Indians of the Four Creeks ever received any of that beef?

Answer. Nothing further than that I was told so by the traders at the Fresno. I have no proof of it.

Question 11. How far is the Fresno from the Four Creeks?

Answer. Eighty miles.

Question 12. Do you not know that, in some instances, the traders who issued and the contractors for the supply of the beef were the same men?

Answer. I do.

Question 13. Were the contracts made by you verbal, or written?

Answer. With Mr. Norris my contract was simply a verbal one: with Messrs. Savage and Haler it was, on my part, the acceptance from them of a proposition, which I understood was the same as a contract.

I have sometimes, when on a visit to the reservations, seen the traders killing beef for the Indians, but do not know whether it was the beef furnished by me or not. It was the impression on my mind, however, that it was the beef of the government. I was told it was so.

I acknowledge the above answers as those made to E. F. Beale, in reply to questions put by him, in his official capacity as superintendent of Indian affairs for California.

O. M. WOZENCRAFT

U.S. Indian Agent

Beale also secured the following statement from one Joel H. Brooks who was employed by J. Savage, "an Indian trader on the Fresno." Savage received 1,900 head of cattle (purchased by the government from Col. J. C. Frémont) from the Indian agent, G. W. Barbour, and was supposed to distribute them to Indians for their support. Brooks says, however,

My instructions from Savage were that when I delivered cattle on the San Joaquin and King's river, and to other more southern Indians, I

84

was to take receipts for double the number actually delivered, and to make no second delivery in case any should return to the band; and when to Indians on the Fresno, to deliver one-third less than were receipted for. I also had orders to sell all beef I could to miners, which I did to the amount of $120 or $130, and to deliver cattle to his clerks, to be sold to the Indians on the San Joaquin, at twenty-five cents per pound; and I know that such sales were made to those Indians. In October I received a written order from Savage to deliver to Alexander Godey seventy-eight head of cattle, to be driven to the mines, and there sold to miners and others. I was also requested, in the same communication, to destroy the order as soon as read—which was done, after I had read it aloud in the presence of Godey, P. Rainbolt, Jose de Soto, and Theodore McNabb. In November I received a similar order to deliver to Godey four hundred and fifty head, which was done. . . . About the last of November . . . I moved the cattle in my possession on to the river Fresno, and delivered to P. Rainbolt, a person appointed by Savage to receive them, eight hundred head. I also gave Savage receipts to the number of seventeen hundred head, which I had taken from the Indians.[18]

It will thus be seen that the Indians got very little help from this attempt to provide them with food, and that Barbour, the Indian agent, and Savage, the trader, did very well for themselves.

Pitiable Conditions

. J. Ross Browne was appointed by the federal government in May 1857 to investigate the condition of Indians in California, Washington, and Oregon. He was obviously sympathetic to their pitiable state, and properly attributed this to the generally lawless conditions prevailing and a more or less diffident federal authority in Washington, which did not really know what its agents were doing on the Pacific shore. What he recounts is a tale of exploitation and cruel, heartless suppression of any efforts to better the Indians' condition. We submit a portion of his lengthy, often ironical, discussion of the California Indians:

> The settlers in the northern portions of the state had [an] effective method of encouraging the Indians to adopt habits of civilization. In

18. Ibid., pp. 4–5.

general, they engaged them at a fixed rate of wages to cultivate the ground, and during the season of labor fed them on beans, and gave them a blanket or a shirt each; after which, when the harvest was secured, the account was considered squared, and the Indians were driven off to forage in the woods for themselves and their families during the winter. Starvation usually wound up a considerable number of the old and decrepit ones every season; and of those that failed to perish from hunger or exposure, some were killed on the general principle that they must have subsisted by stealing cattle, for it was well known that cattle ranged in the vicinity, while others were not unfrequently slaughtered by their employers for helping themselves to the refuse portions of the crop which had been left in the ground. It may be said that these were exceptions to the general rule; but if ever an Indian was fully and honestly paid for his labor by a white settler, it was not my luck to hear of it; certainly it could not have been a frequent occurrence.

The wild Indians inhabiting the Coast Range, the valleys of the Sacramento and San Joaquin, and the western slope of the Sierra Nevada, became troublesome at a very early period after the discovery of the gold mines. It was found convenient to take possession of their country without recompense, rob them of their wives and children, kill them in every cowardly and barbarous manner that could be devised, and when that was impracticable, drive them as far as possible out of the way. Such treatment was not consistent with their rude ideas of justice. At best they were an ignorant race of Diggers, wholly unacquainted with our enlightened institutions. They could not understand why they should be murdered, robbed, and hunted down in this way, without any other pretense of provocation than the color of their skin and the habits of life to which they had always been accustomed. . . . The idea, strange as it may appear, never occurred to them that they were suffering for the great cause of civilization, which, in the natural course of things, must exterminate Indians. Actuated by base motives of resentment, a few of them occasionally rallied, preferring rather to die than submit to these imaginary wrongs. . . .

The federal government, as is usual in cases where the lives of valuable voters are at stake, was forced to interfere. Troops were sent out to aid the settlers in slaughtering the Indians. By means of mounted howitzers, muskets, Minie rifles, dragoon pistols, and sabres, a good many were cut to pieces. But, on the whole, the general policy of the government was pacific. It was not designed to kill any more Indians than might be necessary to secure the adhesion of the honest yeo-

86

manry of the state, and thus furnish an example of the practical work-ing of our political system to the savages of the forest, by which it was hoped they might profit. Congress took the matter in hand at an early day, and appropriated large sums of money for the purchase of cattle and agricultural implements. From the wording of the law, it would appear that these useful articles were designed for the relief and maintenance of the Indians. Commissioners were appointed at handsome salaries to treat with them, and sub-agents employed to superintend the distribution of the purchases. By virtue of this munif-icent policy, treaties were made [in 1851–1852] in which the various tribes were promised a great many valuable presents, which of course they never got. There was no reason to suppose they ever should; it being a fixed principle with strong powers never to ratify treaties made by their own agents with weaker ones, when there is money to pay and nothing to be had in return.

The cattle were purchased, however, to the number of many thousands. Here arose another difficulty. The honest miners must have something to eat, and what could they have more nourishing than fat cattle? . . . So the cattle, or the greater part of them, were driven up to the mines, and sold at satisfactory rates—probably for the benefit of the Indians, though I never could understand in what way their necessities were relieved by this speculation, unless it might be that the parties interested turned over to them the funds received for the cattle. It is very certain they continued to starve and commit depreda-tions in the most ungrateful manner for some time after; and, indeed, to such a pitch of audacity did they carry their rebellious spirit against the constituted authorities, that many of the chiefs protested if the white people would only let them alone, and give them the least pos-sible chance to make a living, they would esteem it a much greater favor than any relief they had experienced from the munificent dona-tions of Congress.

[In 1853 with the establishment of reservations, officials were appointed to provide aid and instruction to the Indians on these tracts.] In order that the appropriations might be devoted to their legitimate purpose, and the greatest possible amount of instruction furnished at the least expense, the Executive Department adopted the policy of selecting officers experienced in the art of public speaking, and thor-oughly acquainted with the prevailing systems of primary elections. A similar policy had been found to operate beneficially in the case of Collectors of Customs, and there was no reason why it should not in other branches of the public service. Gentlemen skilled in the tactics of state Legislatures, and capable of influencing those refractory bodies by the exercise of moral suasion, could be relied upon to deal with the Indians, who are not so far advanced in the arts of civilization, and whose necessities, in a pecuniary point of view, are not usually so urgent. Besides, it was known that the Digger tribes were exceedingly ignorant of our political institutions, and required more instruction, perhaps, in this branch of knowledge than in any other. The most intelligent of the chiefs actually had no more idea of the respective merits of the great candidates for senatorial honors in California than if those distinguished gentlemen had never been born. As to primary meetings and caucuses, the poor Diggers, in their simplicity, were just as apt to mistake them for some favorite game of thimblerig or pitch-penny as for the exercise of the great system of free suffrage. The California delegation made it a point never to endorse any person for office in the service who was not considered peculiarly deserving of patronage. They knew exactly the kind of men that were wanted, because they lived in the state and had read about the Indians in the newspapers. Some of them had even visited a few of the wigwams. Having the public welfare at heart—a fact that cannot be doubted, since they repeatedly asserted it in their speeches—they saw where the greatest difficulty lay, and did all in their power to aid the executive. They endorsed the very best friends they had—gentlemen who had contributed to their election, and fought for them through thick and thin. The capacity of such persons for conducting the affairs of a reservation could not be doubted. If they had cultivated an extensive acquaintance among pot-house voters, of course they must understand the cultivation of potatoes and onions; if they could control half a dozen members of the Legislature in a senatorial contest, why not be able to control Indians, who were not near so difficult to manage? If they could swallow obnoxious measures of the administration, were they not qualified to teach savages how to swallow government provisions? If they were honest enough to avow, in the face of corrupt and hostile factions, that they stood by the Constitution, and always meant to stand by the same broad platform, were they not honest enough to disburse public funds?

In one respect, I think the policy of the government was unfortunate—that is, in the disfavor with which persons of intemperate and disreputable habits were regarded. Men of this kind—and they are not difficult to find in California—could do a great deal toward meliorating the moral condition of the Indians by drinking up all the whisky that might be smuggled on the reservations, and behaving so disreputable in general that no Indian, however degraded in his propensities, could fail to become ashamed of such low vices.

[Speaking of the blankets and clothes which were issued to reservation Indians, Browne has the following to say:] The blankets, to be sure, were very thin, and cost a great deal of money in proportion to their value; but then, peculiar advantages were to be derived from the transparency of the fabric. In some respects the worst material might be considered the most economical. By holding his blanket to the light, an Indian could enjoy the contemplation of both sides of it at the same time; and it would only require a little instruction in architecture to enable him to use it occasionally as a window to his wigwam. . . . Nor was it the least important consideration, that when he gambled it away, or sold it for whisky, he would not be subject to any inconvenience from a change of temperature. The shirts and pantaloons were in general equally transparent, and possessed this additional advantage, that they very soon cracked open in the seams, and thereby enabled the squaws to learn how to sew.[19]

In 1862 William F. Dole, commissioner for Indian affairs, reported as follows to the secretary of the interior:

The condition of the Indians in California is one of peculiar hardship, and I know of no people who have more righteous claims upon the justice and liberality of the American people. Owing to the discovery of its mines, the fertility of its soil, and the salubrity of its climate, that State within a few years past became the recipient of a tide of emigration almost unexampled in history. Down to the time of the commencement of this emigration nature supplied all the wants of the Indians in profusion. They lived in the midst of the greatest abundance, and were free, contented, and happy. The emigration began, and every part of the State was overrun, as it were, in a day. All, or nearly so, of the fertile valleys were seized; the mountain gulches and ravines were filled with miners; and without the slightest recognition of the Indians' rights, they were dispossessed of their homes, their hunting grounds, their fisheries, and, to a great extent of the productions of the earth. From a position of independence they were at once reduced to the most abject dependence. With no one of the many tribes of the State is there an existing treaty. Despoiled by irresistible force of the land of their

19. J. Ross Browne, *Crusoe's Island: A Ramble in the Footsteps of Alexander Selkirk, with Sketches of Adventure in California and Washoe*, pp. 285–292. See also "The Coast Rangers II: The Indian Reservations"; and *The Indians of California.*

fathers; with no country on earth to which they can migrate; in the midst of a people with whom they cannot assimilate, they have no recognized claims upon the government, and are almost compelled to become vagabonds—*to steal or to starve*. They are not even unmolested upon the scanty reservations we set apart for their use. Upon one pretext or another, even these are invaded by the whites, and it is literally true that there is no place where the Indian can experience that feeling of security which is the effect of just and wholesome laws, or where he can plant with any assurance that he shall reap the fruits of his labor. . . . It is now perhaps too late to correct this error by making treaties, and it only remains for us to do voluntarily that justice which we have refused to acknowledge in the form of treaty obligations.[20]

Much has been written about the "Mission Indians" of Southern California and we will not try to summarize this here. The plight of these remnants of once-missionized tribes has been no better or worse than that of other less well advertised survivors scattered in tiny hamlets in out-of-the-way places throughout the state. The reason the Mission Indians are better known is that in 1873 John G. Ames was sent by the commissioner of Indian affairs to investigate the conditions of the Mission Indians, and his report[21] attracted wide attention among the public which was developing a concern for the suffering of these people. In 1875 C. A. Wetmore, special commissioner to the Mission Indians, wrote a more detailed report on conditions, and as we can see from the following excerpt, it was an eloquent one:

The Indians have been forced by superior power to trade their patrimony and their liberties for civilized bubbles blown by the breath of political insincerity; trading by compulsion from bad to worse until they have, as the Mission Indians of California, simply the right to beg. They beg bread of their white neighbors on whose lands they are trespassers; on the roads where they are vagrants; and in the jails which are their only asylums. They have begged in vain for legal rights. Their right to petition to Congress has been ignored.[22]

20. *Report of the Commissioner of Indian Affairs for 1862*, pp. 39–40 (1863).
21. Published in *House Executive Document* 91, 43d Cong., 1st sess., 1873.
22. *Report on the Mission Indians in California*. Washington, D.C., 1875, p. 3.

Helen Hunt Jackson's *A Century of Dishonor* (1881) also helped arouse interest in the Indian's cause, and as a result an improvement of conditions came about.[23]

Legal Rights to Lands

The question of the legal rights of the Indians of California to lands which they had been permitted to occupy by both Mexico and the United States is complex.[24] In 1851 Congress enacted a law which required all claimants to land in California to present their claims within a given time to a board of land commissioners. Most of the mission Indians, unaware of these requirements, failed to comply with the law, and when holders of Spanish or Mexican grants began to force them to move, they brought suit in the California Supreme Court. For a discussion of court decisions on the Indian and the land, see chapter 5 on minorities and the courts.

23. Dale, *Indians of the Southwest*, chap. 6.
24. For the complicated history of the dealings of the federal government with California's Indians after 1846 the reader is referred to Dale, *Indians of the Southwest*, and Ellison, "The Federal Indian Policy in California"; for the larger background of American Indians and their relations with the government, see W. T. Hagan, *American Indians*; W. H. Oswalt, *This Land Was Theirs*; G. E. Simpson and J. M. Yinger, eds., *American Indians and American Life*; U.S., Department of Interior, *Federal Indian Law*.

IV. Constitutional Debate on Race and Rights, 1849

When California fell into the hands of the United States in 1846,[1] life proceeded in much the same way for a couple of years as it had previously under the Mexicans. The event that shook the region out of its lethargy was the discovery of gold at Coloma on January 24, 1848.[2] The word spread and the gold rush began. By April 1848, Col. R. B. Mason, who was commanding officer of the United States forces in California and acting governor of the territory, reported that four thousand men were then mining gold. Within a year one hundred thousand newcomers had arrived. Overnight, as it were, California had secured a substantial population and was producing gold worth tens of millions of dollars. The military forces of the United States were small, and the absence of a government made it imperative that something be done to form one. By 1849 the cities of San Francisco, Sonoma, and Sacramento had begun to establish their own legislatures and

1. California had earlier been American, for the brief period of three days. In October 1842 Commodore Thomas ap Catesby Jones, in command of two ships of the Pacific squadron (*Cyane* and *United States*), seized Monterey, the capital, and accepted the surrender of the Mexican military garrison and civil officials and raised the United States flag. Two days later, convinced at last that he was in error in believing that a state of war existed between Mexico and the United States, he lowered the American flag and restored the town to the Mexicans. J. van Nostrand, *A Pictorial and Narrative History of Monterey, Adobe Capital of California, 1770–1847*.

2. E. L. Egenhoff, *The Elephant as They Saw It*; California Historical Society, *California Gold Discovery: Centennial Papers on the Time, the Site and the Artifacts*.

to frame legal codes. A territorial government did not seem appropriate, and on June 3, 1849, General Riley, commanding the United States forces, issued a proclamation calling a convention to form a state constitution to be submitted to the people, and if approved, to then be presented to Congress with the request for admission as a state into the Union.[3] All of this was done by the forty-eight delegates who were elected from the several districts.

The state constitutional convention met in the fall of 1849, from September 1 to October 13, in Monterey for the purpose of writing a new constitution to be submitted to Congress for approval as a necessary prerequisite to the admission of California as a state. Prior to these debates were the ones that held national attention in Washington. These debates concerned the question of the admission of California to the Union and depicted the anxiety of both the Northern and Southern states over the balance of power in the slavery issue. The task of admitting California as a free state required lengthy debate by America's foremost statesmen at the time and nearly overshadowed the issues that were argued with as much heat and vigor in Monterey.[4]

President James Polk in his annual message of December 5, 1848, referred to the question of slavery in the territory just acquired through the successful conclusion of the Mexican War:

> In organizing governments over these Territories, no duty imposed on Congress by the Constitution requires that they should legislate on the subject of slavery, while their power to do so is not only seriously questioned, but denied, by many of the soundest expounders of that instrument.
>
> Whether Congress shall legislate or not, the people of the acquired Territories, when assembled in Convention to form State Constitutions, will possess the sole right and exclusive power to determine for themselves whether slavery shall or shall not exist within their limits.

3. C. L. Goodman, *The Establishment of State Government in California, 1846–1850.*

4. For an authoritative account of the slave debates in Washington, the reader is referred to R. G. Cowan, *The Admission of the Thirty-first State by the Thirty-first Congress.*

California was admitted to the Union in September, 1850,[5] under a compromise which allowed her to be a free state but left the choice of slavery open in the remainder of the Mexican Territory. The Compromise of 1850 also led to the enactment of a strong fugitive-slave law and prohibited the slave trade in the District of Columbia.

The section in the Declaration of Rights in the California Constitution read: "Neither slavery, nor involuntary servitude, unless for the punishment of crimes, shall ever be tolerated in this State." The delegates voted unanimously in favor of this statement.

The focus of this chapter falls on the discussion which took place in the convention at Monterey between September 1, 1849, and October 13, 1849. The new California Constitution was immediately printed in Spanish and English, circulated as widely as possible, and put to public vote on November 13, 1849. Only 15,000 votes were polled. Of these, 12,061 were in favor, 811 were against, "and from 1200 to 1500 were blanks, in consequence of the failure of the printer to place the words 'For The Constitution' at the head of the ballots."[6]

Bayard Taylor provides us with an eyewitness version of the methods by which the California Constitution was approved by the miners in one of the gold camps on the Mokelumne River:

> [One miner, when voting, said]: "When I left home I was determined to *go it blind*. I went it blind in coming to California, and I'm not going to stop now. I voted for the Constitution, and I've never seen the Constitution. I voted for all the candidates, and I don't know a damned one of them. I'm going it blind all through, I am." The Californians and resident Mexicans who were entitled to vote were in high spirits

5. The first news that California had been admitted to the Union (on September 9, 1850) was brought on the steamer *Oregon*, which arrived at San Francisco on October 18, 1850.

6. J. Ross Browne, *California Constitutional Convention, 1849*, p. xxi. Browne says that those persons eligible to vote to elect delegates were "1. American citizens; 2. Mexicans who had elected under the treaty [of Guadalupe Hidalgo] to become American citizens; and 3. Mexican citizens who had been forced to leave their country in consequence of giving aid and succor to the American arms during the recent war" (p. xx).

in exercising the privilege for the first time in their lives. It made no difference what the ticket was; the fact of their having voted very much increased their self-importance, for the day at least. . . . The inspectors were puzzled at first how far to extend the privilege of suffrage to the Mexicans. There was no copy of the Treaty of Querétaro to be had, and the exact wording of the clause referring to this subject was not remembered. It was at last decided, however, that those who had been residing in the country since the conquest, and intended to remain permanently, might be admitted to vote; and the question was therefore put to each one in turn. The most of them answered readily in the affirmative, and seemed delighted to be considered as citizens. "*Como no?*" said a fat, good-humoured fellow, with a ruddy olive face, as he gave his sarape a new twirl over his shoulder: "*Como no? soy Americano ahora.*" (Why not? I am now an American.)[7]

The California debates, which were reported in full by J. Ross Browne,[8] became the rallying point around which the questions of race and rights turned. Two pressing issues that were warmly argued concerned, first, the right of the California Indian to vote and, second, the right of the free or indentured Negro to migrate to the newly created territory.

The elected delegates to the convention came from different ways of life. Of the forty-eight delegates, nine had been residents of the state for less than one year. The average residence in California for all forty-eight members was about two years. Seven of the members were born in California; five were foreign born; eight had Spanish surnames; sixteen came from slave states; and twenty-one came from free states. The youngest member at the convention was twenty-five years old; the oldest was fifty-two. The full roster of delegates, as listed by Browne, with their ages, origins, length of residence, and professions, is printed in the documents section, p. 226.

Who Shall (Not) Vote?

It is important for us here to follow and to get a taste for

7. *Eldorado, or Adventures in the Path of Empire*, p. 189.
8. *California Constitutional Convention, 1849. Report of the Debates in the Convention of California, on the Formation of the State Constitution in September and October, 1849.*

the subtleties of the arguments that were presented during this important convention concerning the extension of the right of suffrage to different ethnic groups. It was evident from the start of the convention that the Negro was not wanted in the new territory. At all events, it was agreed overwhelmingly that those Negroes already in the territory should not vote. The Indian was already in the state, but he should not be either a citizen or a voter. The fear of the delegates was that large landowners who employed a great many Indians might on election day lead scores of "docile" Indians to the polls. Under the Treaty of Guadalupe Hidalgo in 1848, which followed the Mexican War and where title to California was transferred to the government of the United States, those Mexican citizens who within a year did not elect to retain their original allegiance to Mexico automatically acquired "the title and rights of citizens of the United States."[9] Indians in California were not specified in the treaty as eligible for American citizenship, but since they were Mexican citizens, there was no apparent reason to mention them separately as entitled to acquire American citizenship.

The delegates at Monterey in 1849 remained firm in their convictions that no persons other than whites should play any part in the governing of the state and proceeded to disenfranchise many of those individuals who had originally cast their ballots in the special election that put these very same delegates in their convention seats. Even an amendment that proposed to grant the right to vote to those Indians who had been citizens of Mexico and were taxed as owners of real estate, and expressly excepted all Negroes, was defeated by a vote of 22 to 21. It is interesting to note that before the American invasion of California perhaps not more than two hundred Indians possessed the necessary qualifications to make them potential voters.

9. This treaty, which resolved the issues of the Mexican War, was signed at Guadalupe Hidalgo on March 10, 1848. It was ratified by the president of the United States, James K. Polk, on March 16, 1848, and by the president of Mexico, Manuel de la Peña y Peña. Final ratifications were exchanged between the commissioners of the two republics at Querétaro on May 30, 1848. The treaty was officially proclaimed by President Polk on July 4, 1848.

The American attitude toward Indians before admission to the Union may be gauged by the following, which appeared in the March 15, 1848, issue of the *Californian*: "We desire only a white population in California: even the Indians among us, as far as we have seen, are more of a nuisance than a benefit to the country: we would like to get rid of them."

Who Is White?

The controversy concerning suffrage for different ethnic groups centered around the applicability of the terms of the Treaty of Guadalupe Hidalgo and its exact effect on how the new constitution of the state of California should be constructed. We quote below from Browne, author of the report *California Constitutional Convention, 1849*.

The section under discussion during the convention originally was written:

> SECTION 1. Every white male citizen of the United States, of the age of 21 years who shall have been a resident of the State six months next preceding the election, and the county, in which he claims vote twenty days, shall be entitled to vote at all elections which are now, or hereafter may be, authorized by law.

It was immediately suggested by a delegate that this be amended thus: after the words "United States" and before the word "of" insert "and every male citizen of Mexico, who shall have elected to become a citizen of the United States, under (Article VIII of) the Treaty of Peace, exchanged and ratified at Querétaro, on the 30th day of May, 1848."

The articles of the Treaty of Peace whose interpretation were hotly contested by the delegates were as follows:

> ARTICLE VIII. Those who shall prefer to remain in the said territories, may either retain the title and rights of Mexican citizens, or acquire those of citizens of the United States. But they shall be under obligation to make their election within one year from the date of the exchange of ratifications of this treaty; and those who shall remain in the said territories, after the expiration of that year, without having declared their intention to retain the character of Mexicans, shall be

considered to have elected to become citizens of the United States.

Art. IX. The Mexicans who, in the territories aforesaid, shall not preserve the character of citizens of the Mexican Republic, conformably with what is stipulated in the preceding article, shall be incorporated into the Union of the United States, and be admitted, at the proper time—to the enjoyment of all the rights of citizens of the United States according to the principles of the Constitution. . . .

An amendment that showed the negative feeling which many delegates had for allowing the vote to extend beyond white citizenry was promptly offered by the delegate from Monterey.

His amendment was to insert the word "white" before "male citizen of Mexico." He claimed that the other delegate, his colleague, had left out an exceedingly important word. He hoped it would be the will of the house that no citizen of the United States should be admitted to the elective franchise but white citizens. An objection was raised at this time as to the definition which some of the delegates used for the term *white*.

Mr. Noriego [i.e., Sr. Noriega de la Guerra] desired that it should be perfectly understood in the first place what is the true significance of the word "white." Many citizens of California have received from nature a very dark skin; nevertheless, there are among them men who have heretofore been allowed to vote, and not only that, but to fill the highest public offices. It would be very unjust to deprive them of the privilege of citizens merely because nature had not made them white. But if, by the word "white" it was intended to exclude the African race, then it was correct and satisfactory.

A clarification was then offered by delegate Botts, who had previously expressed his opinion on limited extension of the right of suffrage to only the "white" man.

Mr. Botts then stated that he had

no objection to color, *except so far as it indicated the inferior races of mankind* [emphasis added]. He would be perfectly willing to use any words which would exclude the African and Indian races. It was in this sense the word white had been understood and used—not objectionable for their color, but for what that color indicates.

The question of right and privilege turned on the conditions of the treaty which we have cited. This was carefully brought out by one delegate in an argument which follows.

> Mr. Gilbert hoped the amendment proposed by the gentleman from Monterey (Mr. Botts) would not prevail. He was confident that if the word "white" was introduced, it would produce great difficulty. The Treaty has said that Mexican citizens, upon becoming citizens of the U.S., shall be entitled to the rights and privileges of American citizens. It does not say whether those citizens are white or black, and we have no right to make the distinction. If they be Mexican citizens, it is sufficient; they are entitled to the rights and privileges of American citizens. No act of this kind could, therefore, have any effect. The Treaty is above and superior to it.

From those delegates familiar with Mexican law it was learned that no race of any kind was excluded from voting. Of the Indians in Mexico, very few were actually admitted to the right of suffrage. They were restricted by some property qualification, or by occupation or mode of livelihood, but they were still considered Mexican citizens according to the constitution. It was the feeling of one delegate (Mr. Hastings) that complete exclusion of persons of Indian extraction might be unjust and unfair:

> An Indian in the mountains is just as much entitled to vote as anybody, if Indians are entitled to vote. But men who have Indian blood in their veins are not for that reason Indians. There are, perhaps, many persons resident in this country who have Indian blood, but who are not considered Indian. . . .

Another delegate (Mr. Dimmick), who also urged that the convention members suspend discussion on this question until more information concerning Mexican law could be obtained, expressed the same sentiments:

> At the same time, where there was here and there a good Indian, capable of understanding our system of government, he had no objection to making such provision as would entitle him to vote.

A rebuttal to the proposal that a United States treaty could prescribe action to the delegates to the convention was quickly organized.

Mr. Botts declared that there was one doctrine urged here, that really astonished him—that the Treaty of Peace between the United States and Mexico, or any other Treaty, could prescribe to this convention what persons it should make voters in the State of California! The Congress of the United States could not do it. Were gentlemen not aware of that fact? They ought to be shouting hozannas to liberty, now that they were informed of it. The States of this union are free and sovereign. They prescribe for themselves the right of suffrage. Gentlemen need not look to the Treaty of Peace for authority; it is competent for the people of this country to declare that no man, unless he have black hair, and black eyes, shall vote.

One delegate (Mr. Gilbert) then called attention to the sixth article of the Constitution of the United States, the second section, which gave to the Constitution and laws of the United States and all treaties to be the supreme law of the land.

This Treaty is therefore the supreme law of the land. . . . We cannot go beyond this Treaty and disfranchise any man who is admitted under the Treaty to the rights of citizenship. He wished to make no invidious distinctions as to color, but to abide by the Treaty of Peace and Constitution of the United States.

Mr. Hastings concurred by stating that he

presumed the gentlemen from Monterey (Mr. Botts) would observe that if we do not recognize this Treaty, no Treaty of peace exists. We are then at war with Mexico. . . . If we violate the stipulations of this Treaty, we violate the Constitution. . . . We dare not exclude one human being who was a citizen at the time of the adoption of that Treaty. Every man who was a citizen then, is a citizen now, and will be while he lives in California, unless he declares his intention to remain a citizen of Mexico. Our Constitution must, therefore, conform to the Treaty, or it is null and void.[10]

---

10. Equality of Indians had been granted under the Spanish constitution and various official decrees between 1810 and 1820. The Mexican constitution of 1824 "made the Indians equal in every way to the white man." C. A. Hutchinson, *Frontier Settlement in Mexican California*, pp. 80, 113. "Message from the President of the United States Transmitting Information in Answer to a Resolution of the House of the 31st of December, 1849, on the Subject of California and New Mexico": *Executive Document* 17, ser. 573, 31st Cong., 1st sess., 1850, pp. 139–140.

The reply to this argument was most crucial, for it indicated how the majority of the convention members would resolve the difference between their feeling toward the subject of suffrage and their desire not to do anything which might provide Congress with a reason to reject the new proposed state constitution when it was submitted for approval. At this point Mr. Botts said he

> desired that his own position should be well understood. He maintained that this Treaty, so far as he knew, is binding in every clause because it does not contradict the Constitution of the United States; it does not prescribe who shall be our voters. If it had made citizens of Mexico directly citizens of the United States, it would not have said that they should be voters of the State of California. He granted for the sake of argument, that these Indians are citizens of the United States, because they were citizens in Mexico. The question is still open whether they shall be voters. There are thousands of citizens of the United States who are not voters. Gentlemen should not confound the words. It does not follow that if a man be a citizen of the United States he shall be a voter.

Mr. Dimmick concurred by asking:

> What are the rights of citizens of the United States? Are we to admit them to rights superior to those which we enjoy ourselves? Does any one pretend to assert that we are under obligation to do this? Does it necessarily follow that the right of suffrage is one of these rights? He contended not. It is not necessarily the right of a citizen. He believed that the States in their sovereign capacity have a right to make their own regulations in respect to this matter. . . . He would go as far as any gentleman on this floor, to admit to all the privileges of citizenship such of them as are capable of understanding our institutions, and who are responsible and orderly citizens; but he would be very unwilling to admit the wild Indian tribes of California to the right of suffrage. He did not think such a thing was ever contemplated by the Treaty. Those Indians who have become civilized, and who were entitled by the Mexican government to hold land and pay taxes, are not objectionable. They should be allowed the elective franchise; and as for the mixed race, descended from the Indians and Spaniards, he certainly was in favor of permitting them to enjoy the right of suffrage as liberally as any American citizen. . . . At the same, it is absolutely necessary to embody in this Constitution such a restriction as will prevent the wild tribes from voting.

After the remaining arguments were heard pro and con, the convention was polled to determine the exact feeling of its members on an amendment that would exclude from the right of suffrage Indians not taxed, Africans, and descendants of Africans. A few delegates expressed opinion on this amendment.

> Mr. Hoppe said that his reason for moving to strike out the words "not taxed," was, that the whole Indian race should be excluded from the elective franchise.

> Mr. Wozencraft wished gentlemen to reflect, that there are Indians by descent, as well as full-blooded Indians. He supposed the majority of the members on this floor were not willing to deprive the descendants of Indians of the elective franchise. Many of the most distinguished officers of the Mexican Government are Indians by descent. At the same time, it would be impolitic to permit the full-blooded Indians who held property to vote. Those who held property would, of course, be taxed. Capitalists could, for special purposes, make them purchasers of property. He was, therefore, in favor of the amendment as first proposed—to exclude all Indians.

Who Defends the Indian?

The Indians were not wholly unrepresented by men who had sympathy with their plight. Their defense was ably expounded by several delegates.

> Mr. Noriego desired to say a word in reply to the gentleman from San Jose (Mr. Hoppe) who stated that there were at least 200 Indians in that district, who would become taxable. He (Mr. Noriego) requested that gentleman to place himself in the position of one of those Indians. Suppose he had to pay an equal tax with all other persons, to sustain the expenses of the State? Would it not be most unfair to deprive him of equal privileges when he had to bear an equal burden? The gentleman, he hoped, would readily perceive the great injustice of such a provision in the Constitution.

A vote was then called on the amendment offered by Mr. Botts, to insert the word "white" before "male citizens of Mexico." It was adopted by the convention members.

The next question to be taken up by the convention was the motion to strike out the words "not taxed" in the phrase "Indians not taxed, Africans and descendants of Africans excepted" as those individuals who would not be allowed to vote.

> Mr. Dent observed that it might be a weakness in him, but he had always entertained a peculiar deference for the Indians. They were the original proprietors of the soil. From them we derived it, and from them we derived many of the blessings which we now enjoy. They have already been deprived of their original independence. Why should we pursue them, and drag them down to the level of slaves? It appeared to him that the Indians should enjoy the right of suffrage, and that they should not be classed with Africans.

The following speaker, Mr. Tefft, said

> he could not in justice to his own feelings, allow the motion to pass, without expressing, with the gentlemen from Monterey (Mr. Dent) the deep sympathy he felt for this unhappy race. It might be a prejudice which had grown with his growth, and strengthened with his strength; but from his earliest youth, he had felt something like a reverence for the Indians. He had ever admired their heroic deeds in defense of their aboriginal homes, their stoicism, their wild eloquence and uncompromising pride. He was much pleased, when a resident of Wisconsin, to see incorporated into the Constitution of that State, a provision allowing Indians the privilege of voting. He hoped this question would be considered calmly, and dispassionately in all its bearings, and that gentlemen would not, by acting hastily, exclude all Indians, absolutely and entirely, from the right of suffrage. Were gentlemen aware, that, because a man is two-thirds Indian, he is not an Indian? Had they considered well the feeling that would go abroad among the native population of California, if injustice was done to this class of people? Has not injustice enough already been visited upon the Indian race? They have been driven back from the haunts of civilization into the wilderness, driven from one extremity of the land to the other; shall they now be driven into the waves of the Pacific? Shall we deprive them of the advantages of civilization? Shall we prevent them from becoming civilized? Surely the prejudice against color does not extend so far! He did not desire that the Tulas [the Yokuts tribes of the southern San Joaquin valley], and other savage tribes should vote, but it is not difficult to draw a line of distinction between these wild Indians, and those who have become accustomed to habits of civilization. He considered that this native population was better entitled to the right of suffrage than he was, or a thousand others who came here but yesterday.

The final argument was then heard on this issue:

> Mr. McCarver would vote for striking out the clause allowing Indians who paid taxes the right to vote. . . . He was in favor of giving this class of people all the protection of our laws, but not the right of suffrage. As a general thing the Indian is illiterate, and incompetent to judge of the question presented in an election. . . . By giving him the right to vote, he would in nine cases out of ten, be placed in the power of crafty and designing men.

Final Arguments

A vote was then called for on the motion to strike out the words "not taxed" and this was approved by a vote of 25 to 15. Following this crucial vote, final arguments were heard on the Gilbert amendment as amended. Mr. Sherwood then

> objected to the amendment: "Indians, Africans, and the descendants of Africans, excepted." What is meant by the descendant of an Indian, or the descendant of a Negro? Did the gentleman who offered the proposition mean to say that a man who has the least taint of Indian or Negro blood shall not vote? . . . The word descendant means a person who descends in regular line. He may be of mixed blood or full blood. There is nothing specific in the term "descendant." He did not believe the committee could adopt any better form than the words "white male citizen."

And there the matter rested for the moment, to be taken up for a final vote on October 3. Whatever the final outcome, it was by now apparent that the Indian and African minorities were going to be barred from the right of suffrage.

Shall the Free Negro Be Admitted?

The convention delegates then turned to the question of barring free Negroes from entering the state of California. Delegate McCarver moved as an additional section to the constitution:

> SECTION 39. The legislature shall, at its first session, pass such laws as will effectively prohibit free persons of color from immigrating to and settling in this State, and to effectually prevent the owners of slaves from bringing them into this State for the purpose of setting them free.

This was the matter which many of the delegates considered to be the most important business of the convention, and it continued to be discussed over the period September 19 to October 3, 1849. One delegate after another rose to deliver impassioned warnings on the dangers of California acquiring a population of free blacks who would "degrade labor" and who were "idle in their habits, difficult to be governed by the laws, thriftless, and uneducated." The specter of hordes of Negro slaves brought by their owners from slaveholding states to California where they would be set free after a period of service of one year was repeatedly suggested. Slaveowners desirous of exploiting their chattels in return for the profits secured in a year of gold mining were represented as "monopolies of capitalists." Some delegates pointed out that these fears were unfounded, and that since slavery was prohibited in California no slaveowner would pay the heavy price ($600 to $700) of bringing a slave to California where the latter would automatically become free upon entering the state.

Some delegates argued that free Negroes were as free as any man, and that in California they would serve a useful function as domestic servants. Mr. Dimmick said:

"As this Constitution has been adopted . . . the position in which he [the slaveholder] stands is this: it is not his option to set them free here; the moment they touch this soil they are free by the fundamental law of the land. No matter whether the slaveholder brings them here with the understanding, or under contract, that after they shall have served a certain time in the mines they shall be free; they are free the moment they touch the soil of California. Why, then, introduce this prohibition? What effect can it have? It is perfectly worthless, and stands null, void, and unmeaning in that relation. . . . I am most decidedly opposed, sir, to the introduction of any thing of this kind in the Constitution, because I do contend that free men of color have just as good a right, and ought to have, to emigrate here as white men. I think, too, that the necessities of the territory require them; the necessities of every State in the Union require them. They are required in every department of domestic life; they form a body that have become almost necessary for our domestic purposes; and I see no reason why this Convention should introduce an article here depriving the people of California of the services of a class of men who are required by the people of every State of the Union, and regarded as absolutely essential to the comfort and convenience of domestic life. For this, among other reasons, I shall vote against the resolution. I do not want the people of California to be cut off from the services of any particular body of men. It matters not if they were baboons, or any other class of creatures. I do not speak now, Mr. Chairman, upon the rights of men, of whatever color, as citizens or men. I leave out that consideration entirely, and speak of this as a matter of expediency."

The most eloquent plea, and the most ethnocentric statement to be heard from any member of this convention, was delivered on this subject by delegate Wozencraft:

"Mr. President: We have declared, by a unanimous vote, that neither slavery nor involuntary servitude shall ever exist in this State. I desire now to cast my vote in favor of the proposition just submitted, prohibiting the negro race from coming amongst us; and this I profess to do as a philanthropist, loving my kind, and rejoicing in their rapid march toward perfectability.

"If there was just reason why slavery should not exist in this land, there is just reason why part of the family of man, who are so well adapted for servitude, should be excluded from amongst us. It would appear that the all-wise Creator has created the negro to serve the white race. We see evidence of this wherever they are brought in contact; we see the instinctive feeling of the negro is obedience to the white man, and, in all instances, he obeys him, and is ruled by him. If you would wish that all mankind should be free, do not bring the two extremes in the scale of organization together; do not bring the lowest in contact with the highest, for be assured the one will rule and the other must serve.

"I wish to cast my vote against the admission of blacks into this country, in order that I may thereby protect the citizens of California in one of their most inestimable rights—the right to labor. This right is not only valuable, but it is a holy commandment—'by the sweat of thy brow shalt thou earn thy daily bread.' I wish to inculcate this command, and encourage labor, I wish, so far as my influence extends, to make labor honorable; the laboring man is the *nobleman* in the true acceptation of the word; and I would make him worthy of his high prerogative, and not degrade him by placing him upon a level with the lowest in the scale of the family of man. I would remove all obstacles to his future greatness, for if there is one part of the world, possessing advantages over another, where the family of Japhet may expect to attain a higher state of perfectability than has ever been attained by man, it is here, in California. All nature proclaims this a favored land. The assertion that we would be unjust in excluding that part of the human race from coming here, has no foundation in reason. We must be just to ourselves—by so doing we avoid injustice to others. The African is well fitted for labor, you would say. Why deny him our field? Sir, we do not deny him the right to labor; we are willing that he should have the boundless wastes of his native land for his field— a region where the all-wise Creator, in his wisdom, saw fit to place him; but we are not willing that he should be placed in our field, where, instead of good to either party, evil would come to both. We are not only reasonable but we are just. No one will deny that a free black population is one of the greatest evils that can afflict society. We know it to be so. We have witnessed enough to know it and deplore it. There is not an advocate for the admission of blacks that would be willing to take the negro by the hand in fellowship—that would be willing to extend to him the right of suffrage—that would be willing to admit him on a footing in our political or social confederacy. Is it just, then, to encourage by our silence the emigration of a class of beings who at best are dead weights in society— resting on our social institutions like an incubus of darkness?

"I desire to protect the people of California against all monopolies—to encourage labor and protect the laboring class. Can this be done by admitting the negro race? Surely not; for if they are permitted to come, they will do so—nay they will be brought here. Yes, Mr. President, the capitalists will fill the land with these living laboring machines, with all their attendant evils. Their labor will go to enrich the few, and impoverish the many; it will drive the poor and honest laborer from the field, by degrading him to the level of the negro. The vicious propensities of this class of population will be a heavy tax on the people. Your officers will have to be multiplied; your prisons will have to be doubled; your society will be corrupted. Yes, sirs, you will find when it is too late that you have been saddled with an evil that will gall you to the quick, and yet it cannot be thrown off. You can prevent it now, by passing this section. It should be done now. Do not wait for legislative enactment—the Legislature may, and doubtless will, pass laws effectually to prevent blacks from coming, or being brought here, but it will be an extended evil even at that date. When this Constitution goes forth without a prohibitionary clause relative to blacks, you will see a black-tide setting in here and spreading over

107

the land; you will see a greater curse than the locusts of Egypt. This is no fancy sketch—it is a plain assertion, based on a just knowledge of things, which requires no gift of prophecy to foresee. If you fail to pass this bill you will have cause to revert to my assertions.

"The future, to us, is more promising than that of any State that has ever applied for admission into the Union. The golden era is before us in all its glittering splendor; here civilization may attain its highest altitude; Art, Science, Literature will here find a fostering parent, and the Caucasian may attain his highest state of perfectibility. This is all before us. It is within our reach; but to attain it we must pursue the path of wisdom. We must throw aside all the weights and clogs that have fettered society elsewhere. We must inculcate moral and industrial habits. We must exclude the low, vicious, and depraved. Every member of society should be on a level with the mass—able to perform his appropriate duty. Having his equal rights, he should be capable of maintaining those rights, and aiding in their equal diffusion to others. There should be that equilibrium in society which pervades all nature, and that equilibrium can only be established by acting in conformity with the laws of nature. There should be no incongruities in the structure; it should be a harmonious whole, and there should be no discordant particles, if you would have a happy unity. That the negro race is out of his social sphere, and becomes a discordant element when among the Caucasian race, no one can doubt. You have but to take a retrospective view, and you need not extend your vision beyond our own land to be satisfied of this fact. Look at our once happy republic, now a contentious, antagonistical, discordant people. The Northern people see, and feel, and know, that the black population is an evil in the land, and although they have admitted them to many of the rights of citizenship, the admixture has acted in the political economy as a foreign, poisonous substance, producing the same effect as in physical economy—derangement, disease, and, if not removed, *death.* Let us be warned—let us avoid an evil of such magnitude.

"I will trespass on the patience of the House no further, Mr. President, than to express the wish that this clause may become an article in the Constitution."

The issue was dropped for several days but was revived again with a great deal of lively debate as the convention met as the committee of the whole. Delegate McCarver moved that the committee adopt his amendment. A few other of the delegates expressed their opinions toward this proposal. McCarver himself supported his amendment by saying:

> "No population that could be brought within the limits of our Territory could be more repugnant to the feelings of the people, or injurious to the prosperity of the community, than free Negroes. They are idle in their habits, difficult to be governed by the laws, thriftless and uneducated. It is a species of population that this country should be particularly guarded against."

Mr. Semple expressed his thoughts:

> "And I can assure you, sir, thousands will be introduced into this country before long; if you do not insert a positive prohibition against them in your constitution—an immense and overwhelming population of Negroes, who have never been freemen; who have never been accustomed to provide for themselves. What would be the state of things in a few years? The whole country would be filled with emancipated slaves—the worst species of population—prepared to do nothing but steal, or live upon our means as paupers."

The major argument that was put forth in support of the McCarver amendment concerned the fear that many Southern slaveholders, believing they could do so, would bring their slaves to California to work in the mines and profit by this action. After a certain period of time, the argument ran, these slaves would be set free and would then become a burden on the state. Mr. Semple stated:

> "Suppose you pay seven hundred dollars to get a slave here, and set him free, on condition that he shall serve you for one year. He produces, according to the ordinary rates in the mines, from two to six thousand dollars. There are many of our Southern friends who would be glad to set their Negroes free and bring them here, if they produced only half of this amount."

The opposition, however, charged inconsistency with those delegates who would vote for such an amendment and still affirm the principle of the constitution's Bill of Rights, which guaranteed that the privileges of free institutions would be guaranteed to all classes.

Mr. Dimmick replied: ". . . I am clearly opposed to a provision of this kind in the constitution, on the ground of principle and consistency. What will be said of our Constitution if we assert one thing in our Bill of Rights—extend the privileges of our free institutions to all classes, both from foreign countries and our own and then in another exclude a class speaking our own language, born and brought up in the United States, acquainted with our customs, and calculated to make useful citizens. We even debar them from the privilege of entering upon our soil. The two provisions are inconsistent. . . . But what necessity exists here? Are the slaveholders going to remove their slaves to a state thousands of miles distant, at an enormous expense—an expense equal to the value of the slaves, for the purpose of setting them free? If they wish to set them free, they can do it at much less expense. But we are told that free Negroes will be brought here under indentures. I have yet to learn that there is any law of California by which a free-man can be indentured. The moment they enter our limits they are subject to our laws and cease to be slaves. . . . No man would bring his slaves here for the purpose of working in the mines when he knows they are free the moment they enter our limits. . . . If the legislature should at any future period, find that our interests are endangered by any particular class of population, there will then be justifiable reasons for excluding them. But in the absence of this proof, let our organic law be consistent with the declarations embraced in our Bill of Rights. Let Africans be placed upon the same footing with natives of the Sandwich Islands; Chilians, and Peruvians, and the lower classes of Mexicans. You permit those classes to come here and enjoy the political rights which we enjoy ourselves. Why should we adopt a proscriptive rule with reference to another class speaking our own language, fully as intelligent as they are, possessed of as much physical energy, and better acquainted with our habits and customs? I have no partiality for the Negro race. I have the same personal antipathies which other gentlemen avow; but I desire that we should act with consistency."

A motion was then made by Mr. McDougal, which would require that the first session of the legislature

create enactments against the introduction into this state of any Negro or Negroes who has or have been slaves previously in any of the states of this Union, or of any other country, and who are brought here under bonds or indentures of servitude.

One delegate (Mr. Tefft) was distinctly in favor of stringent, curbing laws that would prohibit free immigration in California of certain groups for several new reasons:

> "I am opposed to the introduction into this country of Negroes, peons of Mexico, or any class of that kind; I care not whether they be free or bond. It is a well established fact, and the history of every State in the Union clearly proves it, that Negro labor, whether slave or free, when opposed to white labor, degrades it. That is the ground upon which I oppose the introduction of this class of persons. . . . All men are by nature free and independent, entitled to certain inalienable rights. Most assuredly I believe that to be so. I believe that all men are free and equally entitled to the enjoyment of liberty and independence. But does it follow that we are to allow certain objectionable classes of men to emigrate here and settle in California. . . . I have always lived in a free state, sir, and I have always seen that of any classes of population, the free Negroes are the most ignorant, wretched, and depraved. . . . Efforts have been made to make better men of them. . . . I lived in New York close by the line, and I know this to be the fact: That where these communities of free Negroes are located on the lands granted to them, they are an idle, worthless, and depraved population. Instead of tilling the soil, they have taken to stealing; they are too indolent to work, and too depraved to be governed by ordinary laws. I have no prejudice against the Negro because of his color. I object to their introduction here because the experience of other states has proved that they are the worst possible class of beings we could have among us—the most idle, disorderly, and unprofitable. I do not believe, Sir, that their nature will undergo a change by coming here."

And with a new twist of logic Mr. Wozencraft spoke in answer to a question asked earlier by Mr. Hastings:

> "I must explain, nevertheless; it can do the gentlemen no harm. It was stated this morning that if we desired that the African should remain free, we had better enact laws to prevent them from coming here. For, depend upon it, sir, so soon as they come among us, though we have a clause prohibiting slavery, they will be slaves to all intents and purposes. The African will always be subservient to the Caucasian. It is his nature to be so—he must be so. If we wish to avoid placing them in a position of servitude, we must exclude them. We must never bring them in competition with our own labor, for if we do, they cannot maintain an equality with the white man; and they will either become slaves in effect, or we must give up our white labor."

Mr. Gilbert, delegate from San Francisco, in answer to some of the more dire warnings expressed by his colleagues about the dangers of admitting Negroes, whether free or slave, to California said:

"I think, sir, that some of the pictures presented to our view by gentlemen on this floor, are drawn from the imagination, and have no substantial existence in fact. We are told that the slaveholders will manumit their slaves and bring them to this country to dig gold; that they will give up their plantations, however lucrative may be their business, and sacrifice their property to accomplish this object; that they will do all this, when they see staring them in the face, in the Constitution of California, that no slavery shall exist here. I do not believe this; it is not credible. There may be exceptions. Some few may do it under particular circumstances—those having a few slaves who are unattached to them, servants who have lived in their families a long time; these may be manumitted and brought here; but that there is any probability of the number being great, I deny. This view of the question, which gentlemen urge upon us with so much vehemence, is over-rated. If you insert in your Constitution such a provision or any thing like it, you will be guilty of great injustice—you will do a great wrong, sir—a wrong to the principles of liberal and enlightened freedom; a wrong to the education and feelings of the American people; a wrong to all the rights of government. You have said in the beginning of your bill of rights, that all men are by nature free and independent, and have certain inalienable rights. You go on to say that all men have the right of pursuing and obtaining safety and happiness; and yet, sir, at the bottom of this you propose to say that no free negro shall enter this territory—that he, a freeman, shall not enjoy the right which you award to all mankind. You have prohibited slavery, and thereby acted in accordance with the dictates of the whole civilized world. Look at the people of Europe. For what are they battling—for what are they shedding their blood? It is to maintain their rights—it is for liberty they contend. Are we to attempt here to turn back the tide of freedom which has rolled across from continent to continent? Are we to say that a free negro or Indian, or any other freeman, shall not enter the boundaries of California? I trust not, sir. Under the former action of this House; under the feelings and principles that have been maintained upon this floor, it would be unjust. Neither slavery nor involuntary servitude, unless for the punishment of crime, shall ever be tolerated in this State; and yet you say a free negro shall not enter its boundaries. Is it because he is a criminal? No, sir—it is simply because he is black. Well might it be said in the words of the revolutionary writer: 'You would be free, yet you know not how to be just.' It has been asserted that our constituents expect us to put such a provision in the Constitution. Gentlemen who know this may be right in advocating it; but I do not believe my constituency expect it, nor do I believe it is the desire of the majority of the people of California. I therefore oppose it. But, sir, we must go a little further than our constituents in settling this question. The people will consider our acts in this Convention, and if they ratify them, those acts will go before the Congress of the United States; and not only there, but before the great public of the United States, and before all the nations of the world. Does any gentlemen here believe, sir, that there is a man who has ever contended upon the floor of Congress for free soil and free speech, and for the universal liberty of mankind, who will sanction a Constitution that bears upon its face this darkest stigma?"

Mr. Gilbert, having thus spoken, was asked if free Negroes were citizens of the states, and answered:

"In the State of New York and in most of the Eastern States they are. I will not say that in the Southern States they are considered citizens, though they are citizens under the spirit and meaning of the Constitution . . . . Entertaining the feelings that I do upon this matter, and I grant that my prejudices against negroes are as strong as any man's can be, for my whole education has tended to make them repugnant to me, yet I am not willing to go this far, and say that a free negro, or any other freeman, shall not enter California. Besides, if we wish to be just here; if, as gentlemen say, we must protect this community from vagrants, murderers, assassins, thieves, and all sorts of criminals, we are doing but half the work. Look at the miserable natives that come from the Sandwich Islands, and other Islands of the Pacific; look at the degraded wretches that came from Sydney, New South Wales— the refuse of the world. Why do you not insert a provision preventing them from polluting the soil of California? If your object is to protect the community from the evils of a bad population, why not include these in your prohibition? Most of them are as bad as any of the free negroes of the North, or the worst slaves of the South. Do not be partial in this matter. You are treading upon the United States' Constitution itself. You must beware how you conflict with its provisions."

Mr. Hastings, delegate from Sacramento, said:

"I shall not detain the House; but to me this is a very dark subject. I have some doubts as to manner in which I shall vote. Perhaps when it is known upon what my doubts are founded, some gentlemen will be kind enough to enlighten me. Mr. Chairman, it is a fundamental declaration made by us in our bill of rights, or whether made by us or not it is true, that all men are free and entitled to certain rights, privileges, and immunities. If this ever reaches the ears of the African race, it occurs to me that they will conceive this country to be a very favorable asylum for the oppressed; especially when they find that to that broad principle, we have added another; that neither slavery nor involuntary servitude shall ever be allowed in this State. It appears to me that I can see them now by thousands on their way here; but when they arrive they are met at the portals and told that they are coming to the wrong place. They are informed that this is not the place where slavery does not exist; where all men are free and independent. It is true we said so, but we did not mean it. You are coming to the wrong place. Now, sir, why say one thing and mean another? By the addition of this resolution the free negro is excluded. This is the difficulty which occurs to me now. If any gentleman will remove it, I shall be prepared to vote for the adoption of the resolution. I am prepared to do so anyhow, because there are various reasons which have occurred to me why negroes should not be introduced into this Territory, as slaves or freemen. But if they are introduced at all, I think they had better be introduced as slaves, for a free negro is the freest human being in God's world. Let us not receive them at all; but if we do, let us receive them as slaves."

Mr. Hastings' arguments were answered in part by Mr. Tefft, delegate from San Luis Obispo, who said:

"As the gentleman has said, when negroes are free, they are the freest of all human beings; they are free in morals, free in all the vices of a brutish and depraved race. They are a most troublesome and unprofitable population."

One final argument was heard, from Mr. Hoppe, delegate from San Jose, which stressed the point of view that intermingling of whites and blacks would always result in violence.

"I have been educated and reared in the slave States, and have held slaves nearly all my life. I have lived in the free States for a short period, and I have seen riots of the most sanguinary and deplorable character arise from the habitation of Negroes among the whites. The two races can never intermingle without mutual injury. I refer especially to the great riot in Cincinnati in 1835. Look at the bloodshed that occurred there. Negroes from all parts of the state were engaged in the conflict, and there was an enormous destruction of property and loss of life. Riots took place also in Illinois, followed by the same melancholy results. What have the people of Illinois done? They have seen the evil consequences that grow out of the intermingling of free Negroes with whites, and they have adopted a provision prohibiting their introduction into the State. Let us now, before we are overrun with that race, exclude them from our boundaries, and we shall avoid those evils which have been experienced by the other free States."

Final Arguments and Votes

As the convention came to a close, those issues which had been debated as the house met as the committee of the whole were discussed, reargued, and then voted on.

Shall the Indian Vote?

The amended section 1 of Article II was reported to the house in this form.

SECTION 1. Every white male citizen of the United States, and every male citizen of Mexico (Indians, Africans, and the descendants of Africans excepted) who shall have elected to become a citizen of the United States under the Treaty of Peace exchanged and ratified at Querétaro on the 30th day of May, 1848, of the age of twenty-one years, who shall have been a resident of the State six months next preceding the election, and the county or district in which he claims his vote thirty days shall be entitled at all elections which are now or hereafter be authorized by law.

New debate again sprang up, with some members favoring the proposed section and others opposing it. One delegate, Mr. Noriego, through his Spanish interpreter, made an impassioned plea for the Indian cause.

By the proposed amendment, all Indians were excluded while at the same time it allowed all foreigners who might choose to come to California and reside for a few years, to become citizens. You allow the Kanaka to come within your territory and admit them to citizenship, when he is ignorant and as foolish as any Indian in California, and yet you exclude the native Indians from enjoying equal privilege with him. It had been asserted by some members that Indians are brutal and irrational. Let those gentlemen cast their eyes back for three hundred years and say who were the Indians then. They were a proud and gifted race, capable of forming a government for themselves. If they were not so much enlightened as now, it was not for want of natural gifts, but because the lights of science were not then so bright as now, even in Europe; and they could fall but dimly upon the natives of the soil. And he would say to those gentlemen who had sneered at the Indian race, that there might still be Indians in the territory of California who were equally as rational and gifted as highly by nature as those who had depreciated them. He would not carry their recollections back three centuries, but bid them to look back but half a century. All the work that was seen in California, was the work of Indians led by some foreigners. If they were not cultivated and highly civilized, it was because they had been ground down and made slaves of. They were intelligent and capable of receiving instructions and it was the duty of the citizens to endeavor to elevate them and better their condition in every way, instead of seeking to sink them still lower. ... If it was the will of the Convention to exclude the body of Indians, he hoped exceptions might be made, and that those who were the holders of property and had heretofore exercised all the rights and privileges of freemen, might still be permitted to continue in the exercise of those rights.

An amendment was then offered similar to the one that had been voted down previously in the committee of the whole. The amendment read:

> Insert in the 1st section, after the words "United States" and before the words "of the age" the following: "and every citizen of Mexico (Indians, not taxed as owners of real estate, and Negroes excepted) entitled to the right of suffrage at the ratification of the Treaty of Guadalupe Hidalgo, and who shall have elected to become a citizen of the United States, under the provisions of said Treaty."

This amendment, like its predecessor, was rejected by a vote of 21 to 22. The matter was then put aside for two days. This issue was finally concluded by the approval of an amendment proposed by delegate Vermeule, which omitted the clause "Indians, Africans, and the descendants of Africans excepted" and substituted the following proviso, which was subsequently adopted by the delegates by a unanimous vote:

> Provided: That nothing herein contained shall be construed to prevent the legislature, by a two-thirds concurrent vote, from admitting to the right of suffrage Indians, or the descendants of Indians, in such special cases as such a proportion of the legislature body may deem just and proper.

(The first legislature, however, immediately placed itself on record as restricting the right of suffrage of citizens of California to white citizens alone.)

Shall the Negro Be Admitted?

Shortly after the debate had closed on the question of the Indian vote, arguments were renewed in the convention over the question of the admission of Negroes into California.[11] Several new amendments were introduced. The first new amendment attempted to reconcile the section with Article IV, section 2, of the Constitution of the United States, concerning the rights of citizens. Delegate McCarver offered the following:

> The legislature shall, at its first session, pass such laws as will effectively prohibit free persons of color from immigrating to and settling in this State, and to effectively prevent the owners of slaves from bringing them to this State for the purpose of setting them free: Provided, that voting in the Constitution shall be construed to conflict with the provisions of the first clause of the second section of the fourth article of the Constitution of the United States.

Again we hear the same arguments which had previously been debated in the committee of the whole. Mr. Jones said:

> "Yet I am decidedly of opinion that . . . it has become universally conceded, that the States have a right to protect themselves from such an evil as that class of population. If, by an act of Congress, we are prohibited from protecting ourselves against free Negroes, we will soon be completely overrun by them. Suppose an act was passed in Maryland turning all her Negroes free, and setting them upon the shores

11. In 1847 the population of San Francisco was 321, of whom 10 were Negroes. In 1850, a "census" showed fewer than 1,000 Negroes in the state.

of Massachusetts, do you suppose the people of Massachusetts would pay their expenses and sustain them.

"Sir, in the mining districts of this country we want no such competition. The labor of the white man brought into competition with the labor of the Negro is always degraded. There is now a respectable and intelligent class of population in the mines, men of talent and education, men digging there in the pit with the spade and pick, who would be amply competent to sit in these halls. Do you think they would dig with the African? No, sir, they would leave this country first."

After the debate had subsided, the question "Shall the main question be now put?" was then taken and put off so that the amended motion offered by Delegate McCarver could be considered. This was defeated by a vote of 9 to 33. Delegate McDougal then offered the following substitute motion:

> The legislature shall at its first session, create such laws as will prohibit the introduction into this state, of any negro or mulatto who was previously a slave in any of the United States, or of any other country, and who is brought here under bonds of indenture; and any bond or indenture given and executed in this State, by any negro or mulatto who was previously a slave, shall be void.

This amendment was considered and rejected also. The question recurring on the adoption of the section as reported by the committee of the whole was then considered and rejected by a vote of 8 to 31.

The final blow to the proposed section 39 of Article II came when the delegates rejected a final amendment which was introduced as a new section.

> The legislature shall pass such laws as may be deemed necessary, either prohibiting the introduction and emigration of free negroes to the state, or presenting the conditions upon which the introduction and emigration of such persons may be allowed.

Those individuals previously in favor of similarly worded sections rejected this offer as having no effect. (One delegate offered and consequently withdrew an amendment which illustrated his argument: "Resolved, that the legislature shall do just as they please on the subject of free Negroes." This delegate hoped that the time of the house would not be consumed in discussing such propositions.) The final vote was taken and the amendment considered was rejected 6 to 27.

Thus were concluded the debates that centered on the issue of race and rights. Only for expediency was the section concerning the admission of Negroes to California rejected, and for the same reason the question of suffrage for Indians was sidestepped and referred to the legislature when it should meet. The risk of having Congress refuse to approve the California Constitution was, in the end, considered too great if such provisions were part of the document.

V. Minorities and the Courts

The Anglo-American racism that had been developing as a result of Negro slavery was not invoked until the American annexation of California in 1846.[1] In the Sierran gold region (the "Mother Lode") as white Americans increased in number and the richest placers were worked out, the feelings against all "colored" people (Mexican, Negroes, Indians) was increasingly expressed. The tenor of the debates that took place during the California constitutional convention of 1849 made it clear that one of the strongest objections to the presence of peoples of minority groups in California was that their competition on the labor market would "degrade" the white worker forced to work alongside the Negro, the Oriental, or the Indian.

The matter of numbers of nonwhites was certainly a fundamental cause for concern for certain groups of white men. While the number of Indians in California diminished, the Negro population increased at a slow rate (between 1850 and 1860 from about 1,000 to 4,000, one percent of the white population, and to only about 21,000 by 1910), and the Chinese population grew rapidly in the latter half of the nineteenth century (from 10,000 in 1850 to 47,000 in 1860, and 75,000 in 1880).

The greatest attraction for all these groups to California, and the principal cause for the Chinese immigration of the 1850s and

1. For Afro-Americans in California before American annexation see J. D. Forbes, *Afro-Americans in the Far West: A Handbook for Educators*; R. M. Lapp, "The Negro in Gold Rush California"; S. B. Thurman, *Pioneers of Negro Origin in California*.

1860s, was the discovery of gold in the foothills of the Sierra Nevadas on January 24, 1848.[2] Thousands of Chinese were attracted to the mining camps in the foothills of the Sierra Nevada, and their poor treatment at the hands of the miners and responsible individuals in mining towns is established record. In 1850 the California legislature established a license tax of twenty dollars a month for all foreigners working in certain nonspecified occupations. The state supreme court in the decision rendered in *People* v. *Naglee* in 1850 supported the legislature's enactments by claiming that the state had the power to require the payment by foreigners of a license fee for the privilege of working the gold mines in the state, and that the legislature could prohibit foreigners from working in the mines except on payment of an established fee for that privilege. The court, in a lengthy decision, examined whether the state legislature's act was in conflict with the federal constitution, treaties with foreign nations, the Treaty of Guadalupe Hidalgo, the Bill of Rights, and the California Constitution. While the Chinese and Mexicans were not specified, it was well known that the "license fee for the privilege of working the gold mines in the state" was aimed at them. The court, finding no conflict between the state license fee regulation and other constitutions or treaties, upheld the regulation.[3]

Fugitive Slave Law, 1852–1858

During the debates at the state constitutional convention one delegate after another warned that if Negroes were allowed to enter California's territory, they would be brought here under indentures by enterprising whites wishing to exploit cheap labor in the goldfields. In many instances such claims were well founded

2. For firsthand accounts of what life was like during the gold rush, see J. T. Brooks, *Four Months among the Gold-Finders in California*; E. G. Buffum, *Six Months in the Gold Mines*; L. A. K. S. Clappe, *The Shirley Letters from the California Mines*; O. C. Coy, *In the Diggings in "Forty-Nine"*; E. de Massey, *A Frenchman in the Gold Rush: The Journal of Ernest de Massey, Argonaut of 1849*; T. T. Johnson, *Sights in the Gold Regions, and Scenes by the War*; B. Taylor, *Eldorado, or Adventures in the Path of Empire*.

3. *Cases in the Supreme Court*, San Francisco, December 1850, pp. 232–255.

in spite of the constitutional provision declaring slavery illegal. The legislature passed a bill requiring the return of runaway slaves to their master under the Fugitive Slave Act passed on April 15, 1852, and the courts early affirmed the constitutionality of that act in the case of Carter Perkins and Robert Perkins on habeas corpus in October 1852. In the majority opinion the court established the principle that by virtue of its police power, the state has the jurisdiction to arrest and restrain fugitive slaves and to remove them from their borders.

It is clear from a great deal of evidence such as the Indian indenture law and the disenfranchisement of all nonwhites, that California sympathy lay more with the slaveholding South than the non-slaveholding North. In the decision written by Chief Justice Murray in the Perkins case there are remarks about "this obnoxious class of population" and "the pernicious consequences necessarily resulting from this class [free Negroes] of inhabitants." These are sufficient to show how little consideration Negroes could expect to receive from the higher courts.

Carter Perkins, Robert Perkins, and Sandy Jones, all black. were brought as slaves to California in 1849 by their master, C. S. Perkins. This action was perfectly legal. The three men claimed to have entered into an agreement with their master to work for a certain period of time and then be granted their freedom after this period of service. C. S. Perkins returned to Mississippi, leaving his three former slaves as free men, but on passage of the fugitive slave act of 1852, he saw an opportunity to reclaim his former property and issued an order for their arrest, with a request for a certificate authorizing him to remove them to Mississippi under terms of the act of 1852. The three men were arrested in Placer County and taken before a justice of the peace in Sacramento, who issued a certificate for their removal. When the county court refused to release them on habeas corpus, the three men appealed to the California Supreme Court. Chief Justice Murray (who was to hand down the decision two years later in *People v. Hall*) ordered that the writ be dismissed and the slaves remanded to their owner. Chief Justice Murray cited a number of instances

in support of his contention that the state had concurrent jurisdiction in slavery legislation through its police powers. Chief
Justice Murray's own opinion shows in the following excerpt of
the decision:

> This subject [return of fugitive slaves] as well as the increase of free
> negro population, has for some time in the past been a matter of
> serious consideration with the people of this State, in view of the
> pernicious consequences necessarily resulting from this class of inhab-
> itants; so much so as to become the subject of a message from the
> Executive of the State more than a year and a half ago. Although I
> have no doubt that the section of the act now under consideration,
> was originated for the purpose of securing the rights of the master, yet
> I am satisfied the desire to purge the State of this class of inhabitants,
> who, in the language of a distinguished jurist, are "festering sores upon
> the body politic" entered largely into the consideration of the Legis-
> lature in passing this act.[4]

A supporting opinion by Justice Anderson stated that the
temporary residence of slaves in free territory (or states) had no
effect on the legality of a slave's servitude. Furthermore, he held
that since California had failed to emancipate slaves at the time of
admission to the Union, the masters of those slaves retained the
right to their services. The mere fact that the state constitution
prohibited slavery was not considered, or was considered irrelevant, since this had never been made a matter of legislative
enactment.

California's first governor, P. H. Burnett, had earlier been a
legislator in Oregon, where he had introduced an act providing
that any free Negro who failed to leave the state within the time
prescribed in the act was to be arrested and flogged at intervals
of six months until he complied with the law by departing from
Oregon. In his inaugural address in 1849 Burnett took a strong
stand against bringing indentured Negroes into California, and
pointed out that since the laws of the state gave them few rights
and classed them as an inferior race, they would therefore have
no incentive "to improve their characters." Although bills were

4. 2 Cal. 429–459 [1852].

introduced in 1850 and 1851 "to prevent the emigration of free negroes and persons of color," these failed to pass, and only in 1852 did the fugitive slave act become law.

Many Negroes were brought to California by their masters, but it was invariably claimed that these were personal servants and not slaves. If they were not slaves, it is clear that their persons and labor were controlled. Schemes by Southerners were proposed to establish Negro colonies in California according to newspaper reports.[5] One man in a letter to the *Pacific*, April 23, 1852, argued that Negro labor in California farming was essential because poison oak was so prevalent that it was impossible for white men to clear and develop the land.

Attempts were made by proslavery legislators as early as 1851 to divide California in two; the southern half, thus reverting to the status of a territory, would have been open to slavery if it so chose, according to the provisions of the Compromise of 1850. In order for this to be done, a revision of the constitution was required, and for a number of years a great amount of effort was devoted to trying to bring the matter of constitutional revision to the voters of the state. This was finally accomplished in 1857, but when the voters failed to provide the necessary majority, the matter ended.

The fugitive slave law, we may safely assume, was not really aimed at the return of escaped slaves, for there could have been at best a very limited number of these in California. The cost to a fugitive slave of securing passage on a ship or making the overland trek undetected would not have allowed many such escaped slaves to get to California. The real, but hidden, aim of the law was to enable a master to retain, or remove from the state, his former slave. Before 1852 there had been a number of cases where the owner of a slave attempted, through the courts, to remove his former slave. Some of these suits were allowed and others were denied. Even though California prohibited slavery, the operation of the fugitive slave act from 1852 to 1858 was such that former slaves could be held, though perhaps not used as such

5. *Pacific*, April 23, 1852; *Daily Evening Picayune*, February 11, 1852.

openly. Many of the owners of black slaves sold their human property in California in such a way that their manumission was secured.[6] In June 1852, the following advertisement appeared in the *Democratic State Journal*, a Sacramento newspaper:

> Negro for Sale.—On Saturday the 26th inst., I will sell at public auction a Negro Man, he having agreed to said sale in preference to being sent home. I value him at $300, but if any or all of his abolition brethren wish to show that they have the first honorable principle about them, they can have an opportunity of releasing said Negro from bondage by calling on the subscriber, at the Southern House, previous to that time and paying $100. I make this great sacrifice in the value of the property, to satisfy myself whether they prefer paying a small sum to release him, or play their old game and try to steal him. If not redeemed, the sale will take place in front of the Southern House, 87 J St., at 10 o'clock of said day.

Between 1852 and 1858 no free black person was really safe in California. He might be claimed as a fugitive slave and thus be liable for removal by a former master if he could not prove with a legal document that he was in fact a free man. He could secure his freedom by laboring for an agreed period in the free state of California, or by purchase, as in the case of the man who was advertised for sale for a hundred dollars in Sacramento in 1852. In 1855 a similar event occurred as attested by the following record taken from Coy:[7]

> *State of California*
> *County of Mariposa*
> Know all men to whom these presents shall come, that I, Thomas Thorn of the state and county aforesaid, being the rightful owner of the Negro man Peter Green and entitled to his services as slave, during his life, have this Day released and do by these presents release him, from any further service as a slave, and I do, by these presents for myself, my heirs, executors and administrators, declare him, the said, Peter Green, to be free to act for himself, and no longer under bonds as a slave, provided however, that said Peter Green, shall pay to me the sum of one thousand dollars, good and lawful money, or

6. L. M. Eaves, *A History of California Labor Legislation,* p. 99.
7. "Evidences of Slavery in California," pp. 1–2.

work for and serve me, from the present time until one year from and after the first day of April next (being until the first day of April, A.D. 1854). In testimony whereof, I have here unto affixed my hand and scroll for seal at Quartzburg this 5th day of February, A.D. One Thousand and Eight Hundred and Fifty Three.

THOMAS THORN

In presence of Benj. F. Rop, P. Codell Jr., Jos. A. Tiry. I hereby notify that the above obligation has been complied with and that Peter Green was legally discharged. Given under my hand at Quartzburg, this 7th day of August, A.D., 1855.

JAS. GIVENS, *Justice of the Peace*

While California was technically a free state, it was never-theless sufficiently understanding of the problem which a slave-owner faced when he found it expedient to dispose of a piece of black property to allow the following advertisement to appear in the *Sacramento Transcript*, April 1, 1850, addressed "To Families":

For Sale—a valuable negro girl aged 18, bound by indentures for two years. Said girl is of amiable disposition, a good washer, ironer and cook. For particulars apply at the Vanderbilt Hotel of J. R. Harper.

The last fugitive-slave case in California was tried in 1858. Archy Lee, a young black, was the property of C. V. Stovall, who had come to California overland by ox-team in 1857. After about a year Stovall, whose ventures at farming and operating a private school in Sacramento had not prospered, decided to return to Mississippi with his slave, Archy. The latter, however, probably through having his education improved by contact with free blacks in California, hid out in order to avoid being taken back to the South. On being apprehended, he was brought before the county court, where Judge Robinson decided that Archy was not a fugitive from labor according to state or federal laws, and ruled that his former master, by reason of the length of his sojourn in California and his having engaged in business, could not claim to be a transient. The judge said:

Comity can never extend to strangers anything beyond the rights and privileges which a State extends to its own citizens. Now if a man retain his citizenship in the State of Mississippi and sojourn here two months and work his slave, why may he not stay twenty years and work twenty slaves? The principle is precisely the same. The law would not permit a citizen of this State to hold and work a slave against his consent, and what it does not allow its own citizens to do, it cannot be reasonably expected to sustain strangers in so doing.[8]

No sooner was Archy released than he was once more arrested and placed in jail, and the case then came before the state supreme court. The chief justice, P. H. Burnett (a former governor of California) was a man of well-known prejudice against blacks, and while his decision in the case was no surprise, his reasons for reaching this were so outrageous that a great public outcry resulted. The chief justice wrote:

> From the views that we have expressed, it would seem clear that the petitioner [Stovall] cannot sustain either the character of traveler or visitor. But there are circumstances connected with this particular case that may exempt him from the operation of the rules we have laid down. This is the first case and under the circumstances we are not disposed to rigidly enforce the rules for the first time. But in reference to all future cases, it is our purpose to enforce the rules laid down strictly according to their true intent and spirit.[9]

While the Supreme Court of California thus upheld the right of Stovall to remove Archy by suspending its own rules, the newspapers reacted in loud protest at the decision.[10]

It was learned that Stovall had taken his manacled slave from San Francisco to Stockton, and would soon return to San Francisco to take steamer passage for Panama. A large number of San Francisco blacks set up a waterfront patrol to rescue Archy, and warrants charging Stovall with kidnapping, and a writ of habeas corpus authorizing the apprehension of Archy, were

8. Quoted from Eaves, p. 100, who cites *Sacramento Daily Union*, January 27, 1858.
9. Ibid., and the *San Francisco Bulletin*, January 28, 1858.
10. *Sacramento Daily Union*, February 12, 1858; *San Francisco Bulletin*, February 13, 1858; *Alta California*, February 14, 1858.

secured, together with the services of officers to serve these. Stovall, who had heard of the plans to rescue Archy, tried to make his getaway by boarding the ship in the bay after it was under way, but the ship was boarded by the officers, the papers were served, and Archy was thus rescued. The case then went to the county court of San Francisco, which referred it to the United States commissioner. After hearing testimony from both sides, the commissioner ruled that Archy was a free man. A great celebration by free blacks was held in San Francisco that night. The case attracted so much public attention, and was so favorable to the cause of black freedom, that it appears to have marked, as Eaves says, "a turning point in the history of negroes in California."[11] This was the last fugitive-slave case tried under the act of 1852. Soon to follow was the Civil War, after which came the Reconstruction legislation aimed at the improvement of blacks under the law. And only during the Civil War, when California became dominated by the Republican party, did Negroes obtain (in 1863) the right to testify in court cases involving whites.

The Nonwhite Barred as a Witness

The right of members of nonwhite groups to testify in cases where white men were accused of crimes against them was early abridged by state statute, a point which we have examined in a previous chapter. This issue was early challenged in the courts in a case involving a murder of a San Francisco Negro barber, Gordon Chase. Testimony given by a witness, Robert Cowles, was discredited because an examination of Cowles's hair was said to prove that he was one-sixteenth African. Efforts were made by the Negro population in California to overturn the antitestimony legislation. This legislation, however, as we have noted, was primarily aimed at *all* minority group populations of the time, most of which were much larger than the Negro group. However, efforts by Negroes and other minority groups for reform went almost completely unnoticed by the white majority, which con-

11. P. 103.

sidered the particular resources of California to be reserved for "Americans."

A historic decision involving the right to testify was set down in 1854 in *People* v. *Hall*.[12] From this record it is known that one George W. Hall was convicted of murder on the testimony of Chinese witnesses. This conviction was appealed, and the original judgment reversed (with the single dissenting opinion of Justice Wells) by arguing that since the American Indians are of Asiatic origin, they are not really different from Chinese and that it was the intent of the legislature in framing section 394 of the Civil Practice Act of 1850 to exclude Chinese as well as Indians from testifying as witnesses against whites.[13] In the words of the court, "the evident intention of the act was to throw around the citizen a protection for life and property, which could only be secured by removing him above the corrupting influence of degraded castes." In California one hundred years ago, we can conclude, it was more desirable to release a Caucasian convicted of murder through the testimony of witnesses than it was to permit any deviation in the established policy of white supremacy.[14] The opinion of the supreme court is quoted in full in the documents section, p. 229.

The present authors, as anthropologists, find the reversal of the original decision in the Hall case of particular interest because of the use of an ethnological argument to prove that Chinese and American Indians are racially related on the presumption that the American Indians belong to the Mongoloid race and originally migrated to the New World from Asia. The problem of the origin of the American Indians, whose existence was quite unsuspected prior to their discovery in 1492 by Columbus, became a much debated topic after these people were first seen. Neither the Scriptures nor classical authors made any reference to them, and they

12. 4 Cal. 399.
13. The prohibition of Chinese giving testimony against whites was repealed by omission from the *California Code of Civil Procedure*, 1872.
14. Cf. Eaves, pp. 113–114.

needed to be accounted for. Joseph de Acosta in 1589 was the first person to propose that the Indians came by land from Asia[15] and this theory was accepted by many.[16]

Some voices of protest were heard as court decisions following *People* v. *Hall* reveal. A San Francisco newspaper of September 17, 1857, cites an incident which may have contributed to the reversal two years later of the decision of the California Supreme Court in *People* v. *Hall*:

> In the Twelfth District Court, yesterday, the defendants introduced a native of Manilla [Philippine Islands] as a witness. The plaintiff objected that the witness was an "Indian," in the meaning of the law of California, and could not be admitted to testify. Judge Norton said that it was evident to him that the legislature, by the word "Indian" meant only American Indians, but as the Supreme Court had held Malays, Polynesians and Chinamen, to be included under the term Indians, he would have to be governed by their decision. The witness was accordingly excluded.[17]

In 1859 in *People* v. *Elyea* the state supreme court determined that the color of a man's skin is not an infallible test of the competency of a witness, under previously enacted antitestimony legislation excluding as witnesses blacks, mulattoes, and Indians.[18] The opinion of the court is printed in the documents section, p. 235.

15. L. E. Huddleston, *Origin of the American Indians: European Concepts, 1492–1729*; S. Jarcho, "Origin of the American Indians as Suggested by Fray Joseph de Acosta (1589)," *Isis* 50 (1959):430–438.

16. We do not know what authorities were cited in 1854 to support the argument of the Asiatic origin of the American Indians, but some of the following sources may have been cited: J. H. McCulloh, *Researches on America, Being an Attempt to Settle Some Points Relative to the Aborigines of America*; J. MacKintosh, *The Discovery of America by Christopher Columbus and the Origin of the American Indians*; S. L. Mitchell, "The Original Inhabitants of America Shown to be of the Same Family and Lineage with Those of Asia." For other citations to pre-1854 writings which held this view, see Bancroft, *History of California*, 5:30–55; R. F. Heizer, "Civil Rights in California in the 1850's—a Case History"; L. E. Huddleston, *Origin of the American Indians*; J. Imbelloni, *La segunda esfinge indiana*; J. Winsor, *Narrative and Critical History of America*, 1:369.

17. Quoted from a dated clipping in the authors' possession. Name of newspaper is not known.

18. 14 Cal. 144.

In April 1857 Manuel Dominguez appeared in a San Francisco courtroom as a witness for the defendant. Dominguez was a "mestizo" of Mexican-Indian ancestry. He had been a delegate to the constitutional convention of 1849 and was one of the signers of that document. In 1857 he was a wealthy landowner and a Los Angeles County supervisor, but before he took the stand the lawyer for the plaintiff pointed out that his Indian blood barred him from giving testimony, and the judge, agreeing, dismissed him as a competent witness.[19]

Two incidents as reported in newspapers in 1851 and 1865 illustrate the helplessness of the Indian because he did not have the right to testify against whites. Usually incidents of this sort, when reported in the newspapers, are accompanied by reportorial or editorial comments to the effect that the Indians are a nuisance and deserve the violence which they receive. Only rarely do we have a comment which indicates compassion for the unhappy condition of the Indian. From the *Sacramento Union*, November 14, 1851, under the headline "Murder in Santa Barbara":

> An Indian was murdered in Santa Barbara, recently, under circumstances which call loudly for the establishment of a Vigilance Committee in that place. He was called from his house by a Sonorian, whose name we did not learn, and who without any provocation whatever, plunged a knife into his heart, killing him instantly. Some four or five Indians were present, witnesses to the transaction, and they pursued the murderer, caught him and carried him before a magistrate. Will it be believed that he was almost immediately released from custody, because our laws will not allow an Indian to testify against a white man? The Indians in this part of the State, in the main a harmless race, are left entirely at the mercy of every ruffian in the country, and if something is not done for their protection, the race will shortly become extinct.

And from the same newspaper, on November 21, 1865, headed "Horrid Murder of an Indian Boy":

> The *Shasta Courier* of November 18 [1865] describes a recent tragedy in its county as follows:

19. L. Pitt, *The Decline of the Californios: A Social History of the Spanish-speaking Californians, 1846–1890*, p. 202.

Near North Fork on Cottonwood, week before last, a most cowardly and barbarous murder was committed. It seems that two white barbarians went to an Indian rancheria in that neighborhood for the purpose of getting possession of an Indian girl about ten years old. This attempt at forcible possession was resisted by the mother of the child, assisted by a crippled Indian boy, the only one in the rancheria. The resistance of this poor cripple so exasperated the villains that one of them seized him by the top of the head, while with his knife he first cut his throat and then stabbed him to the knife hilt, and to wreak his vengeance fully, turned the knife in the wound several times, then withdrawing it, again stabbed his victim, turning the knife as before, repeating the act until life was extinct. While this butchery was going on, the girl and her mother made their escape. In a few days after the fiends burnt the rancheria. There is nothing but the dead body and Indian testimony to prove the above, and though it is convincing, it is not enough, under the law, to punish the miscreants. White men who live with Indians habitually should do so subject to Indian testimony; and we think a law to that effect would be wise and proper.

We have seen that in 1854, in the case *People* v. *Hall*, the supreme court of the state of California reached the decision that Chinese persons were not different from Indians or Negroes. A recent newspaper item from the state of Massachusetts shows that nothing remains static. In 1966 the Boston School Committee officially ruled that Chinese are whites, in a controversy over balancing the racial composition of the city's schools. The following is reprinted from the *National Observer* of October 24, 1966:

A senior at a Boston high school, Walter J. Lee, 17, is puzzled because he has officially been declared a member of the white race. Walter is Chinese.

The young Mr. Lee is not alone in his confusion. Confusion, in fact, is the only sure result that can be expected from the variety of schemes devised to reduce "racial imbalance" in our cities. Even more confusing, the decision to classify Walter Lee and Boston's other Chinese pupils as whites is quite logical in its own way.

Massachusetts has a law requiring that state funds be withheld from school districts with racially imbalanced schools, such a school being defined as one with more than half its enrolment nonwhite. Unless you assume that the state's lawmakers were interested in merely assuring a pleasant proportion of hues in Massachusetts classrooms, it is apparent that they had some great social purpose in mind.

Sure enough. The idea is to let Negro children from poor Negro neighborhoods be exposed to non-Negro children from not-so-poor neighborhoods. Somehow this improves the education of Negro youngsters, or at least it is supposed to broaden the experience of both Negroes and whites.

Boston's School Committee, or school board, hasn't been taken with the idea, and the state has held back funds from the city's schools because the city hasn't done enough balancing. Two of the unbalanced Boston schools have predominantly nonwhite enrolments, but the non-whites are Chinese. Boston school folk have quite logically concluded that the spirit of the state's balancing act applies to Negroes, and that the Chinese-Bostonians are not suffering because they learn alongside other Chinese-Bostonians. So, for balancing purposes, youngsters in Chinatown are now deemed white, and the school committee has now declared the two schools balanced—or, at least, not unbalanced.

There are some Chinese, though, who think that logic dictates otherwise, and it would be hard to quarrel with them. Maybe more white children should indeed see more yellow children.

What makes all this logic illogical is the failure of the balancers to remember what schools really are for. Logically, they are for teaching children. It is only a tenuous theory that mixing and matching races, as one would do with items in a wardrobe, has anything to do with the teaching process. It is far more likely that politicians' obsession with color co-ordination confuses the process. The lesson young Walter Lee learned last week is but a trifling example.

Minority Rights to Schooling

Before 1870 most children of minority group parents were sent to schools maintained at public expense for their separate education. No mention is made of educational facilities that were qualitatively on a par with those provided for whites. Thus, the "separate but equal" doctrine was not the issue at this time. Schooling for Negroes, Orientals, and Indians, when available, was segregated by local policy adopted by local school boards or county ordinance under the supervision of state legislative enactments passed in 1863–64.[20] However, in 1860 the state legislature refused state funds to any school district not segregated,[21]

20. *Statutes of California*, 1864:213.
21. *Cal. Stats.*, 1860, chap. 329, pp. 321–326.

and in 1870 the legislature formally established the statewide segregated school system providing for separate schools for "children of African and Indian descent."[22]

In 1874, in a historic case before the state supreme court, a Negro, A. J. Ward, on behalf of Mary Francis Ward, his daughter, sued the principal of a San Francisco public school for her admittance into the school.[23] The court in its decision determined that the legislature cannot, while providing a system of education for the youth of the state, exclude children from its benefits merely because of their African descent. However, the court was quick to note that the law providing for the education of Negro children in separate schools, provided at the public expense, was not in conflict with the Constitution of the United States or the Thirteenth and Fourteenth amendments, and that colored children may in fact be excluded from schools established for white children when schools provided for colored children are established, but "if such schools for colored children are not established, they cannot be excluded from the schools kept for white pupils."

Harriet A. Ward, mother of Mary Frances Ward, submitted a petition before the supreme court for a writ of mandamus allowing Mary to enter Broadway Grammar School in San Francisco. The text of the petition and the reply of the defendant, Noah F. Flood, are printed in the documents section, p. 237.

The court then proceeded, in its opinion, to argue for the legality under state and federal statutes then existing of the "separate but equal" principle in public education. The arguments are printed in the documents section, p. 241.

Indian Rights to the Land

In 1886, after several years of litigation, the case of *Thompson* v. *Doaksum*[24] made its way to the state supreme court, which ruled that where land was covered by a grant which specifically reserved the Indian right of occupancy and such a grant was pre-

22. *Cal. Stats.*, 1869–70:838.
23. 48 Cal. 36 [1874], pp. 36–57.
24. 68 Cal. 593; 10 Pac. 199 [1886].

sented to the land commissioners, the confirmatory patent of the United States, even though it made no mention of reserved Indian rights, could not be construed to destroy the Indian's right of occupancy. The court referred to the act of Congress of March 3, 1851, stating that Congress has the exclusive right of preemption to all Indian lands lying within the territories of the United States, and that lands in California in the occupancy of Indian tribes at the date of the Treaty of Querétaro (i.e., Guadalupe Hidalgo) in 1848 became a part of the public domain, and subject to preemption, if no claim therefore for verification of legal title under Mexico was presented by the occupants to land commissioners within two years after the date of the act. Needless to say, few of the mass of uneducated Indians presented their claims for the land which they have occupied for thousands of years. The decision in the case of *Thompson* v. *Doaksum* is printed in the documents section, p. 244, as an example of how Indians could lose their land.

In 1888 the court changed its opinion somewhat, in the case of *Byrne* v. *Alas* et al., when it stated:

> Mission or pueblo Indians, who by themselves and their ancestors have been in continuous use, occupation, and possession of lands included within the exterior limits of a Mexican grant from a time prior to the establishment of the Mexican government have the right to remain in the occupancy thereof as against the patentee from the United States government and his grantees, notwithstanding they never presented their claim to the lands to the board of land commissioners appointed by the Act of Congress of March 3, 1851, to ascertain and settle private land claims in California. Under Section 15 of the Act of March 3, 1851, the patent issued in pursuance of the degree confirming the Mexican grant was conclusive only as between the United States and the claimant, and did not determine the relation between him and the Indians. Under this section the rights of the Indians were preserved *without* presenting their claims, and the patentee took the legal title in fee, subject to their right of occupancy.[25]

The dispute over rights to land grew to such proportions that several cases reached the United States Supreme Court. In

25. 74 Cal. 628 [1888].

1889, in the case of *Botiller* v. *Dominguez*, that Court overthrew the state supreme court conclusions reached in *Byrne* v. *Alas* and held that all claims without exception, whether to title or to occupancy, ought to have been presented for confirmation, and that failing presentation and confirmation, the claims were invalid.[26] Thereupon the state supreme court felt constrained to overrule its earlier decision in favor of the Indian's right of occupancy,[27] and this decision was reaffirmed in 1901 in the United States Supreme Court.[28]

As a postscript we may note that Congress on May 18, 1928, passed the California Indians Jurisdictional Act, which authorized the attorney general of California to sue the federal government in the Court of Claims for compensation for "all claims of whatsoever nature which the tribes or bands of Indians of California may have against the United States."[29] The suit, pressing mainly on the eighteen unratified treaties of 1850–1851 and the abortive reservation system, received in 1944 a judgment of $5,025,000, from which was subtracted $28,000 for court expenses incurred by the state of California.

The Indian Claims Commission Act (H.R. 4497) was passed August 13, 1946. Any Indian tribe in the United States was permitted, under this act, to sue the government for redress for any past action which was approved as arguable.[30] The Indians of California were among the 152 plaintiff groups,[31] and in September 1968, President Lyndon B. Johnson signed a bill to provide for a per capita distribution of a judgment of $29,100,000 awarded as compensation for the taking of the lands properly belonging to the California Indians. One of the main points in the Indians' case was the failure of Congress to ratify the eighteen treaties of 1850–1851.

26. 130 U.S. 238 [1889].
27. See *Horney* v. *Baker*, 58 Pac. 692; 126 Cal. 262 [1899].
28. See 181 U.S. 481.
29. R. W. Kenny, *History and Proposed Settlement of Indian Claims in California.*
30. N. O. Lurie, "The Indian Claims Commission Act."
31. For details see O. C. Stewart, "Kroeber and the Indian Claims Commission Cases."

Indians and Alcohol

Besides the curtailment or outright denial of most of the basic civil rights to all minority groups in California, certain legislative enactments specified prohibitions against certain occupations and enjoyment of certain kinds of entertainment by members of certain groups. In the case of *People* v. *Bray* in 1894, the old frontier principle of prohibiting the selling or giving of "firewater" to the "redskin" was supported in an appeal case.[32] The court ruled that "laws restricting the sale of liquors and forbidding such sale to certain classes of persons, who are peculiarly liable to be injured or demoralized by indulgence in alcoholic beverages are constitutional and valid." This decision lent judicial support to the state legislative act passed on February 14, 1872, and based on an act passed in 1850 entitled Sale of Liquors to Drunkards and Indians.[33] Amended in 1893,[34] the act remained legal until it was repealed in 1920. The decision observes that the denial of liquor to Indians "was intended to apply to Indians as a class, and was enacted in view of their well-known race peculiarities and their relations to society." The court's decision in the case of *People* v. *Bray* is printed in the documents section, p. 248.

32. 105 Cal. 344 [1894].
33. *Cal. Stats.*, 1850:409.
34. *Cal. Stats.*, 1893:98.

VI. The Mexican Californians

Historical Perspective

When Mexico secured her independence from Spain in 1821 the Spanish nationals who remained in California automatically became Mexican citizens. No great events occurred in California to mark the transfer of sovereignty. The anticlerical bent of Mexico led, after a delay of some years, to the secularization of the twenty-one Franciscan missions in California. This event is dated traditionally in 1834, but the process of disestablishment was proceeding before this date, and was not finally concluded until 1845. The mission Indians, of which there were about 15,-000 in 1834[1] were suddenly free to do whatever they wished. Many moved into the interior to live in purely native villages on wild foods; some established new villages, where they grew maize and beans and thus continued an economic way of life which they had been taught in the missions. Others simply camped in the abandoned mission buildings and lived by their wits. The development of large ranchos by Mexicans who could secure land grants for the asking offered to Indians a means of livelihood as cattle and ranch hands, and most of the ranchos had a number of Indian laborers attached to them in what was in many, perhaps most, instances a system of peonage. We have good descriptions of life in Mexican California in the 1830s and early 1840s written by American residents and visitors.

The Mexican Californians were often described by Ameri-

---

1. S. F. Cook, *Population Trends among the California Mission Indians.*

can visitors before 1846 in somewhat disapproving terms, perhaps with the idea that they were as unadmirable as the people
of Mexico itself, on whom little love was lost.[2] Typical of this
attitude is T. J. Farnham's characterization:

> That part of the population which by courtesy are called white, are
> the descendants of the free settlers from Mexico and the soldiers of
> the garrisons and Missions, who were permitted by his most Catholic
> Majesty to take wives. Their complexion is a light clear bronze; not
> white, as they themselves quite erroneously imagine; and, withal, not
> a very seemly color; nor remarkably pure in any way; a lazy color; and
> for that reason, rather out of place, associated as it is, with large dark
> flashing eyes, a finely chiselled Roman nose, and teeth as clear and
> sound as a pearl. Looking at the mere exterior of these men, the ob-
> server would most probably come to the conclusion that they were
> somewhat humanized. The speaking gait, the bland gesture of com-
> plaisant regard, the smile, that ray of the soul, all seem civilized—
> truly Castilian. The wide-brimmed and conical-crowned sombrero also,
> with its rope-like silver cord band, well be-tasselled, shoes and shoe-
> buckles, pantaloons well opened at the side seams, showing the snow-
> white flaunting drawers, the snugly-fitted roundabout, with its spher-
> ical silver buttons, and the largely proportioned vest, swinging loosely
> in the wind, the keen Spanish knife sitting snugly in its sheath along
> the calf of the leg, all would indicate to the sojourner of the day among
> them that these Castilianos [Californios] were accustomed to be men
> fulfilling some of the important ends of existence, in a worthy and
> gentlemanly way. And so they do, as understood in the Californias.
> They rise in the morning, that is to say, before noon-day, from their
> couches of blankets or bull's hides, and breakfast upon broiled or
> boiled beef and fried beans. After breakfast, they muster a tinder-box
> from the pocket, strike fire, light cigars made of tobacco rolled up in
> little slips of paper, till the ignited weed burns and discolors their
> thumb and forefinger aristocratically, and then betake themselves to
> their napping again. Thus stands or lies their humanity till the dinner
> hour. . . . And having eaten and drunken liberally, Senor crosses him-
> self reverently over his gastric apparatus, lays himself carefully upon
> his couch, and gives himself and his digestion to his guitar, till choc-
> olate comes at sun-set, to bedew his inner man for the slumbers of the
> night. Thus we have a glance at *los hombres Californios*. . . .

2. L. Pitt, *The Decline of the Californios: A Social History of the Spanish-speaking
Californians, 1846–1890*, pp. 16–17.

Thus much for the Spanish population of the Californias; in every way a poor apology of European extraction; as general thing, incapable of reading or writing, and knowing nothing of science or literature, nothing of government but its brutal force, nothing of virtue but the sanction of the Church, nothing of religion but ceremonies of the national ritual. Destitute of industry themselves, they compel the poor Indian to labor for them, affording him a bare savage existence for his toil, upon their plantations and the fields of the Missions. In a word, the Californians are an imbecile, pusillanimous, race of men, and unfit to control the destinies of that beautiful country.[3]

There was a feeling widely shared by Americans that it was their destiny to occupy the continent from the Atlantic to the Pacific shore. We can illustrate this point by quoting two accounts. The first is also by T. J. Farnham, written in California in 1840 when that area was still under Mexican control:

No one acquainted with the indolent, mixed race of California, will ever believe that they will populate, much less, for any length of time, govern the country. The law of Nature which curses the mulatto here with a constitution less robust than that of either race from which he sprang, lays a similar penalty upon the mingling of the Indian and white races in California and Mexico. They must fade away; while the mixing of different branches of the Caucasian family in the States will continue to produce a race of men, who will enlarge from period to period the field of their industry and civil domination, until not only the Northern States of Mexico, but the Californias also, will open their glebe to the pressure of its unconquered arm. The old Saxon blood must stride the continent, must command all its northern shores, must here press the grape and the olive, here eat the orange and fig, and in their own unaided might, erect the altar of civil and religious freedom on the plains of the Californias.[4]

Alfred Robinson, an American serving as clerk for a Boston trading company and who lived in California from 1829 on, wrote in his *Life in California* just before American annexation:

Why not extend the "area of freedom" by the annexation of California? Why not plant the banner of liberty there, in the fortress, at the entrance of the noble, the spacious bay of San Francisco? It re-

3. T. J. Farnham, *Life, Adventures, and Travels in California*, pp. 358–359, 363.
4. Ibid., p. 413.

quires not the far-reaching eye of the statesman, nor the wisdom of a contemplative mind, to know what would be the result. Soon its immense sheet of water would become enlivened with thousands of vessels, and steamboats would ply between the towns, which, as a matter of course, would spring up on its shores. While on other locations, along the banks of the river, would be seen manufactories and saw-mills. . . . Everything would improve; population would increase; consumption would be greater, and industry would follow.

All this may come to pass; and indeed, it must come to pass, for the march of emigration is to the West, and naught will arrest its advance but the mighty ocean.[5]

An assessment of the Mexicans and Yankees in the early gold-rush mining camps written by "Dame Shirley," a doctor's wife who lived on the Feather River at Indian Bar in 1851–1852, is informative:

It is very common to hear vulgar Yankees say of the Spaniards, "Oh, they are half-civilized black men!" These unjust expressions naturally irritate the latter, many of whom are highly educated gentlemen of the most refined and cultivated manners. We labor under great disadvantages, in the judgment of foreigners. Our peculiar, political institutions, and the prevalence of common schools, give to *all* our people an arrogant assurance, which is mistaken for the American *beau ideal* of a gentleman.

They are unable to distinguish those nice *shades* of manner, which as effectually separate the gentleman from the clown with *us*, as do these broader lines, which mark these two classes among all other nations. They think that it is the grand characteristic of Columbia's children, to be prejudiced, opinionated, selfish, avaricious and unjust. It is vain to tell them, that such are not specimens of American gentlemen. They will answer, "They call themselves gentlemen, and you receive them in your houses as such." It is utterly impossible for foreigners to thoroughly comprehend and make due allowance for that want of delicacy, and that vulgar, "I'm as good as you are," spirit, which is, it must be confessed, peculiar to the lower classes of our people.[6]

When California was seized by the United States in 1846

5. Pp. 225–226.
6. L. A. K. S. Clappe, *The Shirley Letters from the California Mines, 1851–1852,* pp. 158–159.

during the Mexican War, the Mexican population of the state became a defeated enemy population, and one which the Americans felt little admiration for. During the period of military occupation from 1846 until the discovery of gold in January 1848, California was of no particular importance to the United States beyond being a portion of territory which was to be ceded by Mexico following the end of hostilities and the signing of the Treaty of Guadalupe Hidalgo. The discovery of gold changed everything. The massive migration to California by sea and land was dominated by white Americans. Bayard Taylor's prescient formulation of the "melting pot" theory did not, of course, come to pass. The differences of race and condition, which he imagined would soon be obliterated, became the actual basis for the separation of the Yankee Americans and the Mexican Americans which is still today so evident. Bayard Taylor wrote in 1849 of the Mexican Californians:

> I do not believe, however, that the majority of the native [i.e. Mexican Californian] rejoices at the national change which has come over the country. On the contrary, there is much jealousy and bitter feeling among the uneducated classes. The vast tides of emigration from the Atlantic States thrice outnumbered them in a single year, and consequently placed them forever in a hopeless minority. They witnessed the immediate extinction of their own political importance, and the introduction of a new language, new customs, and new laws. It is not strange that many of them should be opposed to us at heart, even while growing wealthy and prosperous under the marvellous change which has been wrought by the enterprise of our citizens. Nevertheless, we have many warm friends, and the United States many faithful subjects among them. The intelligent and influential faction which aided us during the war is still faithful, and many who were previously discontented are now loudest in their rejoicing. Our authorities have acted toward them with constant and impartial kindness. By pursuing a similar course, the future government of the State will soon obliterate the differences of race and condition, and all will then be equally Californian and American citizens.[7]

7. *Eldorado, or Adventures in the Path of Empire*, p. 110.

The Mexican in the Goldfields

The northern half of the state had far fewer Mexican residents in 1846 than the southern half, and this northern group rapidly became a minority. Mexican Californians from southern California trekked north to the Mother Lode to engage in gold mining, and large numbers of people from Mexico also came to seek their fortune. It is said that ten thousand Sonorans came to the California goldfields in 1849, many of them to spend a season mining and then return to their families. Numbers of Chileans and Peruvians also came, and though distinguished from Mexicans by name, they were much resented. The feeling quickly developed that the gold of California belonged to Americans, by which was meant white Americans who were full citizens. W. Kelly, an early observer of the gold rush, wrote:

> As soon as [the American] got an inkling of the system [of mining gold], with peculiar bad taste and ingenious feeling he organized a crusade against these obliging strangers [the Mexicans] . . . in fact, the Yankee regarded every man but a native American as an interloper, who had no right to come to California and pick up the gold of "free and enlightened citizens."[8]

By late 1849 most of the mining camps in the northern mines (i.e., north of Sonora) had adopted regulations denying foreigners (including Mexicans) the right to hold claims and carry out mining. In the southern mines, extending from Mariposa to Sonora, where water was more scarce and mining was much harder work, the Mexicans were not much bothered in 1848 when about 1,300 went to the mines[9] and worked without notable friction with about 4,000 Yankees. By mid-1849 the picture had changed. There were now nearly 100,000 miners looking for gold, many of the richest placers were worked out, food was often difficult to get, many miners were having no luck at all, and a strong anti-foreign reaction set in. Arguing that California was American, the

8. *A Stroll Through the Diggings of California*, p. 13.
9. L. Pitt, *The Decline of the Californios*, p. 50.

miners resented any other nationals sharing its mineral wealth. By the end of 1849, when 80,000 Yankees, 8,000 Mexicans, 5,000 South Americans, and several thousand Europeans had arrived to seek their fortune, all Spanish-speaking people connected in any way with mining, whether Peruvians, "Chilenos," Mexican immigrants, or resident California Mexicans, were lumped together under the term *greasers* and treated accordingly—that is to say, in the worst possible way. The Spanish-speaking miners knew how to mine gold, worked hard, lived frugally, were often successful, and in this way acquired the resentment of the Yankees, who were inexperienced, required more amenities, and had poorer returns as a group since there were more of them. Mexican peddlers and mule dealers did well also, and their success was resented by Yankee traders, who were perhaps less efficient and asked higher prices. Bayard Taylor, who was in the Mother Lode in 1849, wrote:

> The treatment of the Sonorians by the American diggers was one of the exciting subjects of the summer. These people came into the country in armed bands, to the number of ten thousand in all, and took possession of the best points on the Tuolomne, Stanislaus and Mokelumne Rivers. At the Sonorian camp [Sonora] on the Stanislaus there were, during the summer, several thousands of them, and the amount of ground they dug up and turned over is almost incredible. For a long time they were suffered to work peaceably, but the opposition finally became so strong that they were ordered to leave. They made no resistance, but quietly backed out and took refuge in other diggings. In one or two places, I was told, the Americans finding there was no chance of having a fight, coolly invited them back again! At the time of my visit, however, they were leaving the country in large numbers, and there were probably not more than five thousand in all scattered along the various rivers. Several parties of them, in revenge for the treatment they experienced, committed outrages on their way home, stripping small parties of emigrants by the Gila route of all they possessed. It is not likely that the country will be troubled with them in future.[10]

In the effort to legalize prohibitions against foreigners min-

10. *Eldorado*, p. 79.

ing for gold (the Mexicans being the chief target), the state legislature passed in 1850 the Foreign Miners' Tax. An argument supporting this appears in the California *Senate Journal*:

> The wonderful gold discovery in California is an epoch in the world's history—in its mighty influence upon commerce and emigration such as time has never instanced. While in our country it has unbalanced trade, and partially destroyed all former rates of labor on our notions, if this effect is not so immediate it has excited the wildest cupidity which threatens California with an emigration overwhelming in number and dangerous in character. Tens of thousands have already arrived in our country, and they are the commencement of a vast multitude en route and preparing to come hither, of the worst population of the Mexican, South American states, New South Wales, and the Southern Islands to say nothing of the vast numbers from Europe. Among others, the convicts of Mexico, Chile and Botany Bay are daily turned upon our shores, who seek and possess themselves of the best places for gold digging whether upon their own or on account of foreign employers and carry from our country immense treasure. . . . This bill requires the foreigner upon the plainest principles of Justice to pay a small bonus for the privilege of taking from our country the vast treasure to which they have no right.
>
> The strife and bloodshed which has taken place between the citizen and foreigner is mainly to be attributed to the fact that, while the latter had neither legal nor moral right to come into our country and take away the gold, they were doing nothing for the support of the government whose protection they were looking to. Pass this bill and the foreign proprietor of Chilean, Peru, Chinean, Kanaka, or convict gold diggers from any other nation will have to pay some little tribute for this rich unprecedented privilege—a privilege which no other nation at this or any former period would have granted to the balance of the world.[11]

The combination of the miners' tax and the strong pressure against Spanish-speaking miners (as well as Chinese, of course), led half to three-fourths of these people to leave the southern mines where they were concentrated in 1850.[12] It was then realized that this abandonment of the mines was having a serious eco-

11. First session, 1850, p. 493.
12. J. Heckendorn, *Miners' and Businessmen's Directory for the Year Commencing Jan. 1, 1856* (Columbia, California: Heckendorn and Wilson), p. 183.

nomic effect. The original argument that foreign miners were taking gold out of the country turned out not to be true. Most of the gold was spent in the local districts for food, clothing, and in the gambling and entertainment establishments.[13] Thus, the Stockton merchants who had in 1850 howled so loudly for the miners' tax, passed in 1851 a resolution "that we look upon the inflictions of this tax upon the people of the southern district, as but part of a grand scheme to depress the enterprise of our citizens . . . and to cripple our commerce and destroy our local trade."[14] The repeal of the miners' tax in 1851 had little effect, for the Spanish-speaking miners had endured so much discrimination that they had no desire to remain. The Mexicans apparently did not trust the reaction to the repeal of the miners' tax as stated in the editorial appearing in *Alta California* on March 20, 1851:

> Let our Chilean friends and Mexican neighbors, the Gaul and the Briton, the celestial and the Kanaka hombres from the land of Pizarro and Mynheers from submarine Holland, let them all come and work with us, and become part of us full of confidence that justice and policy will never again be so outraged as in that unfortunate law whose death the governor has proclaimed.

Most of them either returned to Mexico or made their way to the cities and villages, mostly in southern California, where they began the process of fusion with the native-born California Mexicans.

After 1851, when the great gold rush had passed its peak, the richest placers had been worked out, and many hopeful argonauts had given up and returned home or turned to farming or some other activity, quartz mining began. Mexicans and Chilenos were familiar with this kind of mining and were sought after as laborers in the mines and mills, which were operated by Americans with American capital.

The Mexican and Popular Justice

Through the 1850s and 1860s large sections of California

13. W. Colton, *Three Years in California* (New York: A. S. Barnes, 1850), p. 367.
14. Cf. *Alta California*, March 17, 1851; Pitt, *Decline of the Californios*, p. 65.

managed their own law in the form of vigilante organizations and popular tribunals. Summary justice in the form of a mob shooting up an Indian village in retaliation for some supposed act by some unidentified native was a regular thing. Mexicans were a favorite target of this kind of popular justice, which operated without a court or judge or reference to the legal code adopted by the legislature.[15] At the same time we note this, we observe that there is a strong probability that Mexicans did engage in more horse-stealing, highway robbery, assault, and thieving than any other single group of people in California. Why this was so has been debated by many, but perhaps the best explanation is that Mexicans reacted more strongly against the injustices that were directed toward them than other minority groups because California had been a part of Mexico where many of these people had lived before American annexation and they resented their status as a conquered people. The central government of Mexico established after independence in 1821 was weak, and local *caudillos* flourished. In California there was a revival of this form of reaction in the period of the general lawlessness which prevailed after 1848.[16]

The kind of justice that Mexicans could expect in the 1850s in California is illustrated by an account written by Clarence King:

> Early in the fifties, on a still hot summer's afternoon a certain man, in a camp which shall be nameless, having tracked his two donkeys and one horse a half mile, and discovering that a man's track with spur-marks followed them, came back to town and told the boys who loitered about a popular saloon that in his opinion some Mexican had stolen the animals. Such news as this naturally demanded drinks all round. "Do you know, gentlemen," said one who assumed leadership,

15. Bancroft (in *Popular Tribunals: History of the Pacific States of North America*) collected a very large number of instances from various sources of popular justice in the two decades following 1850, and one is impressed by the number of Mexicans hung, whipped, branded, ear-cropped, or banished during this period. See also V. M. Berthold, *The Pioneer Steamer, California: 1848–1849*, pp. 37–42; S. B. Dakin, *A Scotch Paisano*, pp. 174–175; Pitt, *Decline of the Californios*, pp. 70–74.

16. Cf. Pitt, *Decline*, p. 75.

"that just naturally to shoot these greasers aint the best way? Give 'em a fair jury trial, and rope 'em up with all the majesty of the law. That's the cure." Such words of moderation were well received, and they drank again to "here's hoping we ketch that greaser." As they loafed back to the veranda, a Mexican walked over the hill-brow, jingling his spurs pleasantly in accord with a whistled waltz. The advocate for law said in undertone, "That's the cuss." A rush, a struggle, and the Mexican, bound hand and foot, lay on his back in the bar-room. The camp turned out to a man. Happily such cries as "String him up!" "Burn the doggoned lubricator!" and other equally pleasant phrases, fell unheeded upon his Spanish ear. A jury, upon which they forced my friend, was quickly gathered in the street, and despite refusals to serve, the crowd hurried them in behind the bar. A brief statement of the case was made by the *ci-devant* advocate, and they shoved the jury into a commodious poker-room, where were seats grouped about neat green tables. The noise outside in the bar-room by and by died away into complete silence, but from afar down the canon came confused sounds as of disorderly cheering. They came nearer, and again the light-hearted noise of human laughter mingled with the clinking glasses around the bar. A low knock at the jury door; the lock burst in, and a dozen smiling fellows asked the verdict. A foreman promptly answered, "Not guilty." With a volley of oaths, and ominous laying of hands on pistol-hilts, the boys slammed the door, with "You'll have to do better than that!" In half an hour the advocate gently opened the door again. "Your opinion, gentlemen?" "Guilty!" "Correct! You can come out. We hung him an hour ago." . . . When, before sunset, the bar-keeper concluded to sweep some dust out of his poker-room back door, he felt a momentary surprise at finding the missing horse dozing under the shadow of an oak, and the two lost donkeys serenely masticating playing-cards, of which many bushels lay in a dusty pile. He was reminded then that the animals had been there all day.[17]

The Mexican experience in the mines seems to have been the means of reinforcing and amplifying the earlier feelings toward Spanish-speaking people in California, a feeling that had in part been acquired through the American experience in the Mexican War. Thus there developed early a strong feeling of prejudice against Mexicans in California—an attitude which has apparently continued down to the present time.

17. *Mountaineering in the Sierra Nevada*, pp. 284–286.

The Mexican and the Government

Of the forty-eight delegates elected to draw up the constitution of California in 1849, eight were Mexicans, and of these, five had been born in California. The Mexican population of California in that year is calculated at 13,000, the Yankee population at 100,000. One delegate, Manuel Dominguez of Los Angeles, was a mestizo—of mixed Indian and Mexican blood.[18] The Mexican Californians did not always vote as a bloc in the convention, but when it came to the question of suffrage, which was being considered for white males only, they combined their forces, pointed out that approval of such restrictions would be a denial of guarantees contained in the Treaty of Guadalupe Hidalgo, and helped carry the vote that approved the section permitting the state legislature when it met first in 1850 to determine which Indians could vote. It was scarcely possible to allow Dominguez to sign the new constitution if it contained a prohibition against Indian suffrage. A concession to the Spanish-speaking Mexican Californians was the constitutional proviso that the legislature print all its laws in the Spanish language. The state constitution was the only document of importance in whose drafting the Mexican Californians shared. After that event, though some participated in state and local government to some degree, their political influence was negligible.

The Mexican government, through its governors of California, from 1821 to 1846 had been very liberal in issuing land grants to citizens. Most of these lands were used for grazing livestock rather than for intensive farming. California was big, applicants for land grants were not very numerous, and as a result a great deal of land was distributed to a few individuals. Pitt notes that at the end of the Mexican period two hundred California families owned fourteen million acres.[19] With the peak of the gold rush over, the Yankees began to take up farmland. If this land happened to be claimed by some other California citizen,

18. D. E. Hargis, "Native Californians in the Constitutional Convention of 1849."
19. *Decline*, p. 86.

one who had formerly been a citizen of Mexico, the Yankee squatter tended to defend his right to the land on the grounds that he needed it and that the Mexican title was invalid under United States law. In 1851 the federal government established a board of land commissioners to examine all Mexican land-grant titles and to rule on their validity. In 1856, when the board had concluded its deliberations, most of the great Mexican estates in the northern half of California had been preempted by squatters or sold off by their owners to pay the legal fees incurred in trying to have the titles validated.[20] Southern California in the 1850s was still to experience the first phases of its ultimate popularity. Los Angeles remained relatively small—in 1854 its population was about 5,000, of whom 1,500 to 2,000 were resident Yankees and most of the balance Mexicans. The great ranchos of southern California were not overrun by squatters. These continued to operate in much the same fashion as they had operated before 1846, and the cattle raised on them brought good prices in the north. There were Yankees, many of them wealthy landowners who had settled there long before 1846,[21] and they came to dominate the political and business enterprises. These Yankees became Mexicanized— spoke Spanish, at times married Mexican wives, and in general adopted the social customs of the majority group, which remained a majority until the 1870s. A few of the Mexican Californians from the south went to the state capital as elected legislators, but this was rarely a pleasant experience, since they found themselves outnumbered by Yankee politicians who looked down on them. Their best political opportunities lay in their home areas, where they represented the majority element in the population.[22]

At the midpoint of the 1850s California was experiencing an economic depression. Money was short, the great flood of gold

20. C. C. Baker, "Mexican Land Grants in California"; P. W. Gates, "Adjudication of Spanish-Mexican Land Claims in California"; J. S. Hittell, "Mexican Land-Claims in California"; L. Pitt, *Decline of the Californios*, chap. 5; W. W. Robinson, *Land in California*.

21. J. A. Hawgood, "The Pattern of Yankee Infiltration in Mexican Alta California, 1821–1846."

22. Pitt, *Decline,* chap. 8.

was nearly played out, land and cattle prices were down, and banditry was rampant. The state legislature in 1855 passed a number of laws that directly or indirectly were aimed at restricting the freedom of Mexican Californian citizens. These included a law prohibiting operation of any "bull, bear, cock or prize fights, horserace, circus, theatre, bowling alley, gambling house, room or saloon, or any place of barbarous or noisy amusements on the Sabbath," the penalty being a fine of ten to five hundred dollars.[23] Others were a special act controlling gambling;[24] a head tax of fifty dollars imposed on immigrants, aimed primarily at Chinese, but incidentally including Mexicans; and a renewal of the foreign miners' tax set at five dollars per month. The most direct slap at Mexicans was the refusal of the legislature to provide funds for translation of laws into Spanish, and the passage of the antivagrancy act, called the "Greaser Act"[25] because section 2 specified "all persons who are commonly known as 'Greasers' or the issue of Spanish or Indian blood ... and who go armed and are not peaceable and quiet persons." Even though the legislature removed the objectionable reference to "greasers" in an amendment to the act in 1856, the law so read and was applied for a full year.

Through the late 1850s more and more open prejudice was shown to Mexicans who aimed at securing political office either through appointment or election. Pitt has outlined the way in which Antonio Coronel, a Mexican-born, partly black man of means and reputation, was defeated in the Los Angeles mayoralty election of 1856, and how the same man had earlier, in 1853, been denied the post of subagent for Indian affairs in southern California.[26] The southern Californians found themselves allied with those legislators and voters in the northern half of the state in 1859 when the effort to divide the state came to a climax. The hope by the proslavery group wishing to split

23. *Statutes of California*, 1855, p. 50.
24. Ibid., pp. 124–125.
25. *Cal. Stats.*, 1855, chap. 175.
26. *Decline*, pp. 200–201.

California was that the southern half would revert to territorial status (to be called the Territory of Colorado and to include the counties of San Luis Obispo, Santa Barbara, Los Angeles, San Diego, and San Bernardino) and thus be open to slaveholding. The Mexican Californians of the south were less concerned with instituting slavery than they were with getting some relief from state taxes—from which they felt they received very little benefit —and with being able to effectively exercise political influence through a Mexican majority. The issue was put to the voters of the state as a referendum measure and was approved, but the legislature balked at actual separation and voted it down.

During the Civil War there was recruited in California the First Battalion of Native Cavalry, whose volunteer members included a large number of Mexican Californians. Numbering 485 men and serving from 1862 to 1865 in Arizona and New Mexico, it proved to be an effective force in reducing Confederate influence.

Postscript

The end of the Mexican Californian insulation and population majority in the southern half of the state came with the completion of the railroads—in 1876 the entry of the Southern Pacific, and in 1887 the Santa Fe to Los Angeles. The great land-grant ranchos were sold off to land speculators and individual farmers, Americanos finally outnumbered the Spanish-speaking group consisting of native-born Mexican Californians ("Californios") and immigrant Mexicans, and there was set in motion the merging of the Mexican groups with each other and to a lesser extent with the now numerous Yankees. Improved political relations with Mexico made things Mexican once more respectable, and there developed what Pitt calls the "cult of Spanish California"— a kind of romantic revival of the Spanish American past, which was to be the theme of so much art and architecture, so many books, pageants, and movies.

> The "Spanish" cult was . . . comprised of one part aestheticism, one part history, and one part ballyhoo. So popular was this cult by 1890

that one could scarcely recall how recently the Spanish Americans had been in disfavor, or that the real, live ones still were. For only after they had reduced the real-life Spanish-speaking to the status of a foreign minority did the Yankees feel any deep compassion toward Spanish-American culture.

Any effort to assess the impact of the Spanish-Mexican tradition on present-day California is complicated by the lingering romantic tradition. Yet historians now generally agree that the most important Yankee influences consist of innumerable Spanish words, place-names, legal arrangements (as in water rights), architectural forms, and holiday pageantry. Some of these influences have survived easily, others only through deliberate effort.

Yankee hatred [toward Mexicans] has diminished and grown less overt. As one Anglo observed, the Mexican-American in California lives in a kind of limbo; neither accepted nor rejected. The Americano finds the Mexican-American amiable and anxious to please, but does not understand him in his "displaced status." Some Anglo-Saxons at least experience a sense of guilt toward the Negro for past oppressions; toward the Spanish-speaking, few feel any similar sentiments or any vivid emotion at all.[27]

The Mexican Californian who calls himself a Chicano is a member of the largest minority group in California; it numbers over two million and is about 80 percent urbanized and native born. This minority lacks effective political leadership, something which, historically, it did not fight to maintain or affirm after 1850. The Mexican Californian has been remarkably tractable, but the potential political power he holds by virtue of constituting 10 percent of the population of the state is something of which he may become aware in the future.

27. *Decline*, pp. 290–291, 295.

VII. The Early Legal Status of the Chinese

The Chinese in the Goldfields

In the late 1850s the Chinese became the focus of attention of California. They came on British ships; the first arrived in 1848 when three Chinese disembarked on the shores of California. By 1850 there were almost 1,000; two years later (1852) there were 9,800, and in 1860 the census lists 35,000. The peak was reached in 1880 with 75,000. They paid their own way and went to the gold mines as "snipers," laundrymen, cooks, and so forth. In the California goldfields the Chinese were placed in a difficult position. They were excluded from legal protection and were robbed, beaten, killed, and forced out of many towns. They were prohibited in many parts of the Sierras from holding mining claims, and what placering they did was by sufferance in areas that had been worked over and abandoned or otherwise not wanted by white miners who had gone on to more productive locations. In the Sierran slopes where the gold rush occurred there were large numbers of men in the "camps," but these were aggregations of men in search of gold and without any government or law.[1] Local "districts," as they were called, adopted the general policy of holding a mass meeting, electing an alcalde (a Spanish word for the combined mayor and justice of the peace of a town),

1. R. W. Paul, *California Gold.*

154

and adopting a set of mining laws.[2] The miners' laws of 1849 and later mark the beginning of opposition to the Chinese by depriving them of the privilege of mining gold, or even living in some districts.

As early as 1852 the state assembly committee on mines recommended in its report that a resolution be sent to Congress declaring that importation by foreign capitalists of large numbers of Asiatics, South Americans, and Mexicans (referred to as "peons" and "serfs") was "a danger to the tranquility of the mining regions," and that speedy action was required to correct the evil.[3] Governor Bigler responded by sending a special message on Asiatic immigration to the legislature, in which he represented the Chinese as temporary visitors who would depress the standard of labor, a people who retained allegiance to their own country, and who would overwhelm the whites unless some means were found to exclude them. The same arguments and phraseology were to be used for the next thirty years in talking about the evils of Chinese immigration.[4] In 1852 the Columbia District, just north of Sonora, observed a set of mining regulations which included sections stating that "neither Asiatics nor South-Sea Islanders shall be allowed to mine in this district, either for themselves or for others"; "any person who shall sell a claim to an Asiatic or South-Sea Islander shall not be allowed to hold another claim in this district for the space of six months"; "none but Americans, or Europeans who intend to become citizens, shall be allowed to mine in this district, either for themselves, or others."[5] In 1848 the miners in the Agua Fria District, in Mariposa County, passed a resolution that "the regulations which have been in vogue for two and a half years prohibiting Chinese from working within our district shall be the law and rule in this district. Any

2. C. H. Shinn, *Land Laws of Mining Districts;* and *Mining Camps: A Study in Frontier Government.*
3. *Assembly Journal,* 1852, Appendix, Doc. 28.
4. For a survey of racial beliefs about the Chinese see S. C. Miller, *The Unwelcome Immigrant: The American Image of the Chinese, 1785–1882,* pp. 154–159.
5. Shinn, *Mining Camps,* pp. 234–235.

Chinaman who tries to mine must leave on twenty-four hours notice, otherwise the miners will inflict such punishment as they deem proper."[6]

Whether Chinese could carry on mining in a district was therefore a matter of local option. The state legislature did its bit by imposing in 1850 a tax of twenty dollars a month on foreign miners. We have treated the history of the miners' tax in chapter 6.

The "Yellow Peril"

The anti-Chinese feeling which was first generated in the early 1850s in the Sierran goldfields expanded to include Chinese everywhere in California, as well as in other Western states. Two songs of the gold rush period are printed in the documents section, p. 251, as illustrative of attitudes toward Chinese in this period. An "Anti-Coolie Club" was founded in San Francisco in 1862[7] and formed the pattern for others. The purpose of such clubs was to promote anti-Chinese feeling and encourage discriminatory legislation. These feelings reached a peak in the mid-1880s when mass demonstrations were made against Chinese in Washington (Tacoma), Oregon (Portland), and widely in California (Santa Barbara, Pasadena, Santa Ana, Santa Cruz, Healdsburg, Red Bluff, Merced, Placerville, Los Angeles, Sacramento, Yuba City, Redding, Petaluma, Vallejo, Chico, Nevada City, and Oakland).[8] Some counties (Humboldt, Del Norte) evicted all resident Chinese beyond their borders in the late 1880s. The Western anti-Chinese sentiment became, in due course, the attitude of the country, and its first national success came when President Arthur in 1882 signed the Exclusion Act, which completely excluded any further Chinese entry to the United States.[9] The stereotype of the Chinese

6. See L. M. Eaves, *A History of California Labor Legislation*, p. 118.
7. *San Francisco Bulletin*, July 12, 1862.
8. H. H. Bancroft, *California inter pocula*, vol. 35, *The Works of Hubert Howe Bancroft*, pp. 563–580.
9. Eaves, pp. 173–180. Miller takes issue, in *The Unwelcome Immigrant*, with the widely held view that anti-Chinese feeling in the United States was generated in California and spread from there to the rest of the country. He believes that the

as cunning, treacherous, immoral, vice-ridden, subversive, un-scrupulous, inhuman, incapable of acquiring the responsibilities of citizenship, degraded, competing with decent workingmen by laboring for low wages, and altogether unassimilable was to be-come a fixed view. A belief that the Chinese remained loyal to their emperor, and that their presence in California was "the ad-vance guard of numberless legions that will, if no check is ap-plied, one day overthrow the present Republic of the United States,"[10] led to the coining of the phrase "yellow peril." Books written to warn the white citizens of the danger of being over-whelmed by the yellow tide were common.[11]

In the early treaties concluded between China and the United States in 1844 and 1858, the precise status of Chinese immi-grating to the United States was left undefined. It was assumed that Chinese had the same rights enjoyed by other noncitizens. Indeed, the negotiation of the Burlingame treaty in 1868 affirmed this principle in a reciprocal clause which accorded Chinese resi-dents in the United States "the same privileges, immunities and exemptions as citizens," with the proviso that "nothing herein contained shall be held to confer naturalization upon citizens of the United States in China, nor upon the subjects of China in

---

prejudice was more general, and that California cannot be blamed for the anti-Oriental feeling in the United States.

10. H. J. West, *The Chinese Invasion*, p. 5.

11. Among these are *Chinese Immigration and the Physiological Causes of the Decay of a Nation* (1862); *The Coming Struggle: or What the People of the Pacific Coast Think of the Coolie Invasion* (1873); *The Chinese Invasion* (1873); *Short and True History of the Taking of California and Oregon by the Chinese in the Year A.D. 1899* (1882); and *The Yellow Peril in Action* (1907). For more extended treatment of the history of the Chinese in California see G. Barth, *Bitter Strength: A History of the Chinese in the United States, 1850–1870*; B. S. Brooks, *Brief of the Legislation and Adjudication Touching the Chinese Question Referred to the Joint Commission of Both Houses of Congress*; D. and S. Chu, *Passage to the Golden Gate: A History of the Chinese in America to 1910*; M. R. Coolidge, *Chinese Immigration*; R. E. Cowan and B. Dunlap, *Bibliography of the Chinese Question in the United States*; L. M. Eaves, *History of California Labor Legisla-tion*, pp. 105–196; M. R. Konvitz, *The Alien and the Asiatic in American Law*; R. W. Paul, "The Origins of the Chinese Issue in California"; A. L. Sandmeyer, *The Anti-Chinese Movement in California*; J. tenBroek, E. N. Barnhart, and R. W. Matson, *Prejudice, War, and the Constitution*, pp. 15–22.

the United States." However, arguments advanced by influential Californians forced President Garfield to negotiate a new treaty in 1880, which provided:

> Whenever, in the opinion of the Government of the United States, the coming of Chinese laborers to the United States, or their residence therein, affects or threatens the interests of that country, or to endanger the good order of the said country or of any locality within the territory thereof, the Government of China agrees that the Government of the United States may regulate, limit, or suspend such coming or residence, but may not absolutely prohibit it. The limitation or suspension shall be reasonable and shall apply only to Chinese who may go to the United States as laborers, other classes not being included in the limitations.[12]

National Legislation to Exclude Chinese

With the new treaty in hand, restrictive legislation on Chinese immigration could now be passed, and this was soon effected. In 1882 the California legislature, with the intent of showing Congress the feelings of the people of California, declared a legal holiday to encourage public demonstrations against admission of Chinese to the United States, and it is said that these rallies drew in some cases as many as 30,000 persons.[13] In 1882, over the objections of President Arthur, Congress enacted legislation suspending Chinese immigration for ten years. Subsequent amendments tightened even further the restrictions against Chinese entry.[14] After the passage of the exclusion measure of 1882, violence and discrimination against Chinese reached such intense levels that nearly every major city in California either passed ordinances severely curtailing the civil rights of Chinese, or reacted to the Chinese presence by attempting to burn down their housing and business districts. In 1888 Congress passed the Scott Act, which prohibited the reentry of 20,000 persons of Chinese

12. Published in *Senate Executive Documents*, 48th Cong., 2d sess., vol. 1, pt. 2, ser. no. 2262, 1882.
13. Eaves, *Labor Legislation*, pp. 141, 178.
14. Eaves, pp. 180–188.

descent who had temporarily left the United States.[15] In 1892 the Congress of the United States, not content with previous restrictions, passed the Geary Act, which continued the suspension of immigration for another ten years, prohibited bail to Chinese in habeas corpus proceedings, and required that all Chinese possess certificates of residence.[16] Being apprehended without such certificates could result in the deportation of the offender.

The Fifty-third Congress in 1893 found itself faced with a Chinese problem. The registration requirement in the Geary Act was tested and upheld as valid by the United States Supreme Court.[17] Only 12,243 Chinese had registered, and it was calculated that about 85,000 Chinese who had failed to register were subject to deportation. The secretary of state asked for an estimate of the cost involved in trying and deporting Chinese convicted of failing to register. When it was learned that the cost would be in excess of ten million dollars, Congress found that after all it had been too hasty, and on November 3, 1893, repealed the requirement to execute the deportation.[18] In 1902 and 1904 Congress, partially as a result of the lobbying of the California Oriental Exclusion League, indefinitely extended the prohibition against Chinese immigration and denied to Chinese the right of naturalization.[19] The Immigration Act of 1924 again barred aliens, especially Chinese ineligible for citizenship, and prohibited American citizens of Chinese descent from bringing alien Chinese wives into the United States.

As Coolidge pointed out, "No small part of the persecution of the Chinaman was due to the fact that it was his misfortune to arrive in the United States at a period when the attention of the whole country was focused on the question of slavery."[20] McWilliams makes the point clearer:

15. *27 U.S. Statutes 476.*
16. *27 U.S. Stats. 25.*
17. *Fong Tue Ting v. U.S.,* 149 U.S. 698 [1893].
18. *28 U.S. Stats. at Large 7,* chap. 14.
19. *32 U.S. Stats. 176; 33 U.S. Stats. 428.*
20. *Chinese Immigration;* see also S. C. Miller, *The Unwelcome Immigrant,* p. 15.

Even so we started out to deal with the Chinese on a non-discriminating basis only to discover that this policy conflicted with our own policy toward Indians and Negroes. Every issue affecting the Chinese cut across the whole complex of issues affecting the Negro. Without a single exception the anti-Chinese measures were carried out in Congress by a combination of Southern and Western votes. Southern Bourbons could not tolerate a policy in California that might have unsettling consequences in Alabama.[21]

Attempts by the State to Discourage Chinese Immigration

From 1852 to 1862 a number of state acts prohibiting or inhibiting entry of Chinese into California were passed, but these proved to be either unenforceable or unconstitutional. The rights of states and the federal government regarding entry of foreigners to the United States had been settled in 1849 in the so-called Passenger Cases where the power to regulate commerce was granted to Congress exclusively. Since the transportation of passengers is an act of commerce, it was ruled that states could not levy taxes on such traffic or deny foreigners admission unless they could be shown to be criminals, paupers, or diseased. The California legislature, however, performed as though it had never heard of superior federal authority in this connection. In 1852 the legislature passed an act requiring the owner or master of a vessel bringing foreign passengers to California to post a bond of five hundred dollars for each passenger. This act was not enforced, and was ultimately declared unconstitutional in 1872 in the case of *People* v. *U.S. Constitution.*[22] In 1854 concurrent resolutions were passed by the senate and the assembly instructing the California congressmen to attempt to secure passage in Congress of an act to legalize imposition of a head tax, to be paid by owners or masters of vessels, on each Chinese and Japanese on board with the intention of debarking.[23] Although the legislature, it is assumed, knew that federal authority superseded that of the state in this connection, it proceeded in 1855, without waiting for

21. C. McWilliams, *Brothers Under the Skin*, p. 98.
22. 42 Cal. 578, 590.
23. *Statutes of California*, 1854:230.

the act of Congress which it had hoped its members would secure, to pass the capitation tax act of fifty dollars for each passenger landed,[24] only to have it promptly be declared unconstitutional.[25]

In 1858, despite what must now have been clearly impossible on constitutional grounds, laws were again enacted in California which prohibited further immigration of Chinese ("Mongolian") people into the state. An act entitled An Act to Prevent the Further Immigration of Chinese or Mongolians to this State was approved on April 26, 1858.[26] The first section of this act was explicit in its wording:

> Any person or persons, of the Chinese or Mongolian races, shall not be permitted to enter this state, or land therein, at any port or ports thereof, and it shall be unlawful for any man, or persons . . . to knowingly allow or permit, any Chinese or Mongolian . . . to enter any of the ports of this state.

The second section warned:

> The landing of each and every Chinese or Mongolian person shall be deemed . . . a separate offense.

This statute carried with it as a penalty the charge of a misdemeanor, with fines from four hundred to six hundred dollars, or imprisonment in the county jail for three months to one year, or both fines and imprisonment. This act was declared unconstitutional in an unpublished decision.[27]

Four years later, on April 26, 1862, the second of a series of discriminatory statutes enacted against the Chinese was passed. Entitled An Act to Protect Free White Labor Against Competition with Coolie Labor and to Discourage the Immigration of Chinese into the State of California,[28] the act legalized what was termed the Chinese Police Tax, which enabled the state government to tax all Chinese who were engaged in a nonagricultural occupation.

24. *Cal. Stats.*, 1855:19.
25. *People v. Downer*, 7 Cal. 170.
26. *Cal. Stats.*, 1858:295.
27. 20 Cal. 534.
28. *Cal. Stats.*, 1862:462.

SECTION 1. There is hereby levied on each person, male and female of the Mongolian race, of the age of eighteen years and upwards, residing in this state, . . . licenses to work in the mines, or to prosecute some kind of business, a monthly capitation tax of $2.50 . . . provided that all Mongolians exclusively engaged in the production and manufacture of the following articles, shall be exempt . . . sugar, rice, coffee, tea.

The consequences of not paying such a tax were severe, and the injustices many. The tax delinquent had no legal recourse to the courts and came completely under the jurisdiction of the tax collector.

SEC. 4. The collector shall collect the Chinese Police Tax provided for in the act, from all persons liable to pay the same, and may seize the personal property of any such person refusing to pay the tax, and sell the same at public auction, by giving notice by proclamation one hour previous to such a sale.

Tax evasion was difficult, for the law was clear that

should any person, liable to pay the tax imposed in this act, in any county in this state, escape into any other county, with the intention to evade the payment of such tax . . . it shall be lawful for the collector to pursue such person and enforce the payment of such tax.

Each month that the tax was collected, a certificate of payment was issued to the person paying the tax. The law also stipulated that a discount could be made to those persons who paid the tax in advance.

And any Mongolian so paying said tax to the Treasurer of the County, if paid monthly, shall be held responsible for the payment of the tax due from each person so hired.

A state supreme court decision made this act invalid by declaring the act in violation of the provision of the Constitution of the United States which gave Congress the power to regulate the commerce with foreign nations.[29] The decision stated that

the Chinese may be taxed as other residents, but they cannot be set apart as special subjects of taxation, and be compelled to contribute to the revenue of the state in their character as foreigners.

29. In *Lin Sing* v. *Washburn*, 20 Cal. 534 [July 1862].

This decision overthrew several previous court decisions to which the reader is referred.[30]

To Hinder and Restrict

New legislation continued to pour from the state capital. The next series of enactments attempted to hinder the Chinese in his everyday life. An act entitled An Act for the Suppression of Chinese Houses of Ill-Fame was approved March 31, 1866.[31] Though obviously a discriminatory measure on its face, it no doubt caused many innocent Chinese people a great deal of legal trouble. This law removed most of the common legal procedures for gathering evidence and establishing the proof of guilt or innocence of the accused:

> SECTION 1. All houses of ill fame, kept, managed, inhabited or used by Chinese women for the purposes of common prostitution are hereby declared to be public nuisances, and common repute shall in all such cases be received as competent evidence of the character of the house.

Under the supposition that property might be used for illegal purposes, a landlord could deny to any Chinese the use of his property:

> SEC. 2. Every lease or demise of any house, land, or premises occupied . . . for the purpose aforesaid, shall be unavailable.

The law also encouraged and made profitable the giving of information to officials about these alleged establishments.

> SEC. 3. The court trying the case shall adjudge one-half thereof to the person giving information of the offense, and/or the witnesses or evidence thereof. . . . And in all such actions Chinese men and women shall be competent witnesses.

This act was amended on Feb. 7, 1874,[32] by deleting the word

---

30. *The People* v. *Naglee*, 1 Cal. 237 [December 1850]; *Crosby* v. *Patch*, 18 Cal. 438 [July 1861]; and *The People* v. *Coleman*, 4 Cal. 46 [January 1854], which affirmed the position that "the Legislature, in its discretion, may, therefore discriminate in the imposition of taxes on certain classes of persons, occupations, or species of property, taxing some and exempting others."

31. *Cal. Stats.*, 1866:641.

32. *Cal. Stats.*, 1874:84.

"Chinese" before "women" in the introductory sentence. "All houses of ill-fame kept and managed, inhabited or used by women for the purpose of common prostitution . . ." eliminated the discriminatory aspect of the law and applied it to all persons engaged in this ancient enterprise.

While hindering the pursuit of life and happiness of the Chinese already in the state, the state legislature in 1870 came up with new legislation aimed at further restricting the influx of immigrants from the Orient. In essence, these two laws assumed that all Oriental females coming into the state were doing so in order to engage in "criminal and demoralizing" purposes; that all children had been kidnapped; and that all males were either criminals or indentured slaves, unless they could prove otherwise to the satisfaction of the immigration authorities.

An act entitled An Act to Prevent the Kidnapping and Importation of Mongolian, Chinese, and Japanese Females for Criminal or Demoralizing Purposes was approved on March 18, 1870, and was the first California statute to mention specifically by name people of Japanese origin.[33]

> PREAMBLE. Whereas the business of importing into this state Chinese women for criminal and demoralizing purposes has been carried on extensively during the past year, to the scandal and injury of the people of this state, and in defiance of public decency: and whereas many of the class referred to are kidnapped in China, and deported at a tender age without their consent and against their will; therefore in exercise of the Police Power . . .

> SECTION 1. It shall not be lawful, from and after the time when this act takes effect [immediately] to bring . . . from any ship . . . into this state any Mongolian, Chinese, or Japanese females . . . without first presenting to the Commissioner of Immigration evidence satisfactory to him that such female desires voluntarily to come into this state, and is a person of correct habits and good character, and thereupon obtaining from such Commissioner of Immigration a license or permit particularly describing such female and authorizing her importation or immigration.

33. *Cal. Stats.*, 1870:330.

This act was followed twenty-three years later by a similar statute (chapter 182) entitled An Act to Prevent Compulsory Prostitution of Women and the Importation of Chinese or Japanese Women for Immoral Purposes and to Provide Penalties Therefore, which was approved March 23, 1893.[34] This act made it a misdemeanor for anyone to bring into the state of California women of "Oriental descent" with the intent of placing them in charge of any other person against their will.

A few years later, on March 16, 1901, the Code Commission Act was enacted, and again it was made a crime to import Oriental females to California for the same reasons listed in the act of 1893. This enactment was subsequently declared to be unconstitutional by the state supreme court, but it was nevertheless reenacted by the legislature on March 21, 1905.[35]

Enacted also on March 18, 1870,[36] was chapter 231, An Act to Prevent the Importation of Chinese Criminals and to Prevent the Establishment of Coolie Slavery. The curious fact about these two acts of 1870 is that the main body of each of these pieces of legislation is introduced by an explanatory preamble, not unknown but not generally in use, in the main body of legislation. It appears that if the explanatory preamble had been omitted from the act, it would have been difficult to understand why the act was passed at all.

> PREAMBLE. Whereas: criminals and malefactors are constantly imported from Chinese seaports, whose depredations upon property entail burdensome expense upon the administration of criminal justice in this state; and whereas: by the importation of such persons a species of slavery is established and maintained which is degrading to the laborer and at war with the spirit of the age, ...

The statute continues in the first section much as did its companion bill, forbidding the landing of Chinese or Mongolian males unless evidence is presented to the immigration authorities

34. *Cal. Stats.*, 217.
35. *Stats. and Amdts.*, 1905:656.
36. *Cal. Stats.*, 1870:332.

indicating that the immigrant has come into the state voluntarily and is a person of moral habits and good character. Penalties for infractions of this statute were severe. Any ship's master found guilty of violation of the provisions of the act was charged with a misdemeanor and punished by a fine of $1,000 to $5,000 or imprisonment from two to twelve months.

The People Speak and the Legislature Acts

In the last half of the decade beginning in 1870 a large number of statutes were passed and legislative resolutions were affirmed concerning Chinese immigration. An act to ascertain and express the will of the people of the state of California on the subject of Chinese immigration was approved on December 21, 1877.[37] This act provided for a vote by the people of the state, at the next general or special state election, that would enable the voters to express their viewpoint as to the continuance or prohibition of Chinese immigration, and required the governor to note the question submitted to the voters and the final result, and to send copies thereof to the president, vice-president, each cabinet minister, senator, and representative at Washington, and the governor of each state and territory. A California ballot was taken in 1879 on authorization of the legislature to determine public sentiment on Chinese immigration. It is reported that 900 voted in favor of continuing immigration and 150,000 voted against.[38] The nature of the ballot was such, however, that it is not possible to say that this was a true expression of the sentiment of the California voters. In order to cast a vote for continuing immigration the balloter was required to cross out "Against" and write in "For" in a line in very small type at the bottom of the ballot reading "Against Chinese Immigration." Any ballot that did not have a check for this line was automatically counted as a vote against immigration, apparently on the assumption that anyone not for was against further immigration.

37. Cal. Stats., 1877–8:3.
38. Coolidge, Chinese Immigration, p. 123; tenBroek, Barnhart, and Matson, Prejudice, War, and the Constitution, p. 17.

Chilians

"The Chilian men almost as invariably wear a cast of countenance
indicative of a desire that the Yankees would just mind their own business, and let him and his mind theirs. The number of Chilians in California are less numerous than they were three or four years ago, and
are annually decreasing, which can hardly be said of any other race of
people among us, except the aborigines." [*Hutchings' Illustrated California Magazine* 1 (9):387, March 1857.]

Mexicans

"With his fondness for horses and field sports, the resident native Californian combines many traits of a social nature that would be deemed commendable in any people, and among these, to the fullest extent of his means and ability are generosity and hospitality; and yet while remarking this of the few it is equally our positive belief that from the migratory portion has arisen more of robbery, rapine and deeds of blood, than from any other class of our population." [*Hutchings' Illustrated California Magazine* 1 (9):389, March 1857.]

Chinese

"Now permit us to introduce to your acquaintance celestial John and his lady, types and shadows of the empire of China—a large majority of whom are doubtless from the lower orders or coolies; exhibiting a cringing, abject sense of servility, to that degree that it appears a fixed trait of character in all but a few of the more intelligent and wealthy. Unlike other Oriental nations, the Chinese have sent hither swarms of their females, a large part of whom are a depraved class; and though with complexions in some instances approaching to fair, their whole physiognomy but a slight removal from the African race." [*Hutchings' Illustrated California Magazine* 1 (9):385, March 1857.]

Chinese Gambling House

"With the exception of the leading Chinese merchants we have had opportunity to observe only most unfavorable specimens of this race. Amongst the throngs of coolies and degraded women transported to our shores are displayed the most revolting features of Chinese life. We do not wonder at the prejudice felt against them by our citizens, when we consider that such are their habits that in whatever locality they establish themselves, public opinion renders it imperative that the neighborhood be abandoned to them." [*Hutchings' Illustrated Magazine 5* (7):329, January 1861.]

In 1876 F. M. Pixley, speaking in behalf of California before a joint congressional committee charged with investigating Chinese immigration, said:

> The Chinese are inferior to any race God ever made. . . . I think there are none so low. . . . Their people have got the perfection of crimes of 4000 years. . . . The Divine Wisdom has said that He would divide this country and the world as a heritage of five great families: that to the Blacks He would give Africa; to the Red Man He would give America; and Asia He would give to the Yellow race. . . . The White race is to have the inheritance of Europe and America and . . . the Yellow races are to be confined to what the Almighty originally gave them and as they are not a favored people, they are not to be permitted to steal from us what we have robbed the American savage of. . . . I believe that the Chinese have no souls to save, and if they have, they are not worth saving.[39]

This rhetorical appeal to divine authority as endowing California to the whites is echoed years later in an editorial in the March 1920 issue of the *Grizzly Bear*, journal of the Native Sons of the Golden West, calling for the impeachment of Governor Stephens for his refusal to call the legislature into special session to promulgate anti-Japanese legislation. His impeachment would "impress upon the yellow-Japs and their white-Jap admirers and hirelings the knowledge that white voters predominate here, and that they are going to see to it that California remains what it has always been and God Himself intended it shall always be—the White Man's Paradise."

Other legislative enactments in the form of resolutions during this period called for the senators and representatives from California in Washington to secure the speedy passage of a bill to restrict Chinese immigration by levying a per capita tax of $250 on each immigrant. This resolution was adopted by the legislature on December 11, 1877.[40] Ten days later a similar request in the form of a resolution called for a modification of all treaties between the United States and Oriental empires so that all immigra-

39. tenBroek, Barnhart, and Matson, p. 21.
40. *Cal. Stats.*, 1877–8:1056.

tion from Asia to California might be totally restricted.[41] A few months later, on February 2, 1878, a further resolution called for the stoppage of federal subsidies granted to those steamship companies running vessels between California and China.[42] Seven days after the passage of this last resolution an additional plea from the legislature[43] requested a modification in existing federal treaties so as to terminate the immigration of Chinese to the United States. And again, in 1880,[44] the legislature, through Senate Concurrent Resolution No. 14, resolved

> that a Joint Committee of six . . . be appointed to memorialize the President of the United States and Congress, to modify the Burlingame Treaty, so as to prohibit the further immigration of Chinese to this country.

Another act, which is of interest as an example of nuisance legislation, was entitled An Act to Protect Public Health from Infection Caused by Exhumation and Removal of the Remains of Deceased Persons and was approved April 1, 1878.[45] Though general in its application, it was primarily directed at the Chinese, who were accustomed to remove the bones of their dead for shipment to and final burial in China. The well-known reverence of the Chinese for their ancestors lay behind this practice of returning the bones of the dead to the homeland for final burial, but the legislative act referred to seems to be aimed more at expressing distaste for the "barbaric" custom than at protecting the health of white citizens. But even this custom showed the total lack of regard for America by Chinese, according to one California congressman, who, in an address, charged the Chinese with bringing to California "slavery, concubinage, prostitution, the opium-vice, the disease of leprosy, the offensive and defensive organization of clans and guilds, the lowest standard of living known and a detes-

41. Ibid., p. 1058.
42. Ibid., p. 1062.
43. Ibid., p. 1063.
44. *Cal. Stats.*, 1880:246.
45. *Cal. Stats.*, 1877–8:1050; *Penal Code*, sec. 297.

tation of the people with whom they live *and with whom they will not even leave their bones when dead."*

In the May 1880 issue of the *Californian*, a popular monthly magazine, the following editorial assessment of one aspect of the current social situation in California appeared. The statement can be judged by what the reader has encountered earlier in this chapter.

> California prejudice, *a propos* of the Chinese question, is a fruitful subject of Eastern criticism. We are met with the charge of race antipathy whenever we attempt to show what is and must always be the result of the unlimited influx of a people who will neither assimilate with nor contribute to any of those things in which we take pride as forming a part of our civilization. Now race prejudice is the outgrowth of a fixed state of society, where the population receives no acquisitions from the outside. It is most strongly developed in districts where the people have been undisturbed for several centuries. The moment men commence to associate with their fellow-men they discover traits to admire, and the old antipathies give way. Hence it is, that whenever the population is homogeneous, and has remained undisturbed for a considerable period of time, race prejudices will be found; and whenever the population becomes cosmopolitan, this antagonism will disappear. Commerce, literature, marriage, and a thousand influences begin their work of assimilation, which no mere prejudice can withstand. Now, as a matter of fact, California has one of the most cosmopolitan populations in the world. . . . Speaking of the population as an entirety, and not of individuals, it is safe to assume that nowhere in the known world is there less of that very feeling which is now so clamorously charged against us. This is apparent from the hospitable way in which the Chinese were themselves first received. They were welcomed in every possible manner, by every grade of society. It was only when the real character of this immigration was discovered that the protest came. Race prejudice comes before acquaintance, and thaws after it. But this protest did not come until long years of observation had forced a reluctant conclusion.

Obstacles to a Livelihood

Another enactment, also designed for its nuisance value, sought to hinder the livelihood of Chinese immigrants. Chapter

116, approved April 23, 1880, was entitled An Act Relating to Fishing in the Waters of this State.[46] Section 1 provided that

> all aliens incapable of becoming electors of this state are hereby prohibited from fishing, or taking any fish, lobster, shrimps, or shell fish of any kind, for the purpose of selling, or giving to another person to sell. Every violation of the provisions of this act shall be a misdemeanor, punished upon conviction by a fine of not less than 25 dollars or by imprisonment in the County Jail for a period of not less than thirty days.

This statute was declared unconstitutional in 1880 by a state supreme court decision involving a Chinese defendant, Ah Chong.[47]

The legislature, continuing with its policy of providing annoyance toward Oriental immigrants, approved a modification of the fish and game acts (originally authorized in the Penal Code on April 11, 1872) on March 23, 1893.[48] This statute changed section 636 in that it did not specifically prohibit aliens from carrying on fishing occupations in the waters of the state, but did prohibit the use of alien *techniques* in these endeavors:

> Every person who shall set . . . any pound, weir, set net trap . . . for catching fish in the waters of this state . . . Every person who shall cast . . . any seine or net . . . in any river . . . of this state which shall extend more than 1/3 across the width . . . Every person who shall cast . . . "Chinese sturgeon lines" or "Chinese shrimp or bag nets" or lines or nets of similar character . . . is guilty of a misdemeanor.

Punishments for violations were severe:

> Every person convicted of a violation of any of the provisions of this chapter shall be punished by a fine of not less than one-hundred dollars nor more than $500 and/or imprisonment in the County Jail (from sixty days to a maximum of 12 months).

A companion bill to the act relating to fish and game passed on April 23, 1880, was approved eleven days earlier, and was en-

46. *Cal. Stats.*, 1880:123.
47. 5 Pacific Coast Law Journal, 1880:451.
48. *Cal. Stats.*, 1893:215.

titled An Act to Prohibit the Issuance of Licenses to Aliens Not Eligible to Become Electors of the State of California. The wording of these two bills is at first curious, but becomes clear when Article II of the California Constitution is reviewed, where the only class of people listed as aliens and also as not eligible to vote were the Chinese. The clause was modified from prohibiting the vote to the Indian, whose numbers were rapidly dwindling and were no longer of significant consequence to the white man, to prohibiting the vote to the Chinese, whose population, to some whites, was becoming dangerously large. In the constitution, the clause read:

> provided no native of China, no idiot, insane person or person convicted of any infamous crime, and no person hereafter convicted of the embezzlement or misappropriation of public money, shall ever exercise the privileges of an elector of this state.

This act, passed on April 12, 1880,[49] read as follows:

SECTION 1. No license to transact any business or occupation shall be granted or issued by the state, or any county, or city, or city and county, or town, or any municipal corporation, to any alien not eligible to become an elector.

SEC. 2. A violation of the provisions of section one of this act shall be deemed a misdemeanor, and shall be punished accordingly.

It had become more and more apparent to Orientals already in the state that with the pleas and resolutions of the state legislature attempting to halt entirely further Oriental immigration, the members of the legislature were making it more difficult to procure a livelihood or to join with the rest of the citizens of the state in engaging in full and productive lives. The legislature cinched up the knot even tighter by passing an act to amend the Penal Code of 1881 (sections 178, 179). Orientals, who had previously been prohibited from obtaining licenses to conduct their own businesses, were now also prohibited from being employed in certain capacities.[50] The code, two sections of which are of in-

49. *Cal. Stats.*, 1880:39.
50. In the state constitutional convention in Sacramento in 1878 there was a great

171

terest, came into effect on February 13, 1880. Section 178 prohibited the officers of corporations from employing Chinese, and section 179 forbade the hiring of Chinese by any corporation:

> SECTION 179. Any corporation now existing or hereafter formed under the laws of this state that shall employ directly or indirectly in any capacity any Chinese or Mongolian shall be guilty of a misdemeanor and upon conviction thereof shall for the first offense be fined not less than $500 nor more than $5000 and upon the second conviction shall in addition to said penalty forfeit its charter and franchise and all its corporative rights and privileges.

The rest of the history of this act[51] is interesting, for it remained in effect until the Code Commission Act of March 16, 1901, which revised the Penal Code, repealed these sections. Sections 178 and 179 were also held to be unconstitutional and were finally dealt a deathblow when they were repealed again by a specific act of the legislature on March 21, 1905.[52]

Last Major State Act of Discrimination

The last major piece of legislation that discriminated against the Chinese was passed in 1891. The scope of this act was essen-

---

deal of discussion on the question of restricting employment of Chinese. Sections 2 and 3 of Article 19 of the Constitution of the State of California ratified in 1879 provided that Chinese could not be employed "on any state, county, municipal, or other public works" or by corporations. The convention delegates in 1878 considered a recommendation that would prohibit any employment of Chinese in the state of California. Senator J. F. Miller, chairman of the Committee on Chinese Questions, characterized the proposed measure as "starvation by constitutional enactment," with the further observation: "If the Chinese are not to be employed by anybody, are not permitted to labor, they cannot live, and if you deprive them of the right to labor they must starve. That is the logical consequence of the position assumed by the advocates of this prohibition against the labor of these people. It is indefensible, for it deprives the prohibited people of the right of life." The measure did not pass, but the fact that it was introduced and seriously considered shows the feelings of some of the state legislators. See *Debates and Proceedings of the Constitutional Convention of the State of California,* Convened at the City of Sacramento, Saturday, September 28, 1878. Sacramento, 1880. Pp. 77, 80, 82.

51. *Code Amdts.,* 1880, *Amdts. to the Penal Code:*1.

52. *Stats. and Amdts.,* 1905:652.

tially the same as that of the preceding statutes passed in 1858 and 1862. Entitled An Act to Prohibit the Coming of the Chinese Persons Into the State, Whether Subjects of the Chinese Empire or Otherwise, and to Provide for Registration and Certificates of Residence and Determine the Status of All Chinese Persons Now Residents of the State and Fixing the Penalties and Punishments for Violations of This Act and Providing for the Deportation of Criminals, it was approved March 20, 1891.[53] This statute was most specific in its provisions.

> SECTION 1. From and after the passage of this act, it shall be unlawful for any Chinese person . . . whether subjects of the Chinese Empire or otherwise, as well as those who are now within the limits of the State, and who may hereafter leave this State and attempt to return, and those who have never been here, or having been here have departed from this State (save and excepting only the following . . .) to come to or within or to land at or remain on any part or place within this State.
>
> SEC. 3. It is hereby made the duty of all agents of transportation . . . when applied to by any Chinese . . . for the passage from one station, town, city, . . . to another . . . or to any other state, . . . and before selling such ticket, to demand of said person applying permission to see and shall, before selling a ticket, examine the "certificate of residence" of the applicant.

Agents of transportation were charged with the enforcement of the provisions of the act:

> SEC. 4. . . . and should any such Chinese person refuse or fail to produce, on demand, said certificate, . . . it shall be the duty of said agent or conductor . . . to arrest and confine such Chinese person until such time as he shall be able to deliver over such person in a court having jurisdiction.

Section 5 provided for the penalties for any person bringing into the state any Chinese not lawfully entitled to emigrate and increased the charge of the crime from a misdemeanor to a felony. Section 6 dealt with the consequences that would befall the Chi-

53. *Cal. Stats.*, 1891:185.

nese person found in the state without proof that he was legally entitled to be there. All Chinese, in effect, were deemed guilty of this offense until they could prove themselves innocent.

Sec. 6. . . . any Chinese person found guilty of being unlawfully within this state shall be caused to be removed therefrom by judgment of the court, to China, unless the defendant shall prove that he is a citizen of some foreign country other than China. . . . The burden of establishing citizenship shall rest upon the defendant. In every case, when established that such Chinese person is not lawfully in this state, then the judgment of the court shall be deportation to the country of his citizenship at the cost of said person so to be deported. . . . If [the cost is] collected [it is] paid into and credited to the Chinese Fund, and if not, paid out of the Chinese Fund or [the person may be] imprisoned in the state prison for a term not less than one nor more than 5 years, and on termination . . . shall be deported to China.

Section 11 outlined the provisions for the Chinese certificate of residence, and section 15 made it mandatory that all Chinese legally residents of the state contribute to a Chinese Fund which in turn, as provided in section 6, would enable the state to finance the deportation of Chinese not legally residents of the state, and to pay informers on whose testimony such deportation would depend.

Sec. 15. Each Chinese person who shall apply to the Commissioner of the Bureau of Labor Statistics shall pay into the State Treasury to be credited to the "Chinese Fund" the sum of $5.00.

Sec. 19. The Governor of this state is authorized and required, at the expiration of one year from the passage of this act, to offer a reward of twenty-five dollars to any person . . . as informants who shall produce the necessary testimony for the conviction of any Chinese person for a violation of this act. . . . [The reward] shall be paid from the . . . "Chinese Fund."

Again the penalty for altering or changing a certificate of residence was increased to a felony, and upon conviction the defendant could be charged one thousand dollars and be imprisoned in the state prison for a period of up to five years.

In an important state supreme court decision in 1894,[54] the act of March 20, 1891, was declared unconstitutional.

> The act . . . to prohibit Chinese persons from coming into the state, and prescribing terms and conditions upon which those residing in the state shall be permitted to remain or travel therein, is in excess of the power of the state and in conflict with the Constitution of the United States, which gives exclusive power to regulate commerce with foreign nations; and Congress, in the exercise of its constitutional powers, having prescribed the terms upon which the Chinese now here shall be permitted to remain within the United States, it is beyond the power of the state to impose any further conditions.

Segregation

Chapter 65 provided "for the removal of Chinese whose presence is dangerous to the well-being of the communities, outside the limits of cities and towns in the state of California."[55] This law in effect established and made legal Chinese ghettos which physically separated the Chinese from the other citizens of the state:

> SECTION 1. The Board of Supervisors . . . are hereby granted the power . . . to pass and enforce all acts . . . necessary to cause the removal without the limits of such cities or towns . . . of any Chinese now within . . . such limits provided that they may set apart certain prescribed portions of the limits of such cities or towns . . . for the location therein of such Chinese.

In 1870 the legislature formally established the statewide segregated school system, which provided for separate schools for persons of "African or Indian descent."[56] In 1885 in the case of *Tape* v. *Hurley*[57] the court ruled that a Chinese child could be excluded from a San Francisco school only if he were "filthy, vicious, or diseased." In 1885, the legislature amended section

54. Ex Parte Ah Cue on Habeas Corpus, 101 Cal. 197.
55. *Cal. Stats.*, 1880:114.
56. *Cal. Stats.*, 1869–70:838.
57. 66 Cal. 473.

1662 of the Political Code "to establish separate schools for children of Mongoloid or Chinese descent." In 1921 the legislature once more amended section 1662 of the Code to include, along with Chinese, children of Japanese descent, at the same time noting that this section did not apply to Indians. Negroes had earlier acquired this right in 1890 in the test case of *Wysinger* v. *Crookshank*,[58] which ruled that Negro children had to be admitted to any school. Thus in 1921, Negroes and Indians were not required to attend segregated schools, but Chinese and Japanese children were. The School Code of 1929 repealed sections 1517–1894 (including the discriminatory section 1662) and specifically provided that all children, regardless of race, should be admitted to all schools. Thus was ended in 1929 the legally segregated school system of California, which had prevailed for eighty years.

Postscript

During the Second World War, China fought with the Allies against the Japanese. In recognition of this service the United States repealed the Chinese Exclusion Acts on December 17, 1943, and permitted the admission of 105 Chinese per year—not a significant change in terms of numbers, but significant as an expression of goodwill, and a token that discrimination was officially only a matter of history.

The bar on immigration in 1882 and natural deaths in the aging resident population, together with the return of many Chinese to their homeland, led to a sharp decline in numbers of Chinese in California. At last the Golden State was saved from the invasion of the "yellow hordes" and the threat was removed of an overthrow of the Republic by the "heathen Chinese." But this feeling of security was not to last long. The Japanese, now permitted to emigrate from their homeland through removal of this prohibition by the newly restored emperor, began to cross the Pacific, and there was a ready acceptance of them in Cali-

58. 82 Cal. 592 [January 1890].

fornia as supplements to the cheap Chinese labor, which was in short supply. Within a few years the Chinese stereotype was shifted to the Japanese, and with it all the prejudice plus a new body of discriminatory legislation. This new group, sent, it must have seemed, by Providence, would now receive the full force of racism.

VIII. Words and Acts
Against the Japanese

Immigration to California of people from the islands of Japan did not begin until 1868 when Japan in a treaty with the United States formally abandoned its closed-door policy. In 1880 there were 86 Japanese recorded in the United States census as residing in California. By 1900 there were 10,000; by 1910 there were 41,000, and by 1920 the number had increased to 72,000. By 1940 a total of 300,000 Japanese had been admitted to the United States.

Sources and Nature of Prejudice

Prejudice against the Japanese sprouted in the rich soil that had nourished anti-Chinese attitudes shortly before. As the Chinese declined in numbers after 1892 the discrimination of the Japanese began. For some years Chinese and Japanese were lumped together as "Asiatics," "coolies," "Mongolians," or people of "yellow race." There seemed little to distinguish them in the views of Californians, since they all came from across the Pacific, they were a source of cheap labor, and in any case one "could scarcely tell them apart." In 1900 the San Francisco journal *Organized Labor* editorialized:

> Chinatown with its reeking filth and dirt, its gambling dens and obscene slave pens, its coolie labor and blood-thirsty tongs, is a menace to the community; but the sniveling Japanese, who swarms along the streets and cringingly offers his paltry services for a suit of clothes and

a front seat in our public schools, is a far greater danger to the laboring portion of society than all the opium-soaked pigtails who have ever blotted the fair name of this beautiful city.

In some degree the dislike of Japanese residing in California was justified by reference to the Russo-Japanese War of 1904–1905, which the Japanese won handily. The presence of a naval power in the Pacific, and moreover one with whom we did not have very friendly relations, led to a great deal of alarmist talk about the inevitability of a war between Japan and the United States. There was no basis in this, but the recent Spanish-American War had made us conscious of the Pacific, we were established in the Philippines, and the effectiveness with which the Japanese had handled the Russians provided the stimulus for such speculation. Out of all this arose the idea, still prevalent on December 7, 1941, that all resident Japanese were spies, and even that many were military officers engaged in espionage. The San Francisco journal *Organized Labor* (March 11, 1905) opined, "Drunk with victory and fired by uncontrollable ambitions, these one million Japanese Napoleons will turn their eyes around for new territory to conquer. . . . California in particular is an inviting field, and if they can capture it without powder and shell so much the better."

In 1907, during the incident involving the San Francisco School Board described elsewhere in this chapter, there was another war scare, and among other unjustifiable statements to appear at that time was that of Captain Richard Hobson of Spanish-American War fame, who said, "Japan now has an army of soldiers in the Hawaiian Islands. They made the invasion quietly as coolies, and now we know that they are soldiers organized into companies, regiments, and brigades."

In 1924 the Immigration Act stopped most persons of Japanese origin from coming into California. Those exempted from the provisions of the act included students, tourists, and treaty merchants, who were granted temporary visas. From this point until recently most movement of Japanese persons was now outgoing from the United States.

Representing but 2 percent of the total population, this racial minority may seem too small to have caused such concern, yet Californians worked themselves up to a high pitch of excitement. The fear expressed in these early decades of the twentieth century was that it was altogether likely that California's most difficult task would be to remain American in composition. More than any other immigrant group, the Japanese were regarded as temporary visitors. They were ineligible for citizenship, were classed as nationals of a foreign power, adhered to an alien religion, and largely failed to master English. Many of them, as well, considered their stay in California temporary, and their whole purpose was to make enough money to return to Japan and reestablish themselves advantageously in their homeland.

The citizens of the state, on the other hand, still harbored a remembrance of the long and bitter contest for Chinese exclusion, and many of the arguments that had been applied against the Chinese were used against the "Nipponese" and "Japs," who by skin color, stature, language, and customs gave little promise of being completely assimilable to the society of white California.

Much of the talk about the "menace" of Japanese laborers was merely window dressing. Throughout the 1890s and in the following decade when they were functioning primarily as agricultural laborers, the Japanese were accepted with a minimum of distrust. They did work which white laborers did not want to do, and were not generally regarded as competitors. Later, however, by organizing and demanding higher pay, they incurred the displeasure of their employers. At the same time, they evinced an increasing tendency to switch from farm labor to farm management. This step into the capitalist class put them into competition with established farm producers, and though in the agitation that followed, appeal was made against "coolie labor," the drive was more against the Japanese as producers than as laborers.

More federal legislation came to bear on the Japanese as an alien group than on any other minority who by reason of place of birth or race managed to find itself involved in controversy with the Caucasian majority of California. From 1890 on, there was a steadily increasing feeling against the Japanese, and it was through these attitudes and the acceptance of the Japanese stereotype, "that special blend of fabrication, myth and half-truth on the basis of which, in large part, the wartime evacuation of the Japanese Americans was authorized, executed, and approved."[1]

School Board Controversy and Compromise

A controversy that was to lead the San Francisco Board of Education to a confrontation with President Theodore Roosevelt resulting in new immigration regulations had its beginning on February 23, 1905, when the *San Francisco Chronicle* started a series of sensational and inflammatory articles directed against the Japanese. Japanese as the roots of crime and poverty, as foreign spies, as destroyers of the school system, as a menace to American womanhood, and a dozen other themes were played up in these lurid articles. On March 1, 1905, the state legislature passed, with only two dissenting votes, a resolution urging Congress to exclude entry of Oriental immigrants to the United States. In May 1905, the Japanese and Korean Exclusion League was formed in San Francisco with a membership that soon numbered 80,000.

In San Francisco, Eugene E. Schmitz was elected mayor by running on an anti-Oriental platform of the Union Labor party. Schmitz and his crony, Abe Ruef, a notoriously corrupt politician, were indicted by the grand jury in 1906. On May 6, 1905, the San Francisco School Board had gone on record as favoring segregation of Oriental students in the city schools, but had postponed final action until a later date. It was not considered to be wholly coincidental that on October 11, 1906, on the eve of the grand jury's indictment of Schmitz and Ruef, the school board suddenly ordered all Oriental students to attend a segregated school in Chinatown. Some 95 Japanese students, out of the total school population of 20,000, were affected by this order.

1. J. tenBroek, E. N. Barnhart, and F. W. Matson, *Prejudice, War, and the Constitution,* p. 22.

The government of Japan reacted rapidly and made strongly worded protests. President Roosevelt dispatched U. H. Metcalf, secretary of commerce and labor, to San Francisco to make an investigation. While Secretary Metcalf was so engaged, the president sent a message to Congress condemning the action of the San Francisco School Board as "a wicked absurdity." When Secretary Metcalf made his report, on December 18, 1906, he advised that there was no legal justification whatever for the action of the San Francisco School Board, and detailed a number of instances of unprovoked physical attacks on Japanese. This report was transmitted to the Congress over the president's signature and is reprinted in the documents section, p. 255, along with three of many personal reports of physical violence. There were debates in Congress on this matter, and the California congressmen found, as might be expected, strong supporters among Southern senators and representatives. The South was quite aware of the need to affirm states' rights in regard to segregated schools.

In San Francisco, Mayor Schmitz, having for the moment successfully diverted public interest from the grand jury's indictment to the more emotional question of school segregation of Orientals, made speeches defying the federal government and claimed that the reason for his indictment was not the criminal acts he was charged with (these being pure invention), but rather his anti-Japanese views.

And there the matter stood, with Mayor Schmitz shouting defiance of federal authority in San Francisco and President Roosevelt under heavy pressure from the Japanese government to bring a speedy end to the actions against its nationals that were in clear violation of treaty stipulations.

The president then invited the San Francisco School Board to come to Washington to discuss the problem. Mayor Schmitz, though not included in the invitation, went anyway. While the mayor and the school board were in Washington, there was introduced in the state legislature a new series of anti-Japanese bills. To quiet this additional element of difficulty, President Roosevelt personally requested Governor James Gillett to have these bills tabled for at least the time he was talking with the San Francisco School Board. In the end the president extracted a promise from the school board to rescind the order to segregate Japanese school children, and in return agreed to negotiate with the Japanese government for an agreement suspending further immigration. The school board acted on March 17, 1907; the Southern senators in Congress howled that they had been sold out by the Californians; and on March 14, 1907, the president issued his executive order barring further entry of Orientals. This is printed in the documents section, p. 258. Later in 1907 the combined federal departments of Commerce and Labor, and the Bureau of Immigration and Naturalization established immigration regulations specifically aimed at halting Japanese movement into the United States. Rule 21 entitled Japanese and Korean Laborers[2] was created for the purpose of giving effect to the president's executive order. That restriction was not the end of the matter, and the culmination was not to come until 1924 with the passage, in the Coolidge administration, of the federal immigration bill, which carried a provision for exclusion of Japanese.

Political Pressures and New Laws

In California, primarily under the heavy pressure of the lobby of the Asiatic Exclusion League, new laws were passed in addition to the ones already on the statute books limiting Oriental immigration.

In 1908 local California platforms of both the Republican and Democratic parties had planks favoring to one degree or another Asiatic exclusion. In Fresno on May 19, 1908, the Democrats stated:

> We favor the total exclusion of all Asiatic laborers from this country by extending the provisions of the Geary Act to Japanese, Koreans and all other Asiatics and the strict enforcement of all other existing laws upon that subject.

2. *Immigration Regulations of July 1, 1907*:36–37.

The national platform had a similarly worded plank. The Republicans in Sacramento on May 14, 1908, approved this local plank, which had no comparable counterpart in the national platform:

> We insist upon the continuance of the policy of exclusion of Asiatic labor by the rigid enforcement of the present exclusion laws and the enactment of other laws or by effective diplomatic arrangements.

Enacted into law on March 8, 1909, was a statute directly aimed at people of Japanese origin, entitled An Act to Provide for the Gathering, Compiling, Printing and Distribution of Statistics and Information Regarding the Japanese of the State and Making an Appropriation Therefor.[3] Section 1 determined:

> Upon this act becoming effective the governor shall direct the State Labor Commissioner to immediately undertake and complete as soon as possible the gathering and compiling of statistics and such other information regarding the Japanese of this state as may be useful to the governor in making a proper report to the President of the United States and to Congress, and in furnishing to the people of this state and elsewhere a comprehensive statement of such conditions as actually exist.

Such documents were published by the Bureau of Labor Statistics of the State of California twice a year, and listed in tabular form the occupations and the numbers of Japanese for each, and wages per hour, per day, per week, and per month.

A "Clipping Bureau" of Reasons for Exclusion

A great deal was written about the Japanese, and many reasons were given why the Japanese as a people should be excluded from California. The Asiatic Exclusion League carefully collected these many reports and in its *Proceedings* devoted an entire section of several pages each month to the "Clipping Bureau," which used for its theme the following:

> That the sentiment for the exclusion of Japanese immigrants is not dying out and that the people of California are almost a unit in condemning the practice of employing Japanese while American laborers

3. *Statutes of California*, 1909: 134–227.

are seeking employment, is demonstrated by the following editorial excerpts.[4]

A selection of articles from California newspapers taken from the *Proceedings of the Asiatic Exclusion League* in 1908 follows.

(*Oroville Mercury*) Those who have kept in touch with the sentiment regarding the exclusion of Chinese and Japanese labor know how strong is the feeling against the letting down of the bars and admitting a class of laborers against which no American can compete, and which would lower his standard of living to such a degree that civilization would be turned backward at least two hundred years. California workingmen will not consent to the free admission of Asiatic labor, and no man who openly espouses such a policy should be elected to public office.

(*Pasadena Star*) The Japanese are too busy fighting the tax collector to get up another war scare.

(Note, on this subject, from the Asiatic Exclusion League: From the innumerable instances on record in this office, it is apparent that the Japanese are the most determined tax dodgers and persistent lawbreakers on the whole Pacific Slope.)

(*Winters Express*) The Florin district of Sacramento County affords one of the most convincing examples of the bad effects of the Japanese invasion. Formerly it was inhabited wholly by white men and their families, who built up a large strawberry industry and planted numerous small vineyards. Irrigation by means of wells and wind mills enabled a family to obtain a comfortable living on from ten to twenty acres, and from the fact that the land was in small holdings there was much neighborly intercourse and the district was noted for its social advantages. But gradually the Japanese crept in, first as laborers then as renters, until nearly all the white growers of berries either rented to Asiatics or sold out entirely, in either case usually leaving the district. The result has been a great change for the worse. The Japanese have dominated the berry industry, having acquired and planted nearly all the acreage devoted to berries.

Their wretched, unsightly shacks are blots on the face of the country where there should be flower decked homes of American families. And so hundreds of alien unmarried Asiatics, caring nothing for

4. *Proceedings of Asiatic Exclusion League*, December 1908.

the land or its future, have robbed the district of what was once its enviable attractiveness.

(*Monrovia News*) The present surplus of white labor has given the orchardists and fruit-growers of this section the long-looked-for opportunity of ridding themselves of Japs, who for months have controlled the labor situation in the fruit districts.

The insolence of the Japs was almost unbearable, and many small growers were coerced into leasing or selling their holdings to the aggressive Asiatics. The outlook was decidedly gloomy for the growers, as the demands of the Japs were constantly growing.

The latest of the Growers Association to declare against the employment of Japs is the Colton Association (San Bernardino Co.), the members of which agreed to not employ the Asiatics in their orchards. The movement is spreading like wild fire throughout the fruit districts, and for the first time in years the working and harvesting of the crop will be done with white labor.

(*Los Angeles Times*) From Lexington down to Appomattox there are lying in the trenches American soldiers whose first breath was drawn in the British Isles, in Germany, Russia, France and nearly all the countries of the world. But, if Japan and the United States were to go to war tomorrow, or at any time beyond, almost every Jap in the land would hie himself away to Nippon to shoulder a gun against us. Everybody knows this to be true; there is no denial of it from any source. It is not a pleasant fact to think of and it really explains why the Jap is not liked.

(*Collier's Weekly*, October 10, 1908) Asiatic immigration is the direct source of the bubonic plague—the most terrible and swift of fatal scourges known to modern science. It is a human disease and the rodent family against which the war is now being carried on, is really the victim of human agencies. Since the United States has practically excluded the Chinese, we must open our eyes to the unwelcome fact that the influx of Japanese coming in a steady and unbroken stream from parts where the plague is always raging, is the direct cause of the alarming spread of the disease in the United States. While as a nation to nation we should maintain the best of relations with our Japanese neighbors, it has now become apparent that immigration from Japan must positively cease.

(*Los Angeles Tourist*) The report that Mr. Levy has disposed of all his Jap help in his big cafe on Main Street is a step in the right direction and should be followed by other restaurant and hotel proprietors of our city. There are so many idle American help parading our streets, aimlessly looking for honest work, which they seem to be unable to obtain, while the Jap a foe to our country, is filling the lucrative positions about the hotels and restaurants in Los Angeles. The Jap receives his salary, makes his necessary purchase from the Jap dealers, and the balance of his income, over his living expenses, which are generally small, he sends back to Japan. Little, or none of the American earned dollars are used here in the interest of the city or state, while the American help spends his salary freely in the support of his family, pays taxes on his property, and in every way his income goes to the general interest of the community in which he lived.

(*Redlands Review*) Now is the time when some of the ranchers hereabout might with much advantage to all concerned, and not the least of this advantage to themselves, by any means, discharge any Japanese they may have in their employ as farm hands and give the work to the many unemployed white men in this city. There are a dozen good, hard working white men hereabouts for every job. They are bone of our bone and flesh of our flesh, and every dollar they make they will spend with us. It may be some trouble to the rancher to break in new men to do the work, but his duty in the case is very clear.[5]

Other complaints relate the "facts" that the Japanese are clannish, have no honor, are cunning, and all look alike. The public press at this time worked diligently to establish these criteria for the Japanese stereotype.

(*Hanford Sentinel*) Some deputy assessors in this valley are having troublesome experiences with Japanese. The fact that the home of a Jap does not amount to much, is one of the troubles in the country. They are hard to identify, and may give one home today and another tomorrow. Several out on the little Lucerne Vineyard refused to give any homes today, and they will be arrested. People who have never run up against this Japanese question in America are often radical in their views of friendliness to the Japs, but did they understand the true situation they would do differently. The Japs are smart and cunning and they take advantage of a situation that often enables them to protect their race in a manner that in this country amounts to abuse of privilege and a violation of all ethics of justice.[6]

5. Reprinted in *Proceedings*, Asiatic Exclusion League, April 1908.
6. Ibid., December 1908.

(*Alameda Times*) The experiment made in Santa Clara County of running canneries with Japanese men and white women under the direction of Chinese overseers has resulted in failure. In the first place, the Chinese overseers favored the Japanese by giving the women the hardest work to do; when the white women objected, some of the Japanese retaliated by spitting in their faces, pulling their hair and offering other indignities, which in Alviso almost resulted in the Japanese being mobbed. It did result in the white women going on strike, and a nasty scandal, which forced some of the canneries to get rid of their Japanese laborers.[7]

In an effort to stem Japanese immigration many white growers, canners, and others refused to give jobs to the Japanese. Another editorial urged even further action.

(*Visalia Times*) The feeling against allowing Japanese to get a foothold in this country can hardly be said to have died when real estate agents refuse to make deals with the sons of the Mikado. Yet that is what happened here in Visalia the other day. A Japanese made an application to a prominent local real estate man for the purchase of a tract of land, which he had on the market, and was told that no Japanese need apply. The sooner they are prohibited from owning property at all in the United States, the sooner will this part of the country be satisfied. "California for the white man" is a pretty good motto for all real estate men to remember. There will be plenty of buyers of a desirable class along this way before long and land should be held for them.[8]

Asiatic Exclusion League: Purposes and Proceedings

A good portion of the racist attacks on the Japanese came from or were sponsored by the Asiatic Exclusion League of North America. Their avowed purposes were clear when the first annual convention of the league met in Seattle, Washington, on February 4, 1908, and adopted the following memorial, which was forwarded to the president, the Senate, and the House of Representatives:

The first annual convention of the Asiatic Exclusion League of North America, in regular session assembled, Seattle, Washington, Feb. 4, 1908, do hereby most respectfully:

7. Ibid.
8. *Proceedings*, April 1908.

REQUEST the immediate passage of a law which will exclude, absolutely and emphatically, all Asiatics from the mainland and insular possessions of the United States, and your memorialists do hereby emphatically

PROTEST, against the administrative and executive officers of the United States entering into any agreement which will permit the ruler of any foreign country to make stipulations as to what class of persons and in what numbers shall leave said foreign country for the purpose of immigrating to the United States; and your memorialists

DECLARE, that any such agreement with a foreign power is a subversion of the traditions and policies of the United States, and a betrayal of the rights of American citizens. And your memorialists further

PROTEST, against the employment of Asiatics on board vessels flying the American flag, to the exclusion of American seamen and in violation of American law; therefore, your memorialists pray for the speedy enactment of a law which will prohibit the employment of Asiatics upon all vessels flying the American flag, or in any branch or department of the public service. Your memorialists again emphatically

PROTEST, against the continuance of Asiatic immigration upon the grounds of American patriotism, for the reasons—

FIRST, that these Asiatics come to the United States entirely ignorant of our sentiments of nativity and patriotism, and utterly unfit and incapable of discharging the duties of American citizenship.

SECOND, the introduction of this incongruous and non-assimilable element into our national life will inevitably impair and degrade, if not effectively destroy, our cherished institutions and our American life.

THIRD, these Asiatics are alien to our ideas of patrotism, morality, loyalty and highest conceptions of Christian civilization.

FOURTH, their presence here is a degrading and contaminating influence to the best phases of American life.

FIFTH, with their low standard of living, immoral surroundings and cheap labor, they constitute a formidable and fierce competition against our American system, the pride and the glory of our civilization, and unless prohibited by effective legislation, will result in the irreparable deterioration of American labor.

SIXTH, the living in our midst of a large body of Asiatics, the greatest number of whom are armed, loyal to their governments, entertaining feelings of distrust, if not hostility, to our people, without any allegiance to our governments or institutions, not sustaining American life in times of peace, and ever ready to respond to the cause of their own nations in times of war, make these Asiatics an appalling menace to the American Republic, the splendid achievements wrought by the strong arms and loyal hearts of Caucasian toilers, patriots and heroes in every walk of life.

These were the general themes upon which meeting after meeting expounded. As we explore the minutes of the proceedings themselves, the eloquence of the prose as it was written in the above memorial is hardly equaled, though the themes remain the same, as the following illustrate:

> Merchants getting tired of Japanese: Men of standing in the community who employ Japanese and have no race prejudice apparently, and who are distinctly opposed to labor unions, largely on account of the opposition of the latter to Orientals, declare the Japanese dishonest and inferior in this regard to the Chinese. When the Japanese arrived in the Pajaro Valley they were welcomed by the merchants; today the merchants bitterly complain that the Japs have become their very close competitors.[9]

> Philosophers and philanthropists may preach about the common fatherhood and brotherhood of all races, but between the white American and the Asiatic there is no common tie whatever. There is no community of thought, nor of feeling, nor of sympathy. The character of an Oriental population degrades the idea of labor, as did the chattel slavery of the South. The Asiatic is looked upon with contempt, even by his employer, but they in turn reciprocate thoroughly the race contempt which the whites feel for them. Even the second generation of Asiatics will develop a less desirable class than are the immigrants who come directly from the rice fields of Nippon. The two races are separated by every possible bar. In race history, or traditions there is nothing in common. They differ in their spiritual ideas, religious beliefs and in their conception of female virtue and morality. They differ wholly in their social conventions, their philosophy and habit of thought. The second and succeeding generations of these Asiatics, however much they may conform to American social and business customs, will remain alien in thought, sympathy and loyalty and will be in consequence unable to properly perform the duties of American citizenship. Such being the result of citizenship inherent by birth on

9. From *Digest of Report of California Bureau of Labor Statistics*, Third Annual Meeting of the Asiatic Exclusion League, May 1908; reprinted from *Proceedings*, 1908, p. 24.

American soil, what shall be said of the proposition to confer upon them the privilege of naturalization.[10]

And in the best racist prose the following:

> The Sandwich [Hawaiian] Islands are an object lesson to us: Australia, New Zealand, Canada, and South Africa do not want them, and must we to please somebody, open our doors? Must we be forced to become a Japanese colony? Must we allow a foreign power to dictate to us who shall land on our shores? Will we be sacrificed to the greed and rapacity of Eastern Commercialism? Will we become a nation of nondescripts? Have we not already enough race questions within our doors? Will you permit your daughter to marry a Jap coolie? Do you want him for a citizen? What would you think of a Jap governor or a Supreme Court Judge? . . . It is time we should cease being the common dumping ground of all the adventurers of the Earth. We desire to preserve our Americanism and institutions to the end. We want the best of all nations or nothing.[11]

An "address" by Mr. A. Sbarboro, president of the Italian Bank, to the Asiatic Exclusion League in San Francisco in 1908 represents the attitude of one California pioneer who by his own proud admission worked vigorously first against the Chinese and later the Japanese in the state. One of his chief complaints appears to be that the Japanese were thrifty, enterprising, and industrious, and he was much put out that Japanese grape-pickers left off their work at "our" Italian-Swiss Colony for jobs with better pay. One supposes that if the attitudes toward Japanese as expressed here were shared by Mr. Sbarboro's associates in the Italian-Swiss Colony, the pickers may not have found this employment ideal and, quite naturally, were interested in working for some other grower. The address is printed in the documents section, p. 259.

Two Views of the Japanese

As was the case with other minority groups, there were some individuals within the white community who attempted a defense

10. *Proceedings*, May 1908, pp. 33–34.
11. *Proceedings*, 1908. Said to be an address by William Temple, LL.B., Harvard, 1874.

of their differently colored brother. We reprint the following "defense of the Japanese character" by M. M. Scott, principal of the Honolulu high school, offered in evidence in the United States Supreme Court in *Takao Ozawa* v. *United States* in October 1918:

> The Japanese people are classed as Mongolians by those who know absolutely nothing about physical anthropology. Those physical anthropologists that have studied bodily characters of the Japanese, all agree that they do not belong to the Mongolian race, whose main habitation is in Central Asia. Kaemper, Titsignh, Von Rein, Morse and Bachelor, who were all skilled anthropologists, feel sure that whatever mixture there may be in their racial stock, Mongolian blood is not the predominant, nor even a large element in the Japanese. Not one of them would be rash enough to say what element of blood is the predominant one. . . . In no one physical character do the Japanese people correspond to a like physical character of the true Mongolian. Neither in color of skin, nor pigment, nor stature, nor in measurement of limbs, above all, in "cephalic index," the surest character to determine race, can the Japanese be called Mongolians.
>
> First as to color of skin. In certain parts of Japan regarded by their own ethnologists, the skin and pigment therein are more nearly white than yellow or brown. . . . They are whiter than the average Italian, Spaniard or Portuguese. . . .
>
> As to the possibility of assimilation to American standards of government and all other things American, I regard the Japanese as one of the most assimilable of all the races of man. . . . Truth to tell, since the Japanese have become a settled people, ethnically homogeneous, they have been assimilating everything they were shown from other nations. For a thousand years, with no intercommunication, except slight ingress and egress with China and Korea, they borrowed from China and Korea letters, literature and the art of porcelain making. They have improved by their peculiar genius on everything they borrowed from these two places.
>
> Since the opening of Japan by Commodore Perry in 1854, treaties and communications with Western Nations have enabled the Japanese to assimilate science, industries, commerce, and politics with a rapidity that no other nation has ever shown. Their students are great admirers of American governmental forms, and even social forms. There is an immense body of men today in Japan urging a democratic and constitutional government on the model of that of the United States. There is no question but in a brief time their forms of government will be as

liberal and democratic as those of England and the United States. They are immensely loyal—loyal to properly constituted government. Those Japanese born and nurtured in Hawaii are as much American as the children of the descendants of the Pilgrim Fathers that came to this country to Christianize the Hawaiians. Let me repeat, and I measure my words in so doing, with nearly a half a century of study and association with the Japanese, that I am persuaded that they will make as loyal and patriotic American citizens as any that we have.[12]

That the intensity of feelings against the Japanese continued, however, is illustrated in a message of Governor W. D. Stephens (1917–1923) to the secretary of state, in which the following occurs:

> The people of California are determined to repress a developing Japanese community within our midst. They are determined to exhaust every power in their keeping to maintain this state for its own people. This is a solemn problem in affecting our entire Occidental civilization. California does not wish the Japanese people to settle within her borders and to develop a Japanese population. Without disparaging these people of just sensibilities, we cannot look for inter-marriage or that social interrelationship which must exist between citizens of a contented community. It may be an exquisite refinement, but we cannot feel contented at our children imbibing their first rudiments of education from the lips of the public school teacher in classrooms crowded with children of a different race.
>
> California wants peace. But California wants to retain this commonwealth for its own peoples where they may grow up and develop their own ideals. California is making this appeal primarily, of course, for herself, but in doing so she feels that the problem is here solely because of her geographical position on the Pacific Slope. She stands at the gateway for Oriental immigration. Her people are the first affected and unless the race ideals and standards are preserved here at the gateway the conditions that will follow must soon affect the rest of the continent.

A California Senator said in Congress in 1921:

> The reason that we in California are calm in the presence of this crisis

12. Japanese Naturalization Case no. 21, Supreme Court of the United States, October term 1918. No. 222. Takao Ozawa v. United States. Brief for the Petitioner. Quoted M. M. Scott.

is: first, because we know we are right; second, because we hope to convince our countrymen that we are right; third, that if we fail to convince them, we will, whatever they do or say, do what we know to be right.

This part of the story of the Japanese in California closes with the 1924 Immigration Act.[13] But the legacy of hatred and violence resulting from this discrimination continued for many years. The story of the treatment of American citizens of Japanese ancestry during World War II is one which we shall do no more than mention in passing as inherited from this earlier clash at the beginning of this century. For the important details the reader is referred to tenBroek, Barnhart, and Matson's work, *Prejudice, War, and the Constitution*.

13. There is a large published literature on the subject of the Japanese in California, and for aspects of the subject which we have barely mentioned, or wholly ignored, the reader is referred to the following: R. L. Buell, "The History of Japanese Agitation in the United States"; C. W. Eliot, *Japanese Characteristics*; H. Holt, *Wanted—A Final Solution of the Japanese Problem*; Y. Ichihashi, *The Japanese in the United States*; H. B. Johnson, *Discriminations against the Japanese in California: A Review of the Real Situation*; R. N. Lynch, "The Development of the Anti-Japanese Movement"; R. D. McKenzie, *Oriental Exclusion*; R. W. Paul, *The Abrogation of the Gentlemen's Agreement*; C. Rowell, "Chinese and Japanese Immigrants—a Comparison"; P. Scharrenburg, "The Attitude of Organized Labor toward the Japanese"; B. J. O. Schrieke, *Alien Americans: A Study of Race Relations*; J. tenBroek, E. N. Barnhart, and F. W. Matson, *Prejudice, War, and the Constitution*; D. S. Thomas, *The Salvage*; E. Tupper and G. McReynolds, *Japan in American Public Opinion*.

IX. Summary

The Indians were a totally alien, stone-age people who held the entire continent before 1492. The California natives first came under Spanish control, and they submitted without much objection to missionization. Control was strict, and often harsh. Many Indians had difficulty in accepting the enforced adaptation to restriction of movement, disruption of family life, regular labor, and new food patterns. Physical rebellion by mission Indians was so rare as to be insignificant. The usual response to mission life by an individual who could not adjust was fugitivism. The soldier guard stationed at each mission undertook to recover runaways, and such expeditions often served as a means to replenish the stock of neophytes by capturing "gentiles" and escorting them under guard to the missions. The Indians thus came to see the Spaniards as dominating through superior force of arms. Indians, though considered to be humans, were at the same time thought to be an inferior kind of people whose souls must be saved. The Spanish view of California Indians, therefore, was that they existed mainly as a means of demonstrating the religious devotion of Spain.[1] If, in addition, the Indians built and maintained the mission establishments that attested to Spain's ownership of California, that was only a secondary benefit. The Indians seem to have learned little that was useful in the missions, and after 1834 (thirteen years after Mexico secured her

1. On the "nature" of Indians, in the Spanish view, see C. A. Hutchinson, *Frontier Settlement in Mexican California*, pp. 49–54.

independence) when the missions were disestablished the released Indians were not prepared to enter into the economic or social or political life of the country, even if they had been encouraged to do so. Many of them exchanged the enforced confinement of mission life for involuntary, or at best semivoluntary, labor on the Mexican ranchos.

The nonmissionized Indians east of the coastal "mission strip" no doubt had all heard of the Spaniards and Mexicans, and probably had no desire to come into contact with them, but they were able to continue to live their old way of life until they were suddenly confronted by the hordes of gold miners that appeared in their midst in 1848. The Americans came with well-developed views about Indians, and none of these were favorable. A veritable slaughter of Indians occurred all over California, and nearly 50,-000 natives died of disease, starvation, or homicide between 1848 and 1870. The California Constitution and the Civil Code gave the Indians no rights or privileges, and their only recognition was in restrictive or discriminatory legislation. The Indian, suffering from deprivation of the land where he hunted and gathered his food, and harassed by armed bands of miners or settlers intent upon killing as many natives as possible, occasionally reacted by killing a miner or a settler, or stealing stock for food, but their attempts to fight back or to exploit their oppressors were feeble, and served only to add to the whites' preconception of Indians as cowardly and treacherous thieves. There were decent whites who spoke out against the treatment of the Indians, but neither the state nor the federal government cared enough to prevent the wanton killing of Indians or to provide the means for protecting them. Occasionally an Indian group would appeal through the courts for justice, but this was rarely if ever granted. Only recently with the development of a national conscience and an attempt to assuage the feeling of guilt and shame of past wrongs has the federal government provided compensation (and little enough at that) for the seizing of the lands of the California Indians. Today the California Indians are the poorest, least educated, worst housed, and most neglected minority in the state.[2]

The Mexicans in 1846 found themselves suddenly under American military occupation. There was no love lost between the two peoples who had so recently been at war with each other. The state constitution drawn up in 1849 acknowledged former Mexican residents as citizens; this was necessary because the Treaty of Guadalupe Hidalgo required it. Mexicans in the Mother Lode, whether newly arrived from across the border or from their California homes, were badly treated. In the northern part of the state where the gold rush occurred the Mexicans were simply overwhelmed by the flood of newly arrived immigrants coming by ship or across the continent. The Mexican gold-seekers were concentrated in the "southern mines," and there they held out for a couple of years, but before long they too were pushed out. In southern California Mexicans were in the majority for some time, and figured prominently in the social and political life of the region. But the southern "cow counties" exercised little influence in state politics, and as Los Angeles became increasingly non-Mexican in population they lost even this nominal eminence and entered the growing group of depressed minorities. The Mexicans indicated early that they were not going to challenge the Americans for leadership, and they have maintained that position to the point where they are today California's largest but most silent minority group.

The Chinese ran afoul of the racist feelings of the American settlers, partly because they were so different in appearance and customs, and partly because they were a source of inexpensive labor. It may be suggested that in the absence of blacks the anti-Negro sentiments of Californians were applied to the Chinese. The combination of the antipathy of the laboring class and the politicians' espousal of the anti-Chinese cause proved too much

2. California State Department of Public Health, Bureau of Maternal and Child Care. *California Indian Health Status*. Mimeographed, 9 pp. Issued at Berkeley, September 1969.

for the Chinese, who were ineligible for naturalization and could not vote. The Chinese fought for their rights, few though they might be, in the courts, but even here they all too often found no sympathy. The Chinese could seek relief in the courts because they had enough money to pay the necessary legal fees, and they were allowed to do this partly because they were a people with whose home government the United States was bound by treaty provisions. Although they were not liked any better than were the Indians, one notes that no indenture act was ever passed to allow them to be bound over as the Indians were from 1850 to 1863. In the end the state of California succeeded in taking its cause before the American public, and when Congress passed the Exclusion Act in 1882, the Chinese were finished. If the effort in Congress in 1870 to entitle them to naturalization had been successful, they might have become an important, even powerful, minority group, but that was not to be.

The Japanese simply succeeded to the position which the Chinese had vacated, and the history of their persecution, though not the bloody one that the Indians experienced, was surely as emotional and intense. The exclusion of the Japanese during the Second World War showed how near the surface the old feelings were, and if another Pacific conflict should arise in our lifetime, one where the Japanese position was anything but "foursquare" for the United States, it is easy to predict that the latent hostility against them would once again manifest itself.

The Negro was unwelcome in California from the days of the gold rush. California was to be a nonslaveholding state, and no blacks were wanted. They were discriminated against in early legislation; they could not give testimony against whites; and the fugitive slave act of 1852 was applied in such a way as to be most unjust. Black population grew slowly, perhaps partly for the reason that California was for long a state with strong Southern sympathies and it thus seemed more hostile than the Northern states. The black population of California seems to have been a peaceful minority that rarely raised its voice.

Of the five minorities considered in this book, it is difficult to say which one got the worst deal. The Indians probably deserve the greatest sympathy. Indians all over the New World seem to have been taken by the European conquerors and colonizers to be a people so alien and unassimilable that in retrospect we see that they never had a chance. Whether it was by direct military conquest, as with Cortes in Mexico, Alvarado in Guatemala, or Pizarro in Peru, even the most advanced and populous of the native cultures simply could not withstand the onslaught of the European armed might. Each culture fell—whether it was a highly developed civilization such as those of the Aztecs and Incas, a lesser one such as the Pueblos or the Natchez, or the simple hunter-collector Neolithic type of society of California or the Plains—and with each surrender there was extinguished one of man's experiments in civilization. The California Indians were one of these extinguishments, and while we may regret the brutality of their subjugation through force of arms and having their souls captured by the Franciscan priests, it is nevertheless true that some (presumably European) power would have imposed its domination had not Spain filled that role. In the absence of Spain, that conquering power most probably would have been England, France, or Russia.[3] The Pacific shore was quite susceptible to seizure until about 1800, and it is, one supposes, largely historical accident that Spain, operating from her base nearby in Mexico, exercised the effort required to reinforce her claim of ownership by establishing actual settlement. It is our guess that the fate of the Indians of California would have been little different had some other European or Asiatic power first settled and succeeded in holding the area. What would have been different is what happened to the later minorities, since under occupation of another power the ones which did develop in California might not have appeared on the scene.

Within the larger, national framework of nineteenth-century racism and slavery, the California attitudes toward nonwhites—regardless of whether they were blacks, Indians, Mexicans, Chileans, Polynesians, Chinese, Japanese, Filipinos, or of some other

3. Hutchinson, *Frontier Settlement*, chaps. 3 and 4.

race or ethnic group—were consistent with those generally observed in the United States. The constitutional convention delegates in 1849 and the first state legislature in 1850 had acted in conscience in prohibiting slavery, yet they took no pains to conceal the racism which the majority of members brought with them from other states after 1848.[4] California was willing to have free nonwhites, but only if they had few or no human rights and if they could be considered without argument to be born inferiors. The benefits of true equality, which might lead to the acquisition of power, were denied to all nonwhite racial or ethnic groups, and only in this condition as nonequals were the latter acceptable. Without rights these discriminated groups had no recourse to law, and they had few champions to defend themselves against the violence and hostility of the whites. Few Americans were ever brought to court to answer for the homicidal (we have dared use the term *genocidal*) acts in killing Indians. No effective voice was ever raised against the 1850 indenture act through which uncounted numbers of Indians were committed to long periods of labor and restriction which came so close to being slavery that it is a semantic question whether to call it that or not.

The kinds of actions directed against nonwhite minorities that occurred in the past in California were aspects of a society that no longer exists. These things will not repeat themselves. Never again will the indenture of Indians or any other minority occur; never again will the Chinese or Japanese in California be treated in such inhuman ways. Federal and state laws such as the United States Nationality Act of 1940 and the 1943 federal laws concerning naturalization now make it possible for many aliens who were earlier barred from citizenship to come under the protection of the federal authority through opportunity to become naturalized. But old prejudices die out slowly, and they can be

4. How these attitudes developed in America, especially with regard to blacks, has been examined in detail in M. P. Banton, *Race Relations,* and in W. D. Jordan, *White over Black: American Attitudes toward the Negro, 1550–1812,* to mention two of a series of recently published studies.

transmitted through the generations for a very long time. One of the main points which Myrdal made in his great study of the Negro problem, *An American Dilemma*, was that the Negro, though freed with Emancipation, continued to be looked upon *socially* as he was in antebellum days, namely as a slave. It is the extraordinary persistence of the century-old beliefs about black inferiority that still prevents the Negro from enjoyment of the equality he was granted so long ago. The tenacity with which people hold convictions about superiority and inferiority permits one to say today that such ideas have not been replaced by alternative and more rational beliefs in equality. The old biases and intolerances still exist in latent form, and they can be aroused when a cause appears.

California as the presently most prosperous and populous state in the Union has come a long way since it was illegally seized by military forces of the United States from a defenseless Mexico in 1846 and settled by the footloose riffraff of the United States. If this evaluation of the settlers seems too strong, compare it with two contemporary assessments of the nature of the argonauts:

> Take a sprinkling of sober-eyed, earnest, shrewd, energetic, New-England-business-men: mingle with them a number of rollicking sailors, a dark band of Australian convicts and cut-throats, a dash of Mexican and frontier desperadoes, a group of hardy backwoodsmen, some professional gamblers, whiskey-dealers, general swindlers . . . and having thrown in a promiscuous crowd of broken-down merchants, disappointed lovers, black sheep, unfledged dry-goods clerks, professional miners from all parts of the world, and Adullamites generally, stir up the mixture, season strongly with gold-fever, bad liquors, faro, monte, rouge-et-noir, quarrels, oaths, pistols, knives, dancing, and digging, and you have something approximating California society in early days.[5]

Hugo Reid, an early European resident of California, wrote:

> Don't go to the mines on any account. They are loaded to the muzzle

5. G. F. Parsons, *The Life and Adventures of James W. Marshall.*

with vagabonds from every quarter of the globe, scoundrels from no-
where, rascals from Oregon, pickpockets from New York, accomplished gentlemen from Europe, interlopers from Lima and Chile,
Mexican thieves, gamblers of no particular spot, and assassins man-
ufactured in Hell for the express purpose of converting highways and
byways into theaters of blood; Then, last but not least, Judge Lynch
with his thousand arms, thousand sightless eyes, and five-hundred
lying tongues.[6]

California politicians have always held the state up as a
model, and as one occupied by an industrious and enlightened
people. But history tells us that no more sorry record exists in the
Union of inhuman and uncivil treatment toward minority groups
than in California. The conscience of the Spaniards and Mexicans
must answer for what they did to the Indians between 1769 and
1846. But in American history—in the shoddy excuses used for
seizing California from Mexico, in the ignoring of the plainly
worded provisions in the Treaty of Guadalupe Hidalgo of 1848
guaranteeing rights to pre-1848 residents, and in the cruel discrimination against Indians, Mexicans, Japanese, Chinese, Negroes, and Filipinos—there is no record to equal that of the people
of the Golden State. The evidence that we have presented here,
partial and selective as it admittedly is, should serve as a warning.
It was not pure accident, we suggest, that the resident Japanese
were evacuated to concentration camps in 1942, but rather it
was that the old prejudices were so easily aroused that there
could occur this infamous "great and evil blotch on our national
history."[7]

6. S. B. Dakin, *A Scotch Paisano*, p. 164.
7. J. tenBroek, E. N. Barnhart, and F. W. Matson, *Prejudice, War, and the Constitution*, p. 325.

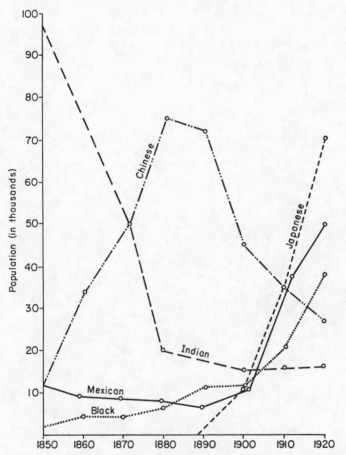

Graph of population numbers of minority groups in California, 1850–1920.

List of Documents

Letter from Governor John Bigler to General E. Hitchcock, April 8, 1852

EXECUTIVE DEPARTMENT
SACRAMENTO CITY, April 8, 1852

To Gen. E. Hitchcock
Commanding the U.S.
Troops in California

SIR:

I have the honor to submit for your examination a letter addressed to me to-day by the Senators and Representatives from the Counties of Trinity, Klamath, Shasta and Siskiyou. You will learn, from a perusal of this communication, that there has been a resumption of hostilities in the North, and that our fellow citizens residing in the northern Counties are suffering the horrors of a predatory war. You are also presented with an aggregate statement of the number of citizens ruthlessly murdered in these counties by Savages within a "very few months" past. Annexed to this melancholy narrative is an aggregate statement of the value of property destroyed by Indians during the same period.

The history of these troubles, as recounted in this despatch, and in other papers before me, show that the acts of these Savages are sometimes signalized by a ferocity worthy of the cannibals of the South Sea. They seem to cherish an instinctive hatred toward the white race, and this is a principle of their nature which neither time nor vicissitude can impair. This principle of hatred is hereditary, and it is transmitted from the live to the Son by example and by injunction. Another infirmity of the Indian character of which we have incontestible evidence is that their respect for treaty stipulations ceases at the moment when the inciting causes—self-interest or apprehensions of punishment—are removed. The character and conduct of these Indians presents an additional illustration of the accuracy of observations repeatedly made—that Whites and Indians cannot live in close proximity in peace; and it seems to confirm the opinion expressed in the inclosed despatch, that an ultimate evacuation of the Northern Counties by the Whites or the Indians will be unavoidable.

In contingencies like these a simple but imperative duty is imposed upon the Executive: to place the State in the hands of the General Government, and to demand from it that aid and protection which the guaranties of the Federal Constitution assure us we are entitled to receive. If the General Government is neglectful of the demand which we make upon it—if it is unmindful of the duty which it owes to us—we have one other alternative—to fight our own battles—to maintain our independence as a sovereign but isolated State, and to protect ourselves from intestine troubles, as well as from the incursions of merciless and Savage enemies. Although we have found it necessary to embrace this alternative hitherto, we have not forgotten our allegiance to the General Government, nor have I forgotten that devoted citizens, who respect their private and political obligations, possess the most sacred and binding claims upon the fostering protection of Government. The interests of a Government and a people are mutually dependant, and there is a line of reciprocal duty upon which a continuance of their mutual relations and interests depends. The citizen cannot absolve himself from this allegiance so long as he claims the protection of the Government, nor can the Government disregard the interests of the citizen in whatever quarter of the globe they may lie.

But, sir, it is my duty, however unpleasant it may be, to express conviction that adequate protection has not been extended by the Government in Washington to American citizens residing in the State of California. I refer particularly to the fact that the number of regular troops detailed for service in California and on the borders of Oregon, have not been proportionate to the demand of the service. The mountain Indians, whose activity, sagacity, and courage has never been surpassed by Indians on the continent of America, are untamed and unconquered. Collissons [sic] between them and American citizens have been frequent, and the number of victims sacrificed to this neglect of the General Government is being augmented every day. The strong and decisive interposition of that Government is now asked: if this reasonable petition is not granted, I am apprehensive that results will ensue which every true friend of the Government must deplore.

I deem it my duty to assure you that unless prompt protection is afforded to the citizens of this State by the General Government I shall feel constrained to resort to the only means left me to defend the frontiers and to conquer a lasting peace. A resort to these means will increase the debt of the State, and add to the burden of taxation imposed upon our citizens. To dispense with such a necessity I indulge the earnest hope that you, as the military representative of the General Government in California will exercise your authority to arrest hostilities and to secure to us the blessings of a permanent peace.

In conclusion, permit me to suggest that if you have not at your immediate disposal a sufficient number of troops to detail for this service, and if you are authorized to state that the General Government will assume and pay expenses incident to a call of volunteers in to the Service, I will promptly issue a call for them whenever you may indicate a desire to have it done.

I have the honor to be, Sir, Your obt. servant

JOHN BIGLER

[United States National Archives, Records of the War Department, RG 98, Letters Received, Pacific Division, 1852. Box No. 4, Vol. 2, Document C 10/12.]

"The Indian War in the North"

The expedition against the Northern Indians is over, and a permanent peace has been established by the capture of the belligerent tribes and their removal to one of the Reservations.

The war was undertaken at the urgent solicitation of many residents of Humboldt and Trinity counties, who averred that their property had been despoiled, and that their lives were in danger. That the lives of many whites had been taken by these roaming, well-armed and ferocious tribes—for they were not like our Diggers—and that their presence, in the hostile attitude they had assumed and were maintaining was a serious drawback to the settlement and prosperity of that entire section. In accordance to this request the Governor, who is ex-officio Commander in Chief of the State forces, ordered mustered into the field a company of eighty men to chastise these Indians, and ordered Gen. Kibee to accompany the expedition for the purpose of supplying it with all needful things and at the cheapest possible rate. The Governor also said in his orders: "The women and children must be spared, and there must be no indiscriminate slaughter of the Indians; humanity demands that no more blood should be shed than is indispensable to open the trail and render travel upon it secure and uninterrupted in the future. You will take care that this order is ready to the company which may be mustered into service."

This does credit to both his head and his heart, for it is not to be denied that Indian Wars conducted by State troops have heretofore, been more like cold blooded massacres than anything else. These orders we are informed, were strictly obeyed wherever it was possible to do so, and the report of the Quartermaster and Adjutant-General, Kibee tells us that but 75 to 100 were killed, a large number wounded and 350 taken prisoners. The campaign commenced in the middle of October last, and was ended in the middle of February. The Indians were scattered over an area of fifty miles square, of an almost impenetrable country. They were watched by day and pursued by night. Their haunts were visited; their hiding-place ascertained and nocturnal descents had to be resorted to as the only means of capturing them. Several old Indian hunters were of the party, and traced the aboriginies everywhere, no matter how guarded were their trails. In this four months expedition in mid-winter against hostile Indians in their own haunts known only to themselves, whose numbers were as six or seven to one, compared with their pursuers, not one of the troop lost his life, and but seven were found wounded. Of these seven four have entirely recovered, and three are yet under medical treatment. The cost of the expedition, not including the pay of the troops, amounted to $32,406.93 which compared to all former expeditions of a like nature, is said to be, and we believe it is very little.

Much credit is given in the report to both officers and men in this expedition and it would seem from all the facts before us that this praise is not undeserved. By this action a large tract of fertile country has been opened up to actual settlers, and the lives and property of those there residing have been protected from future depredations by the Indians. The Governor and Quartermaster General in their reports and dispatches, having spoken well of the troops, we are free to say that from the best information we have on this subject, these two officers are entitled as the directors of the movement, to no less praise that they have bestowed upon others. To conduct such a campaign with such economy and such humanity, is so rare a spectacle among us that those who have inaugurated a new and better era in this respect, should have at least the satisfaction in knowing that their conduct meets approbation somewhere.

[This quotation is taken from a newspaper clipping in the authors' possession. We have not been successful in identifying the name of the paper. A full official report on these and subsequent campaigns in 1859 is in W. C. Kibbe, *Report of the Expedition Against the Indians in the Northern Part of the State.* Chas. T. Botts, State Printer, 1860. 10 pp.]

An Act for the Government and Protection of Indians, April 22, 1850

The People of the State of California, represented in Senate and Assembly, do enact as follows:

1. Justices of the Peace shall have jurisdiction in all cases of complaints by, for, or against Indians, in their respective Townships in this State.

2. Persons and proprietors of land on which Indians are residing, shall permit such Indians peaceably to reside on such lands, unmolested in the pursuit of their usual avocations for the maintenance of themselves and families: *Provided,* the white person or proprietor in possession of lands may apply to a Justice of the Peace in the Township where the Indians reside, to set off to such Indians a certain amount of land, and, on such application, the Justice shall set off a sufficient amount of land for the necessary wants of such Indians, including the site of their village or residence, if they so prefer it; and in no case shall such selection be made to the prejudice of such Indians, nor shall they be forced to abandon their homes or villages where they have resided for a number of years; and either party feeling themselves aggrieved, can appeal to the County Court from the decision of the Justice: and then divided, a record shall be made of the lands so set off in the Court so dividing them, and the Indians shall be permitted to remain thereon until otherwise provided for.

3. Any person having or hereafter obtaining a minor Indian, male or female, from the parents or relations of such Indian minor, and wishing to keep it, such person shall go before a Justice of the Peace in his Township, with the parents or friends of the child, and if the Justice of the Peace becomes satisfied that no compulsory means have been used to obtain the child from its parents or friends, shall enter on record, in a book kept for that purpose, the sex and probable age of the child, and shall give to such person a certificate, authorizing him or her to have the care, custody, control, and earnings of such minor, until he or she obtain the age of majority. Every

male Indian shall be deemed to have attained his majority at eighteen, and the female at fifteen years.

4. Any person having a minor Indian in his care, as described in the foregoing Section of this Act, who shall neglect to clothe and suitably feed such minor Indian, or shall inhumanly treat him or her, on conviction thereof shall be subject to a fine not less than ten dollars, at the discretion of a Court or Jury; and the Justice of the Peace, in his discretion, may place the minor Indian in the care of some other person, giving him the same rights and liabilities that the former master of said minor was entitled and subject to.

5. Any person wishing to hire an Indian, shall go before a Justice of the Peace with the Indian, and make such contract as the Justice may approve, and the Justice shall file such contract in writing in his office, and all contracts so made shall be binding between the parties; but no contract between a white man and an Indian, for labor, shall otherwise be obligatory on the part of an Indian.

6. Complaints may be made before a Justice of the Peace, by white persons or Indians; but in no case shall a white man be convicted of any offence upon the testimony of an Indian.

7. If any person forcibly conveys any Indian from his home, or compels him to work, or perform any service against his will, in this State, except as provided in this Act, he or they shall, on conviction, be fined in any sum not less than fifty dollars, at the discretion of the Court or jury.

8. It shall be the duty of the Justices of the Peace, once in six months in every year, to make a full and correct statement to the Court of Sessions of their county, of all moneys received for fines imposed on Indians, and all fees allowed for services rendered under the provisions of this Act; and said Justices shall pay over to the County Treasurer of their respective counties, all money they may have received for fines and not appropriated, or fees for services rendered under this Act; and the Treasurer shall keep a correct statement of all money so received, which shall be termed the "Indian Fund" of the county. The Treasurer shall pay out any money of said funds in his hands, on a certificate of a Justice of the Peace of his county, for fees and expenditures incurred in carrying out the provisions of this law.

9. It shall be the duty of Justices of the Peace, in their respective townships, as well as all other peace officers in this State, to instruct the Indians in their neighborhood in the laws which relate to them, giving them such advice as they may deem necessary and proper; and if any tribe or village of Indians refuse or neglect to obey the laws, the Justice of the Peace may punish the guilty chiefs or principal men by reprimand or fine, or otherwise reasonably chastise them.

10. If any person or persons shall set the prairie on fire, or refuse to use proper exertions to extinguish the fire when the prairies are burning, such person or persons shall be subject to fine or punishment, as a Court may adjudge proper.

11. If any Indian shall commit an unlawful offence against a white person, such person shall not inflict punishment for such offence, but may, without process, take the Indian before a Justice of the Peace, and on conviction, the Indian shall be punished according to the provisions of this Act.

12. In all cases of trial between a white man and an Indian, either party may require a jury.

13. Justices may require the chiefs and influential men of any village to apprehend and bring before them or him any Indian charged or suspected of an offence.

14. When an Indian is convicted of an offence before a Justice of the Peace punishable by fine, any white person may, by consent of the Justice, give bond for said Indian, conditioned for the payment of said fine and costs, and in such case the Indian shall be compelled to work for the person so bailing, until he has discharged or cancelled the fine assessed against him: *Provided*, the person bailing shall treat the Indian humanely, and clothe and feed him properly; the allowance given for such labor shall be fixed by the Court, when the bond is taken.

15. If any person in this State shall sell, give, or furnish to any Indian, male or female, any intoxicating liquors (except when administered in sickness), for good cause shown, he, she, or they so offending shall, on conviction thereof, be fined not less than twenty dollars for each offence, or be imprisoned not less than five days, or fined and imprisoned, as the Court may determine.

16. An Indian convicted of stealing horses, mules, cattle, or any valuable thing, shall be subject to receive any number of lashes not exceeding twenty-five, or shall be subject to a fine not exceeding two hundred dollars, at the discretion of the Court or Jury.

17. When an Indian is sentenced to be whipped, the Justice may appoint a white man, or an Indian at his discretion, to execute the sentence in his presence, and shall not permit unnecessary cruelty in the execution of the sentence.

18. All fines, forfeitures, penalties recovered under or by this Act, shall be paid into the treasury of the county, to the credit of the Indian Fund as provided in Section Eight.

19. All white persons making application to a Justice of the Peace, for confirmation of a contract with or in relation to an Indian, shall pay the fee, which shall not exceed two dollars for each contract determined and

filed as provided in this Act, and for all other services, such fees as are allowed for similar services under other laws of this State. *Provided*, the application fee for hiring Indians, or keeping minors, and fees and expenses for setting off lands to Indians, shall be paid by the white person applying.

20. Any Indian able to work and support himself in some honest calling, not having wherewithal to maintain himself, who shall be found loitering and strolling about, or frequenting public places where liquors are sold, begging, or leading an immoral or profligate course of life, shall be liable to be arrested on the complaint of any resident citizen of the county, and brought before any Justice of the Peace of the proper county, Mayor or Recorder of any incorporated town or city, who shall examine said accused Indian, and hear the testimony in relation thereto, and if said Justice, Mayor or Recorder shall be satisfied that he is a vagrant, as above set forth, he shall make out a warrant under his hand and seal, authorizing and requiring the officer having him in charge or custody, to hire out such vagrant within twenty-four hours to the best bidder, by public notice given as he shall direct, for the highest price that can be had, for any term not exceeding four months; and such vagrant shall be subject to and governed by the provisions of this Act, regulating guardians and minors, during the time which he has been so hired. The money received for his hire, shall, after deducting the costs, and the necessary expense for clothing for said Indian, which may have been purchased by his employer, be, if he be without a family, paid into the County Treasury, to the credit of the Indian fund. But if he have a family, the same shall be appropriated for their use and benefit: *Provided*, that any such vagrant, when arrested, and before judgment, may relieve himself by giving to such Justice, Mayor, or Recorder, a bond, with good security, conditioned that he will, for the next twelve months, conduct himself with good behavior, and betake to some honest employment for support.

[Chapter 133 of the *Statutes of California*, enacted into law on April 22, 1850.]

Amendments in 1860 to the Act of April 1850

CHAP. CCXXXI—An Act amendatory of an Act entitled "An Act for the Government and Protection of Indians," passed April twenty-second, one thousand eight hundred and fifty. [Approved April 18, 1860.]

The People of the State of California, represented in Senate and Assembly, do enact as follows:

SECTION 1. Section third of said act, is hereby amended so as to read as follows:

SEC. 3. County and District Judges in the respective counties of this State, shall, by virtue of this act, have full power and authority, at the instance and request of any person having or hereafter obtaining any Indian child or children, male or female, under the age of fifteen years, from the parents or person or persons having the care or charge of such child or children, with the consent of such parents or person or persons having the care or charge of any such child or children, or at the instance and request of any person desirous of obtaining any Indian or Indians, whether children or grown persons, that may be held as prisoners of war, or at the instance and request of any person desirous of obtaining any vagrant Indian or Indians, as have no settled habitation or means of livelihood, and have not placed themselves under the protection of any white person, to bind and put out such Indians as apprentices, to trades, husbandry, or other employments, as shall to them appear proper, and for this purpose shall execute duplicate articles of indenture of apprenticeship on behalf of such Indians, which indenturess shall also be executed by the person to whom such Indian or Indians are to be indentured; one copy of which shall be filed by the County Judge, in the Recorder's office of the county, and one copy retained by the person to whom such Indian or Indians may be indentured; such indentures shall authorize such person to have the care, custody, control, and earnings, of such Indian or Indians, as shall require such person to clothe and suitably provide the necessaries of life for such Indian or Indians, for and during the term for which such Indian or Indians shall be apprenticed, and shall contain the sex, name, and probable age, of such Indian or Indians; such indentures may be

216

for the following terms of years: Such children as are under fourteen years of age, if males, until they attain the age of twenty-five years; if females, until they attain the age of twenty-one years; such as are over fourteen and under twenty years of age, if males, until they attain the age of thirty years; if females, until they attain the age of twenty-five years; and such Indians as may be over the age of twenty years, then next following the date of such indentures, for and during the term of ten years, at the discretion of such Judge; such Indians as may be indentured under the provision of this section, shall be deemed within such provisions of this act, as are applicable to minor Indians.

SEC. 2. Section seventh of said act is hereby amended so as to read as follows:

SEC. 7. If any person shall forcibly convey any Indian from any place without this State, to any place within this State, or from his or her home within this State, or compel him or her to work or perform any service, against his or her will, except as provided in this act, he or they shall, upon conviction thereof, be fined in any sum not less than one hundred dollars, nor more than five hundred dollars, before any court having jurisdiction, at the discretion of the court, and the collection of such fine shall be enforced as provided by law in other criminal cases, one-half to be paid to the prosecutor, and one-half to the county in which such conviction is had.

[Chapter 231 of the *Statutes of California*, enacted into law on April 18, 1860.]

Letter from J. A. Sutter to Governor R. B. Mason

His Excellency   NEW HELVETIA Feby 22^d 1848
R. B. Mason
Gov of California

SIR:

By the bearer of this Mr. Charles Bennett, I have taken the liberty of sending for your approval articles of agreement made by Mr. Marshall and myself with the Yalesumney tribe of Indians. Should it meet with your approbation you would confer a special favour by sanctioning it. Mr. Bennett can give a full description of location etc, etc. We have been at great expense in building and settling the place and would like to be protected in our title or claim for the term expressed in the Lease.

The settlement will be of great benefit to the Indians by protecting them against the wild tribes above them, furnishing them with food, clothing etc and teach them habits of industry. It will also be the means of settleing the lands at the base of the California mountains which are of a very superior quality by protecting the settlers against the Indians.

I have the honour to be very
Respectfully you Obt Servt.
J. A. SUTTER [unsigned]

Articles of Agreement Made by Mr. Marshall and Mr. Sutter with Yalesumney Tribe

This indenture made the first Day of January in the year of our Lord One thousand Eight hundred and fourty eight between Pulpuli and Gesu, Chiefs. Colule and Sole, Alcaldes of the Yalesumney tribe on the part of said tribe of the Territory of Upper California of the one part, and John A. Sutter and James W. Marshall of the Territory of Upper California, Sacramento District of the other part. Witnesseth. That the said Pulpuli, Gesu, and Colule & Sole for and in consideration of the yearly rents and covenants hereinafter mentioned and reserved on the part and behalf of the said Pulpuli, Gesu, Colule & Sole as agents for the Yalesumney tribe their heirs, executors and administrators doth rent and lease unto Sutter and Marshall the following described track [tract] of Land for the term of twenty years, beginning at the mouth of a small creek known by the Indian name of Pumpumul where said creek empties into the south branch of the American fork, a tributary of the Sacramento River thence north one mile thence up said fork on the north side at the distance of one mile from said stream to a point three miles above a saw mill building by said Sutter and Marshall thence in a south east direction until it strikes crossing the south branch the said Pumpumel Creek thence down the same to the point of beginning and likewise grant to the said Sutter and Marshall the right and privilege of cutting Lumber at any point on or near the said south fork and to float the same down the said stream and the privilege of making a road from said mill to New Helvetia the same grant being made for the following purposes and conditions, viz. the said Sutter and Marshall to have the right to erect a saw mill and what other machinery necessary for their purpose and to cultivate such land as they may think proper and likewise open such mines and work the same as the said aforsaid tract of land may contain, the said tribe reserving to themselves the individual residence of said tract of land excepting such as may be enclosed by said Sutter and Marshall. The said Sutter & Marshall doth bind themselves to erect one pair of mill stones and to grind the grain for said tribe taking one bushel in eight and to pay on the first day of January each year one hundred and fifty dollars to Pulpuli, Gesu, Colule & Sole their heirs and assigns for the use of said Yalesumney tribe during the term aforesaid said payment to be made in clothing and farming utensils for the common use and benefit of said tribe at the fair market value; and the said Sutter and Marshall of the second part at the expiration of said term agree and bind them selves their heirs and assigns to give quiet and peaceable possession of the aforesaid premises unto the said Pulpuli, Gesu, Colule and Sole their heirs and assigns they paying the said Sutter and Marshall a reasonable price for the mill and buildings that may be put on the said premises by them.

In witness whereof the said parties of the first and second part set their names and seals. Done this the fourth day of February in the year of our Lord one thousand Eight hundred and fourty eight.

WITNESSES   his
CHARLES BENNET   Pulpuli X Chief [SEAL]
WILLIAM SCOTT   mark
                                                   his
                                        Gesu X Chief [SEAL]
                                                   mark
                                                   his
                                        Colule X Chief [SEAL]
                                                   mark
                                                   his
                                        Sole X Alcalde [SEAL]
                                                   mark
                                           J. A. SUTTER [SEAL]
                                        JAMES W. MARSHALL [SEAL]
                          Done in the presence and with my aprobation
                                             J. A. SUTTER
                                                    Sub Indian Agent

[Sutter's letter to Governor Mason, together with the lease, is published in C. Olson, "The Sutter-Marshall Lease with the Yalesumney Indians for Monopoly of the Gold-bearing Lands." *Letters of the Gold Discovery* No. 2, Book Club of California, 1948 (pamphlet of 5 pages). See also J. S. Hittell, *Mining in the Pacific States of North America*, (San Francisco, 1861), pp. 12–14.]

A Typical Treaty Made with the Indians in 1851

(J.) Treaty made and concluded at the fork of the Cosumnes river, september 18, 1851, between O. M. Wozencraft, United States indian agent, and the chiefs, captains, and head men of the Cu-lu, Yas-si, etc., tribes of Indians

A treaty of peace and friendship made and concluded at the fork of Cosumnes river, between the United States Indian Agent, O. M. Wozencraft, of the one part, and the chiefs, captains, and head men of the following tribes, viz: Cu-lu, Yas-si, Loc-lum-ne, and Wo-pum-nes.

Article 1. The several tribes or bands above mentioned do acknowledge the United States to be the sole and absolute sovereign of all the soil and territory ceded to them by a treaty of peace between them and the republic of Mexico.

Art. 2. The said tribes or bands acknowledge themselves jointly and severally under the exclusive jurisdiction, authority and protection of the United States and hereby bind themselves hereafter to refrain from the commission of all acts of hostility and aggression towards the government or citizens thereof, and to live on terms of peace and friendship among themselves and with all other Indian tribes which are now or may come under the protection of the United States; and furthermore bind themselves to conform to, and be governed by the laws and regulations of the Indian Bureau, made and provided therefor by the Congress of the United States.

Art. 3. To promote the settlement and improvement of said tribes or bands, it is hereby stipulated and agreed that the following district of country in the State of California shall be and is hereby set apart forever for the sole use and occupancy of the aforesaid tribes of Indians, to wit: commencing at a point on the Cosumnes river, on the western line of the county, running south on and by said line to its terminus, running east on said line twenty-five miles, thence north to the middle fork of the Cosumnes river, down said stream to the place of beginning; to have and to hold the said district of country for the sole use and occupancy of said Indian tribes forever. *Provided*, That there is reserved to the government of the United States the right of way over any portion of said territory, and the right to establish and maintain any military post or posts, public buildings, school-houses, houses for agents, teachers, and such others as they may deem necessary for their use or the protection of the Indians. The said tribes or bands, and each of them, hereby engage that they will never claim any other lands within the boundaries of the United States, nor ever disturb the people of the United States in the free use and enjoyment thereof.

ART. 4. To aid the said tribes or bands in their subsistence, while removing to and making their settlement upon the said reservation, the United States, in addition to the few presents made them at this council, will furnish them, free of charge, with five hundred (500) head of beef cattle, to average in weight five hundred (500) pounds, two hundred (200) sacks of flour, one hundred (100) pounds each, within the term of two years from the date of this treaty.

ART. 5. As early as convenient after the ratification of this treaty by the President and Senate, in consideration of the premises, and with a sincere desire to encourage said tribes in acquiring the arts and habits of civilized life, the United States will also furnish them with the following articles, to be divided among them by the agent, according to their respective numbers and wants, during each of the two years succeeding the said ratification, viz: one pair of strong pantaloons and one red flannel shirt for each man and boy, one linsey gown for each woman and girl, four thousand yards of calico and one thousand yards brown sheeting, forty pounds Scotch thread, two dozen pairs of scissors, eight dozen thimbles, three thousand needles, one two and a half point Mackinaw blanket for each man and woman over fifteen (15) years of age, four thousand pounds of iron and four thousand pounds of steel, and in like manner in the first year, for the permanent use of the said tribes, and as their joint property, viz: seventy-five brood mares and three stallions, three hundred milch cows and eighteen bulls, twelve yoke of work cattle with yokes and chains, twelve work mules or horses, twenty-five ploughs, assorted sizes, two hundred garden or corn hoes, eighty spades, twelve grindstones. Of the stock enumerated above, and the product thereof, no part or portion shall be killed, exchanged, sold, or otherwise parted with, without the consent and direction of the agent.

ART. 6. The United States will also employ and settle among said tribes, at or near their towns or settlements, one practical farmer, who shall superintend all agricultural operations, with two assistants, men of practical knowledge and industrious habits, one carpenter, one wheelwright, one blacksmith, one principal school-teacher, and as many assistant teachers as the President may deem proper to instruct said tribes in reading, writing, &c., and in the domestic arts, upon the manual labor system; all the above-named workmen and teachers to be maintained and paid by the United States for the period five years, and as long thereafter as the President shall deem advisable. The United States will also erect suitable school-houses, shops, and dwellings, for the accommodation of the school teachers and mechanics above specified, and for the protection of the public property.

In testimony whereof, the parties have hereunto signed their names and affixed their seals this eighteenth day of September, in the year of our Lord one thousand eight hundred and fifty-one.

O. M. WOZENCRAFT
United States Indian Agent

For and in behalf of the Cu-lu
MI-ON-QUISH, his X mark   [SEAL]

For and in behalf of the Yas-si
SAN-TEA-GO, his X mark   [SEAL]

For and in behalf of the Loc-lum-ne
POL-TUCK, his X mark   [SEAL]

For and in behalf of the Wo-pum-nes
HIN-COY-E, his X mark   [SEAL]
MAT-TAS, his X mark   [SEAL]
HOL-LOH, his X mark   [SEAL]
BOY-ER, his X mark.   [SEAL]

Signed, sealed and delivered, after being fully explained, in presence of

FLAVEL BELCHER
J. B. McKINNIE
WILLIAM RHOAD

[From Hearings before a Subcommittee of the Committee on Indian Affairs, House of Representatives, 66th Cong. 2d sess., March 23, 1920. GPO 1920 (pp. 30–31).]

Treaty Between Mohave and Chem-e-Huevis Tribes, 1867

At a convention held at the office of the Arizona Superintendency at La Paz on the 21st day of March A.D., 1867, in presence of G. W. Dent, Superintendent of Indian Affairs, between delegations of the *Mohave* tribe of Indians and the *Chem-e-huevis* tribe of Indians for the purpose of concluding peace between these two bands, and restoring and confirming amity.

The *Chem-e-huevis* were personally present by "Pan Coyer," their Head chief, and certain of his Captains and Headmen—and the *Mohaves* were personally present by "*Iretaba*," their Head chief, and certain of his Captains and Headmen, and after full conference the 2 bands agreed upon the following terms:

To wit:

First—All hostilities heretofore existing between *Mohaves* and *Chemhuevis* cease on and after this day and perpetual amity shall exist between the two bands.

Second—The *Mohaves* shall occupy and cultivate the lands on the left bank of the Colorado River, and the *Chemhuevis* the lands of the right bank of the Colorado River. Provided, that Indians of either tribe may freely visit or travel over either country, and shall not be molested therein either in their person or their property.

Third—It is also agreed between the parties to this agreement that they will use their best exertions to prevent the members of either of [the] tribes from committing an[y] depredations upon the persons or property of American citizens in the country occupied by them, and should any such depredations be committed, that they will endeavor to recover property taken and bring offenders and deliver them to the Superintendent of Indian Affairs at La Paz.

In testimony to the above agreement we have set our hands and our seals at La Paz, Arizona, on the day and year just written.

                           his
        (Signed) Iretaba X Head Chief of Mohaves
                          mark   [SEAL]

                           his
        (Signed) Pan Coyer X Head Chief of Chemhuevis
                          mark   [SEAL]

        Signed and sealed in presence of
            (Signed) J. W. DENT
                                    Special Indian Agent, Colorado River Indians

[Treaty between Mohave and Chem-e-huevis tribes, March 21, 1867. MS Copy,
War Dept., filed with Annual Report of Commander of Dept. of Calif., 1867.]

Delegates to the California Constitutional Convention of 1849

Name	Age	Where born	Of what state last a resident	District in California	Length of residence	Profession
Aram, Joseph	39	Oneida County. N.Y.	Illinois	San Jose	Three years	Farmer
Botts, Ch. T.	40	Spotsylvania County, Va.	Virginia	Monterey	Sixteen months	Attorney at Law
Brown, Eliam	52	Herkimer County. N.Y.	Missouri	San Jose	Three years	Farmer
Carrillo, Jose Anto.	53	San Francisco	California	Angeles	Toda la vida	Laborador
Covarrubias, J. M.	40	California	California	San Luis Obispo	—	—
Crosby, E. O.	34	Tompkins County, N.Y.	New York	Sacramento	Seven months	Lawyer
Dent, Lewis	26	St. Louis County	Missouri	Monterey	Three years	Lawyer
Dimmick, Kimball H.	34	Chenango County, N.Y.	New York	San Jose	Three years	Lawyer
Dominguez, Manuel	46	San Diego	California	Angeles	All my life	Banker
Ellis, A. J.	33	Oneida County	New York	San Francisco	Two years and-a-half	Merchant
Foster, Stephen C.	28	East Machias, Me.	Missouri	Angeles	Three years	Agriculturist
Gilbert, Edw.	27	Dutchess County, N.Y.	New York	San Francisco	Two years and-a-half	Printer
Gwin, W. M.	44	Summer County, Tenn.	Louisiana	San Francisco	Four months	Farmer
Halleck, H. W.	32	Oneida County	New York	Monterey	Three years	U.S. Engineer

Name	Age	Birthplace	State	California Location	Time in California	Occupation
Hanks, Julian	39	Tolland County, Conn.	Connecticut	San Jose	Ten years	Farmer
Hastings, L. W.	30	Knox County	Ohio	Sacramento	Six years	Lawyer
Hill, Henry	33	Virginia	Virginia	San Diego	One year five months	U.S. Army
Hobson, Joseph	39	Baltimore	Maryland	San Francisco	Five months	Merchant
Hollingsworth, J. McH.	25	Baltimore	Maryland	San Joaquin	Three years	Lieut. Volunteers
Hoppe, J. D.	35	Carroll County, Md.	Missouri	San Jose	Three years	Merchant
Jones, J. M.	25	Scott County, Ky.	Louisiana	San Joaquin	About four months	Attorney at Law
Larkin, Thomas O.	47	Charlestown	Massachusetts	Monterey	Sixteen years	Trader
Lippincott, Benj. S.	34	New York	New Jersey	San Joaquin	Three years and-a-half	Trader
Lippitt, Francis J.	37	Rhode Island	New York	San Francisco	Two years seven months	Lawyer
McCarver, M. M.	42	Madison County, Kentucky	Oregon	Sacramento	One year	Farmer
McDougal, John	32	Ohio	Indiana	Sacramento	Seven months	Merchant
Moore, B. F.	29	Florida	Texas	San Joaquin	One year	Elegant leisure
Noriega, de la Guerra	36	California	California	Santa Barbara	—	—
Norton, Myron	27	Birmington County, Vt.	New York	San Francisco	One year	Lawyer
Ord, Pacificus	34	Allegany County, Md.	Louisiana	Monterey	Eight months	Lawyer
Pedrorena, Miguel de	41	Spain	California	San Diego	Twelve years	Merchant

Name	Age	Where born	Of what state last a resident	District in California	Length of residence	Profession
Pico, Antonio M.	40	Monterey	California	Pueblo de San Jose	All my life	Agriculturist
Price, Rodman M.	30	Orange County, N.Y.	New Jersey	San Francisco	Four years	U.S. Navy
Reid, Hugo	38	Cardross	Scotland	Angeles	Sixteen years	Farmer
Rodriguez, Jacinto	36	Monterey	California	Monterey	All my life	Agriculturist
Sansevaine, Pedro	31	Bordeaux	Bordeaux	San Jose	Eleven years	Negotiant
Semple, R.	42	Kentucky	Missouri	Sonoma	Five years	Printer
Shannon, W. E.	27	Ireland (Mayo)	New York	Sacramento	Three years	Lawyer
Sherwood, Winfield S.	32	Sandy Hill Washington Co.	New York	Sacramento	Four months	Lawyer
Snyder, Jacob R.	34	Philadelphia, Pa.	Pennsylvania	Sacramento	Four years	Surveyor
Stearns, Abel	51	Massachusetts	Massachusetts	Angeles	Twenty years	Merchant
Steuart, W. M.	49	Montgomery County, Md.	Maryland	San Francisco	One year	Attorney at Law
Sutter, J. A.	47	Switzerland	Missouri	Sacramento	Ten years	Farmer
Tefft, Henry A.	26	Washington County, N.Y.	Wisconsin	San Luis Obispo	Four months	Lawyer
Vallejo, M. G.	42	Monterey (U.C.)	California	Sonoma	All my life	Military
Vermeule, Thos. L.	35	New Jersey	New York	San Joaquin	Three years	Lawyer
Walker, J. P.	52	Goochland County, Va.	Missouri	Sonoma	Thirteen months	Farmer
Wozencraft, O. M.	34	Clermont City, Ohio	Louisiana	San Joaquin	Four months	Physician

SOURCE: Browne, J. Ross. *California Constitutional Convention*, *1849*, pp. 478–479.

The People v. Hall, Oct. 1, 1854

The People, respondent, v George W. Hall, appellant. Section 394 of the Civil Practice Act provides, "No Indian or Negro shall be allowed to testify as a witness in any action in which a white man is a party."

Section 14 of the Criminal Act provides, "No black, or mulatto person, or Indian shall be allowed to give evidence in favor of, or against a white man."

Held, that the words, Indian, Negro, Black and White, are generic terms, designating race. That, therefore, Chinese and all other people are not white, are included in the prohibition from being witnesses against whites. Mr. Ch. J. Murray delivered the opinion of the court, Mr. J. Heyenfeldt concurred.

The appellant, a free white citizen of this state was convicted of murder upon the testimony of Chinese witnesses. The point involved in this case, is the admissibility of such evidence.

The 394th section of the Act concerning Civil Cases, provides that no Indian or Negro shall be allowed to testify as a witness in any action or proceeding in which a white person is a party.

The 14th section of the Act of April 16th, 1850, regulating Criminal Proceedings, provides that "No Black, or Mulatto person, or Indian, shall be allowed to give evidence in favor of, or against a white man."

The true point at which we are anxious to arrive, is the legal signification of the words, "Black, Mulatto, Indian and White person," and whether the Legislature adopted them as generic terms, or intended to limit their application to specific types of the human species.

Before considering this question, it is proper to remark the difference between the two sections of our Statute, already quoted, the latter being more broad and comprehensive in its exclusion, by the use of the word "Black," instead of Negro.

Conceding, however, for the present, that the word "Black," as used in the 14th section, and "Negro," in 394th, are convertible terms, and that the former was intended to include the latter, let us proceed to inquire who is excluded from testifying as witnesses under the term "Indian."

When Columbus first landed upon the shores of this continent, in his attempt to discover a western passage to the Indies, he imagined that he had accomplished the object of his expedition, and that the Island of San Salvador was one of those Islands of the Chinese sea, lying near the extremity of India, which had been described by navigators.

Acting upon this hypothesis, and also perhaps from the similarity of features and physical conformation, he gave the Islanders the name of Indians, which appellation was universally adopted, and extended to the aboriginals of the New World, as well as of Asia.

From that time, down to a very recent period, the American Indians and the Mongolian, or Asiatic, were regarded as the same type of human species.

In order to arrive at a correct understanding of the intention of our Legislature, it will be necessary to go back to the early history of legislation on this subject, our Statute being only a transcript of those older States.

At the period from which this legislation dates, those portions of Asia which include India proper, the Eastern Archipelago, and the countries washed by the Chinese waters, as far as then known, were denominated the Indies, from which the inhabitants had derived the generic name of Indians.

Ethnology, at that time, was unknown as a distinct science, or if known, had not reached that high point of perfection which it has since attained by the scientific inquiries and discoveries of the master minds of the last half century. Few speculations had been made with regard to the moral or physical differences between the different races of mankind. These were general in their character and limited to those visible and palpable variations which could not escape the attention of the most common observer.

The general, or perhaps universal opinion of that day was, that there were but three distinct types of the human species, which, in their turn, were subdivided into varieties or tribes. This opinion is still held by many scientific writers, and is supported by Cuvier, one of the most eminent naturalists of modern times.

Many ingenious speculations have been resorted to for the purpose of sustaining this opinion. It has been supposed, and not without plausibility, that this continent was first peopled by Asiatics, who crossed Behring's Straits, and from thence found their way down to the more fruitful climates of Mexico and South America. Almost every tribe has some tradition of coming from the North, and many of them, that their ancestors came from some remote country beyond the ocean.

From the eastern portions of Kamtschatka, the Aleutian Islands form a long and continuous group, extending eastward to that portion of the North

American Continent inhabited by the Esquimaux. They appear to be a continuation of the lofty volcanic ranges which traverse the two continents, and are inhabited by a race who resemble, in a remarkable degree, in language and appearance, both the inhabitants of Kamtschatka (who are admitted to be of the Mongolian type), and the Esquimaux, who again, in turn, resemble other tribes of American Indians. The similarity of the skull and pelvis, and the general configuration of the two races; the remarkable resemblance in eyes, beard, hair, and other peculiarities, together, with the contiguity of the two Continents, might well have led to the belief that this country was first peopled by the Asiatics, and that the difference between the different tribes and the parent stock was such as would necessarily arise from the circumstances of climate, pursuits, and other physical causes, and was no greater than that existing between the Arab and the European, both of whom were supposed to belong to the Caucasian race.

Although the discoveries of eminent Archeologists, and the researches of modern Geologists, have given to this Continent an antiquity of thousands of years anterior to the evidence of man's existence, and the light of modern science may have shown conclusively that it was not peopled by the inhabitants of Asia, but that the Aborigines are a distinct type, and as such claim a distinct origin, still, this would not, in any degree, alter the meaning of the term, and render that specific which was before generic.

We have adverted to these speculations for the purpose of showing that the name of Indian, from the time of Columbus to the present day, has been used to designate, not alone the North American, but the whole of the Mongolian race, and that the name, though first applied probably through mistake, was afterwards continued as appropriate on account of the supposed common origin.

That this was the common opinion in the early history of American legislation, cannot be disputed, and, therefore, all legislation upon the subject must have borne relation to that opinion.

Can, then, the use of the word "Indian," because at the present day it may be sometimes regarded as a specific, and not as a generic term, alter this conclusion? We think not; because at the origin of the legislation we are considering, it was used and admitted in its common and ordinary acceptation, as a generic term, distinguishing the great Mongolian race, and as such, its meaning then became fixed by law, and in construing Statutes the legal meaning of words must be preserved.

Again: the words of the Act must be construed in *pari materia*. It will not be disputed that "White" and "Negro," are generic terms, and refer to two of the great types of mankind. If these, as well as the word "Indian," are not to be regarded as generic terms, including the two great races which

231

they were intended to designate, but only specific, and applying to those Whites and Negroes who were inhabitants of this Continent at the time of the passage of the Act, the most anomalous consequences would ensue. The European white man who comes here would not be shielded from the testimony of the degraded and demoralized caste, while the Negro, fresh from the coast of Africa, or the Indian of Patagonia, the Kanaka, South Sea Islander, or New Hollander, would be admitted, upon their arrival, to testify against white citizens in our courts of law.

To argue such a proposition would be an insult to the good sense of the Legislature.

The evident intention of the Act was to throw around the citizen a protection for life and property, which could only be secured by removing him above the corrupting influences of degraded castes.

It can hardly be supposed that any Legislature would attempt this by excluding domestic Negroes and Indians, who not unfrequently have correct notions of their obligations to society, and turning loose upon the community the more degraded tribes of the same species, who have nothing in common with us, in language, country or laws.

We have, thus far, considered this subject on the hypothesis that the 14th section of the Act Regulating Criminal Proceedings, and the 394th section of the Practice Act, were the same.

As before remarked, there is a wide difference between the two. The word "Black" may include all Negroes, but the term "Negro" does not include all Black persons.

By the use of this term in this connection, we understand it to mean the opposite of "White," and that it should be taken as contradistinguished from all White persons.

In using the words, "No Black, or Mulatto person, or Indian shall be allowed to give evidence for or against a White person," the Legislature, if any intention can be ascribed to it, adopted the most comprehensive terms to embrace every known class or shade of color, as the apparent design was to protect the White person from the influence of all testimony other than that of persons of the same caste. The use of these terms must, by every sound rule of construction, exclude every one who is not of white blood.

The Act of Congress in defining what description of aliens may become naturalized citizens, provides that every "free white citizen," &c.&c. In speaking of this subject, Chancellor Kent says, that "the Act confines the description to 'white' citizens, and that it is a matter of doubt, whether, under this provision, any of the tawny races of Asia can be admitted to the privileges of citizenship." 2 Kent's Com. 72.

We are not disposed to leave this question in any doubt. The word

"White" has a distinct signification, which *ex vi termini*, excludes black, yellow, and all other colors. It will be observed, by reference to the first section of the second article of the constitution of this State, that none but white males can become electors, except in the case of Indians, who may be admitted by special Act of the Legislature. On examination of the constitutional debates, it will be found that not a little difficulty existed in selecting these precise words, which were finally agreed upon as the most comprehensive that could be suggested to exclude all inferior races.

If the term "White," as used in the Constitution was not understood in its generic sense as including the Caucasian race, and necessarily excluding all others, where was the necessity of providing for the admission of Indians to the privilege of voting, by special legislation.

We are of the opinion that the words "White," "Negro," "Mulatto," "Indian," and "Black person," wherever they occur in our Constitution and laws, must be taken in their generic sense, and that, even admitting the Indian of this Continent is not of the Mongolian type, that the words "Black person," in the 14th section must be taken as contradistinguished from White, and necessarily includes all races other than the Caucasian.

We have carefully considered all the consequences resulting from a different rule of construction, and are satisfied that even in a doubtful case we would be impelled to this decision on grounds of public policy.

The same rule which would admit them to testify, would admit them to all the equal rights of citizenship, and we might soon see them at the polls, in the jury box, upon the bench, and in our legislative halls.

This is not a speculation which exists in the excited and overheated imagination of the patriot and statesman, but it is an actual and present danger.

The anomalous spectacle of a distinct people, living in our community, recognizing no laws of this State except through necessity, bringing with them their prejudices and national feuds, in which they indulge in open violation of the law; whose mendacity is proverbial; a race of people whom nature has marked as inferior, and who are incapable of progress or intellectual development beyond a certain point, as their history has shown; differing in language, opinions, color, and physical conformation; between whom and ourselves nature has placed an impassable difference, is now presented, and for them is claimed, not only the right to swear away the life of a citizen, but the further privilege of participating with us in administering the affairs of our Government.

These facts were before the Legislature that framed this Act, and have been known as matters of public history to every subsequent Legislature.

There can be no doubt as to the intention of the Legislature, and that if it has ever been anticipated that this class of people were not embraced in the prohibition, then such specific words would have been employed as would have put the matter beyond any possible controversy.

For these reasons, we are of opinion that the testimony was inadmissible.

The judgment is reversed and the cause remanded.

Mr. Justice Wells dissented, as follows:

From the opinion of the Chief Justice, I most respectfully dissent.

[4 Cal. 399.]

The People v. Elyea

The defendant was convicted of murder in the first degree, and the errors assigned relate to the proceedings at the trial.

1. The first point made is, that the Court below erred in the instructions given to the jury. It is not stated in what particular the instructions were erroneous, nor does it appear that they were objected to at the trial. So far as the record is concerned, we are authorized to conclude that they received the assent and approval of the defendant. There is, however, no doubt of their correctness.

They were confined to definition of the offense of murder, given nearly in the language of the statute, and a few simple directions to the jury in relation to their verdict, in which there was no error.

2. The second point is, that a witness for the prosecution was permitted to testify to a particular statement of the defendant, without being allowed to speak of other statements made by him at the same time. This point has no foundation in the record. The counsel here has evidently mistaken the point of the exception in the Court below. The question there, was not whether these statements were admissible, but whether it was competent to prove them by a written memorandum made by the witness at the time, and which he stated to be correct. The Court very properly decided that this paper could not be given in evidence, and to that decision, and to that alone, the defendant excepted.

3. The third and only remaining point, that the Court erred in permitting one Martin to be examined as a witness. It is claimed that he was incompetent under the provisions of our statute (Cr. Pr. Act, sec. 14) precluding negroes and Indians from testifying either for or against a white person. The objection to his competency is based upon his color, and the fact that he is a native of Turkey, and was born of Turkish parents. It is incumbent upon the party alleging a disability of this character to prove it by clear and indubitable evidence. This we conceive has not been done in the present case. The *indicium* of color cannot be relied upon as an infallible test of competency under the statute. It may be a sufficient test in many cases, but only

when it is so decided as to leave no doubt of the particular race to which the witness belongs. If a negro should offer to be sworn, he could be rejected upon the sole evidence of his color. So with an Indian, and so with persons of mixed blood who are obviously within the rule of exclusion. But the color is a mere fact to be received in evidence as tending to establish the conclusion of competency or incompetency, and if alone it is sufficient for that purpose, nothing further is required.

The questions embraced in the decision of this Court in the case of *The People* v. *Hall*, (4 Cal. 399), must be regarded as settled, but we cannot presume that all persons having tawny skins and dark complexions are within the principle of that decision. The statute itself, after declaring that no black or mulatto person, or Indian, shall give evidence, etc., provides that persons having one-eighth or more of negro blood, shall be deemed mulattoes, and persons having one-half of Indian blood, shall be deemed Indians, thus rendering impossible the adoption of any rule of exclusion upon the basis of mere color. We have, in this case, the additional facts of the birthplace and parentage of the witness. But these facts, if material at all, are rather against, than for, the defendant; for, although the population of Turkey is made up, in some degree, of several distinct types of the human race, the Caucasian largely predominates, and constitutes the controlling element.

The judgment of the Court below is affirmed, and that Court will designate a day to carry its sentence into execution.

[State Supreme Court, October Term 1859:142–144.]

The Case of Mary Frances Ward: Petition and Reply

I am the mother of Mary Frances Ward, who is under the age of four-teen years—namely, of the age of between eleven and twelve years. I am the wife of A. J. Ward, and by that marriage the mother of said Mary Frances Ward. We are all of African descent, colored citizens of the United States and of the State of California, and at present and continuously for thirteen years now last past, and now, residing at No. 1,006 Pacific street, in the city and county of San Francisco. The city and county of San Francisco is not now, nor for the year last past has been divided into school districts; but by law, and also by the custom adopted and established by the Board of Education of said city and county, pupils residing therein have a right to be received as such at the public school nearest their residence, in case such school is not full, and they have made sufficient progress to be received therein.

The nearest public school to our said residence in said city and county for six months now last past, and now, is the so-called Broadway Grammar School, on Broadway street, in said city and county, between Powell and Mason streets; a public school under the control of the Board of Education of said city and county, sustained by taxes raised in said city and county for the support of public schools therein, and at the time the application here-inafter mentioned was made, was, and ever since then has been, and is now, in charge of Noah F. Flood as Principal thereof, appointed thereto by, and holding office as such under the said Board of Education.

On or about the 1st day of July, A.D. 1872, by the consent and direction of my said husband, I took the said Mary Frances Ward with me to the said Broadway Grammar School, the same being in session, and there found the said Noah F. Flood, then and there being such Principal of said school, and then and there as such being the proper and only person to whom to make application for the admission of pupils to the same, and presented her to him, as a pupil asking to be admitted as such to said school. The said school then and there was not full, nor was there any good or lawful reason why the said Mary Frances Ward should not be received therein as such pupil, as aforesaid. But the said Noah F. Flood, instead of making inquiries respecting the said Mary Frances Ward, her residence, citizenship, or in any other respect, or examining her as to her proficiency, at once politely, but firmly and definitively declined to entertain the said application, or to admit the said Mary Frances Ward as such pupil, assigning, as the only reason for such action and refusal, the fact that she was a colored person, and that said Board of Education has established and assigned separate schools for such colored persons, and that he was sorry to be compelled for that reason to adopt that course of action on his part. And I aver that the reason so assigned was true in fact, and was in truth and fact the only reason existing for such action and refusal of the said Noah F. Flood.

The said Broadway Grammar School was then and is now of the description called a graded school, which signifies that the pupils in it are classified into several distinct grades, according to the instruction which they may respectively require; those of the lowest grade receiving instructions nearly of a primary character; and those of the highest grade receiving instruction of a somewhat thorough character in arithmetic, grammar, and other studies. The said Mary Frances Ward, at the time of said application, had already received sufficient instruction to enable her to enter the lowest grade of said grammar school, but not the highest grade.

HARRIET A. WARD

[To the above, the defendant, Noah F. Flood, answered:]

Now comes Noah F. Flood, and for his answer in the above entitled action or proceeding, admits that he is and was on or about the 1st day of July, 1872, the Principal of the Broadway Grammar School, in the city and county of San Francisco; admits that Harriet A. Ward, in said action or proceeding mentioned, is the mother of Mary Frances Ward, a minor under the age of fourteen years, and that she is the wife of A. J. Ward; admits that petitioner and her said mother and father are of African descent, and colored citizens of the United States, and admits their residence as stated in the affidavit of Harriet A. Ward in said action or proceeding; admits that the said city and county of San Francisco is not now, nor the year last past has been divided into school districts; and admits that by law, and also by the custom adopted and established by the Board of Education of said city and county, white pupils residing therein have a right to be received as such at the public school nearest their residence, in case such school is not full, and they have made sufficient progress to be received therein, but denies that children of African descent have a right to be admitted into any public school other than those separately organized and provided for them.

Further answering, said defendant admits that the nearest public school to the residence of petitioner has been for six months last past, and now is, the said Broadway Grammar School; and admits that the same is a public school under the control of the Board of Education of said city and county, sustained by taxes raised in said city and county for the support of public schools therein, and was on or about the 1st day of July, 1872, and ever since has been, and now is, in charge of this defendant, as Principal thereof, appointed thereto by, and holding office as such under the said Board of Education.

He admits that on or about the 1st day of July, 1872, the said Harriet A. Ward, by the consent and direction of her said husband, took the petitioner with her to the said Broadway Grammar School, and that the same was then in session; that said Harriet then and there presented the said petitioner to this defendant as a pupil asking to be admitted as such to said school, this defendant then and there being such Principal as aforesaid. He admits that said school was not then and there full, but denies that there was no good or lawful reason why said petitioner should not be received in said school as said pupil as aforesaid, and denies that he had any right or authority to admit her as such pupil, or that she had any right to be admitted as such pupil; but on the contrary, avers that there was a good and sufficient reason in this, that he was appointed as such Principal by the said Board of Education, and in refusing to receive the petitioner as a pupil, he acted under and in accordance with the rules and regulations adopted and prescribed by the said Board, one of which is as follows:

"SEC. 117. Separate Schools.—Children of African or Indian descent shall not be admitted into schools for white children, but separate schools shall be provided for them in accordance with the California School Law."

And this defendant avers that in accordance with said rule and the Act of the Legislature therein referred to, entitled "an Act to amend an Act to provide for a system of common schools," approved April 4th, 1870, two separate schools were and are provided for colored children, with able and efficient teachers, and which afford equal advantages and are conducted under the same rules and regulations as those provided for the education of white children.

Further answering, defendant admits that the said Broadway Grammar School was then and is now of the description called a graded school, which signifies that the pupils in it are classified into distinct grades, according to the instruction which they may respectively require; but this defendant avers that the lowest grade in said Grammar school then was and now is the sixth grade, into which the petitioner had not received sufficient instruction to enable her to enter; and further avers that the said Mary Frances Ward, was, prior to and at the time of her said application, and now is a member of and pupil in a school provided for colored children or children of African descent, under the said Act of the Legislature of the State of California, and in the seventh grade of said school.

And this defendant further avers that the said Mary Frances, in applying for admission into the said Broadway Grammar School, did not present to him as the Principal thereof, any certificate of transfer, as required by the said rules and regulations as adopted by the said Board of Education, one of which rules is as follows:

"Sec. 134. Transfers.—People desiring to be transferred from any school to another shall apply to their principal for a certificate, which shall state their name, age, grade, scholarship, deportment, residence and cause of transfer."

And now, having fully answered, the said defendant asks that the prayer of petitioner be denied, and that said defendant be hence dismissed, with judgment for his costs in this proceeding incurred.

[48 Cal. 36 (1874), pp. 36–57.]

The Case of Mary Frances Ward: The Court's Decision

The opportunity of instruction at public schools is afforded the youth of the State by the statute of the State, enacted in obedience to the special command of the Constitution of the State, directing that the Legislature shall provide for a system of common schools, by which a school shall be kept up and supported in each district, at least three months in every year, etc. (Art. 19, Sec. 3). The advantage or benefit thereby vouchsafed to each child, of attending a public school is, therefore, one derived and secured to it under the highest sanction of positive law. It is, therefore, a right—a legal right— as distinctively so as the vested right in property owned is a legal right, and as such it is protected, and entitled to be protected by all the guarantees by which other legal rights are protected and secured to the possessor.

The clause of the Fourteenth Amendment referred to did not create any new or substantive legal right, or add to or enlarge the general classification of rights of persons or things existing in any State under the laws thereof. It, however, operated upon them as it found them already established, and it declared in substance that, such as they were in each State, they should be held and enjoyed alike by all persons within its jurisdiction. The protection of law is indeed inseparable from the assumed existence of a recognized legal right, through the vindication of which the protection is to operate. To declare, then, that each person within the jurisdiction of the State shall enjoy the equal protection of its laws, is necessarily to declare that the measure of legal rights within the State shall be equal and uniform, and the same for all persons found therein—according to the respective condition of each—each child as all other children—each adult person as all other adult persons. Under the laws of California children or persons between the ages of five and twenty-one years are entitled to receive instruction at the public schools, and the education thus afforded them is a measure of the protection afforded by law to persons of that condition.

The education of youth is emphatically their protection. Ignorance, the lack of mental and moral culture in earlier life, is the recognized parent of vice and crime in after years. Thus it is the acknowledged duty of the parent or guardian, as part of the measure of protection which he owes to the child or ward, to afford him at least a reasonable opportunity for the improvement of his mind and the elevation of his moral condition, and, of this duty, the law took cognizance long before the now recognized interest of society and of the body politic in the education of its members had prompted its embarkation upon a general system of youth. So a ward in chancery, as being entitled to the protection of the Court, was always entitled to be educated under its direction as constituting a most important part of that protection. The public law of the State—both the Constitution and Statute—having established public schools for educational purposes, to be maintained by public authority and at public expense, the youth of the State, are thereby become *pro hac vice* the wards of the State, and under the operations of the constitutional amendment referred to, equally entitled to be educated at the public expense. It would, therefore, not be competent to the Legislature, while providing a system of education for the youth of the State, to exclude the petitioner and those of her race from its benefits, merely because of their African descent, and to have so excluded her would have been to deny to her the equal protection of the laws within the intent and meaning of the Constitution.

But we do not find in the Act of April, 1870, providing for a system of common schools, which is substantially repeated in the Political Code now in force, any legislative attempt in this direction; nor do we discover that the statute is, in any of its provisions, obnoxious to objections of a constitutional character. It provides in substance that schools shall be kept open for the admission of white children, and that the education of children of African descent must be provided for in separate schools.

In short, the policy of separation of the races for educational purposes is adopted by the legislative department, and it is in this mere policy that the counsel for the petitioner professes to discern "an odious distinction of caste, founded on a deep-rooted prejudice in public opinion." But it is hardly necessary to remind counsel that we cannot deal here with such matters, and that our duties lie wholly within the much narrower range of determining whether this statute, in whatever motive it originated, denies to the petitioner, in a constitutional sense, the equal protection of the laws; and in the circumstances that the races are separated in the public schools, there is certainly to be found no violation of the constitutional rights of the one race more than of the other, and we see none of either, for each, though separated from the other, is to be educated upon equal terms with that other, and both at the common public expense.

[The court then quoted the decision of the Supreme Court of Massachusetts in a similar case in 1849 (Roberts v. the City of Boston, 5 Cushing R. 198) and stated:]

We concur in these views, and they are decisive of the present controversy. In order to prevent possible misapprehension, however, we think proper to add that in our opinion, and as the result of the views here announced, the exclusion of colored children from schools where white children attend as pupils, cannot be supported, except under the conditions appearing in the present case; that is, except where separate schools are actually maintained for the education of colored children; and that, unless such separate schools be in fact maintained, all children of the school district, whether white or colored, have an equal right to become pupils at any common school organized under the laws of the State, and have a right to registration and admission as pupils in the order of their registration, pursuant to the provisions of subdivision fourteen of section 1,617 of the Political Code.

Writ of mandamus denied.

[48 Cal. 36 (1874), pp. 36–57.]

Thompson v. Doaksum

The fact relied upon by the defendants as an estoppel were, that on the 26th of September, 1870, one Seagraves, a justice of the peace, believing himself to be authorized by law so to do, went to the land claimed by Blunt, and with his consent, and that of the defendants, set off a portion thereof for the use of the latter; that Blunt thereupon agreed with the defendants that whenever he should procure a government title to the lands, he would deed the tract so set apart to the defendants, and executed a written memorandum to that effect.

Defendants are Indians, belonging to a tribe generally known as the Big Meadows tribe, and called in their own language as the Nahkomas.

The allegations of the answer sought to be sustained by the testimony offered are, in substance and effect, that, at a time unknown to defendants, but which they are informed and believe, and therefore allege, was prior to October 1, A.D. 1492, said lands being vacant, unoccupied, and unclaimed, the ancestors and predecessors of defendants discovered, entered upon, claimed, and occupied said tract of land, and built their dwellings thereon, and that ever since said date defendants and their said ancestors and predecessors have continuously owned, claimed, and occupied said land, and used the same for a village site and burial-place, and for supplies of water, fuel, etc., according to the customs and necessities of their people; that the right thus acquired has never been ceded, sold, granted, transferred, or relinquished to any nation, government, state, or individual, but remains to them by right of discovery and occupation.

That no treaty has ever been made by them with any state or government, for their support, maintenance, or education and no proceedings have ever been had by which their title to said land has been extinguished.

The right or title attempted to be set up by appellants has the merit of age, if no other.

The relation of the Indians to the lands they occupied, their title thereto, their power of alienation, and the mode of its accomplishment were questions much discussed in the earlier days of our government.

On the discovery of America, the leading nations of Europe eagerly sought a foothold upon its soil, and each sought to appropriate all it could discover and occupy.

Its great extent afforded an ample field to the ambition and enterprise of all. To avoid conflicting settlements and consequent war with each other, the principle was established that discovery gave title to the government by whose subjects or by whose authority it was made, against all other European governments, which title might be consummated by possession.

The relations between the discoverer and the natives were to be regulated by themselves.

These relations were to be settled upon the basis of ownership of the soil by the discoverer, with the right of occupancy in the original inhabitants. So long as they remained at peace with the superior race, they were entitled to be protected in their occupancy, but to be deemed incapable of transferring the absolute title to any other than the sovereign of the country.

Congress has the exclusive right of preemption to all Indian lands lying within the territories of the United States (Johnson v. McIntosh, 8 Wheat, 543; Fletcher v. Peck, 6 Cranch, 142).

The United States own the soil, as well as the jurisdiction, of the immense tracts of unpatented lands included within their territories, and of all the productive funds which those lands may hereafter create.

The title is in the United States by the treaty of peace with Great Britain, and by subsequent cessions from France and Spain, and by cessions from the individual states; and the Indians have only a right of occupancy, and the United States possess the legal title subject to that occupancy, and with an absolute and exclusive right to extinguish the Indian title of occupancy either by conquest or purchase.

The *status* of the Indian and his relation to the land by him occupied have received careful consideration at the hands of Chancellor Kent; and his views as expressed in the third volume of his Commentaries, pages 379 and 400, threw much light upon the question under discussion.

It seems, however, unnecessary to discuss the several propositions involved in the foregoing authorities.

The subject in the present case is confined to a narrower limit.

The title to land is dependent entirely upon the law of the nation in which it lies.

Under the English law, the king was the original proprietor or lord paramount of all the land within the kingdom, and the sole source of title.

We have adopted the same principle and applied it to our republican government, and the doctrine with us is settled beyond a peradventure that valid individual title to land within the United States is derived from the grant of our own local governments, or from that of the United States, or from the predecessors of our government.

The lands within the territorial limits of the state of California were ceded to our general government by the republic of Mexico under the treaty of Guadalupe Hidalgo of February 2, 1848.

By that treaty the United States became vested with the title to all the lands in California not held in private ownership by a legal or equitable title.

By the law of nations, private rights were sacred and inviolable, and the obligation passed to the new government to protect and maintain them.

The treaty operated as a confirmation *in praesenti* of all perfect titles to lands in California held under Spanish or Mexican grants (*Minturn* v. *Brower*, 24 Cal. 644).

In the cases of inchoate titles,—cases where an equity only vested in the claimant,—the legal title passed to the United States, which held it subject to the trust imposed by the treaty and equities of the grantee.

The execution of this trust was a political power, to be exercised in such manner as the government might deem expedient (*Leese* v. *Clark*, 18 Cal. 535).

The United States, for the purpose of discharging the obligation resting upon it under the treaty with Mexico, through Congress, the repository of its political power, at the second session of the thirty-first Congress, passed an act to ascertain and settle the private land claims in the state of California.

Under that act a commission was created, for the purpose of hearing and determining the validity of claims to land within the state.

The thirteenth section of the act provided "that all lands the claims to which have been finally rejected by the commissioners in manner herein provided, or which shall be finally decided to be invalid by the District or Supreme Court, *and all lands* the claims to which shall not have been presented to the commissioners within two years after the date of this act (March 3, 1851), shall be deemed held and considered as a part of the public domain of the United States."

There is no pretense that the claim set up by defendants in their answer was ever presented to the commissioners under this act of Congress; and when the time for such presentation expired, the land in question must be deemed and taken as having become a part of the public domain.

Again, the patent to plaintiff's grantor is to be taken as conclusive evidence of title in the grantee, as against those not connecting themselves with the government title, in any collateral attack thereon.

If defendants had any right to the land, it should have been asserted in the land department, pending the application for patent, or by direct proceeding on the part of the government to set aside the patent.

An estoppel *in pais* can have no more force or effect in binding the parties than would a contract including the very subject-matter urged by way of estoppel.

The findings support the conclusion reached by the court below, and the judgment should be affirmed.

FOOTE, C., and BELCHER, C. C., concurred.

THE COURT.—For the reasons given in the foregoing opinion, the judgment is affirmed.

ROSS, J., concurring.—I concur in the judgment, on the ground that whatever right, if any, the defendants have to the land in question, should have been asserted in the land department of the government, pending the application for patent, or by direct proceedings on the part of the government to vacate the patent. As long as the patent exists, it is conclusive evidence of title in the grantee, and his successors in interest, as against those not in privity with the government.

[(1886) 68 Cal. 593, 10 Pac. 199.]

The People v. Bray

The defendant [William Bray] was convicted [in the Superior Court, Sonoma County] of the crime of selling intoxicating liquor to an Indian, named Mary Smith, in violation of section 397 of the Penal Code, which, as amended in 1893 (Stats. of 1893, p. 98), reads as follows: "Every person who sells or furnishes, or causes to be sold or furnished, any intoxicating liquors to any habitual or common drunkard is guilty of a misdemeanor; or who sells or furnishes, or causes to be sold or furnished, intoxicating liquors to any Indian is guilty of a felony." It was admitted upon the trial that the defendant furnished intoxicating liquor to the said Mary Smith, at the time and place stated in the information, and that she "has no other than Indian blood in her veins." It was further shown that her father and mother live in a house of their own, and their said daughter, Mary, resides with them; that the parents and daughter dress like white people, and have adopted the habits and customs of civilized life; that the father of the said Mary owns a horse, wagon, household goods, and other property, and that neither he nor any of his family have ever lived upon a government reservation, "nor have they ever lived in tribal relations, or under or subject to the control of any chief or like authority." Upon this state of the evidence the defendant requested the court to give the following instructions:

"2. Section numbered 397 of the Penal Code, under which the information in this case was filed, is not violated by a sale of intoxicating liquor to an Indian, who at the time of the sale was a citizen of this state."

"4. If you find from the evidence that the Indian in question was born in this state, and at the time of her birth her parents were living separate and apart from any tribe of Indians, and had no tribal relations, and did not live on any Indian reservation, or other land set apart for such purpose, then I charge you that the Indian in question is a citizen of the United States, and you cannot convict the defendant of the crime charged against him in the information, even if you should also find that he did sell or furnish the said Indian intoxicating liquors at the time alleged."

"12. All citizens of this state are entitled to equal protection under the law in person, property, and privileges, and a law which takes from one person, on account of color or race, any privilege which others are legally permitted and allowed to enjoy, is void as to such person."

The court refused to so instruct the jury, and this refusal is assigned as error, and presents all the grounds upon which the defendant claims that the judgment and order appealed from should be reversed; and the counsel for appellant rest their argument for such reversal upon these three propositions: 1. That under the facts shown the person named in the information as the one to whom defendant furnished the intoxicating liquor is a citizen of the United States; 2. That section 397 of the Penal Code, in so far as it relates to Indians, applies only to those Indians who are under control of the general government as dependent communities, living in tribal relation or upon government reservations, and as such deemed wards of the general government; 3. That, if said section is not so limited by construction, it is void, because it discriminates between citizens of the United States, denying to the citizen of Indian birth the privilege of buying intoxicating liquors, which is according to citizens of the white race, and that, in making such distinction, it abridges the privileges and immunities of the former.

By an act of Congress approved February 8, 1887 (24 U. S. Stats. at Large, 390), it is provided that "every Indian born within the territorial limits of the United States who has voluntarily taken up within said limits his residence, separate and apart from any tribe of Indians therein, and has adopted the habits of civilized life, is hereby declared to be a citizen of the United States, and is entitled to all the rights, privileges, and immunities of such citizens, whether said Indian has been or not, by birth or otherwise, a member of any tribe of Indians within the territorial limits of the United States without in any manner impairing or otherwise affecting the right of any such Indian to tribal or other property." It was undoubtedly competent for Congress to thus confer upon Indians the privileges of citizenship (*Elk* v. *Wilkins*, 112 U. S. 94), and it may be conceded that the facts of this case show that said Mary Smith, referred to in the information, is a citizen of the United States within the meaning of the act of Congress from which the foregoing quotation is made, and as such, that she is entitled to the privileges and immunities of such citizens; but we are not able to agree with the further contention of appellant's counsel in their construction of section 397 of the Penal Code. In our opinion that section forbids the sale or giving of liquors to Indians of full blood, without any reference to the question whether they have or have not adopted the habits of civilization, or separated themselves from tribal relations. It was intended to apply to Indians as a class, and was enacted in view of their well-known race peculiarities and their relations to society. There are thousands of California Indians to be found in this state, most of them civilized to a certain degree, and perhaps none of them living under any well-defined tribal government; they live generally by themselves, in small villages or communities, and yet are in constant contact with the white race, most of them, at times, being employed as laborers in the harvest field, and in fishing, or as servants in families, or otherwise. The statute applies to this people as a race, and in its enforcement all inquiry as to the habits or the degree of civilization attained by the individual of such race to whom the intoxicating liquor is furnished, or as to whether he is or is not a citizen of the United States, under the act of Congress before referred to, is irrelevant; and, as thus construed, this section of the Penal Code is not in conflict with any provision of the constitution of the United States or of this state. It is general and uniform in its operation, because it affects in the same manner all persons belonging to the class to which it refers, and does not deprive any citizen of his privileges and immunities as such.

Whatever may be true in respect to particular individuals of that race, it is certainly true that Indians, as a class, are not refined and civilized in the same degree as persons of the white race; and for that reason are less subject to moral restraint, and, therefore, not only less able to resist the desire for such liquors, but also more liable to be dangerous to themselves or others when under the influence of intoxicating liquors. It was, doubtless, in view of considerations like these that, in the judgment of the legislature, it was thought wise to give to persons of the Indian race, as well as the community in which they move, the protecting influence of this statute. Thus viewed, we have no doubt the law under consideration falls within the proper exercise of the police power of the state. It was so stated by Sanderson, J., in *Ex parte Smith,* 38 Cal. 708, and a statute in all respects similar to it was upheld by the supreme court of the territory of Montana as a valid exercise of the police power in the case of *Territory* v. *Guyott,* 9 Mont. 46, the court there saying: "The act under consideration is clearly within the police power of the territorial government, as defined by the courts, and is not inconsistent with the constitution and laws of the United States."

These views dispose of all the questions arising upon this appeal.

Judgment and order affirmed.

[105 Cal. 344, 1894.]

Two Songs of the Gold Rush Period

John Chinaman's Appeal

1

American now mind my song
    If you would but hear *me sing,*
And I will tell you of the wrong,
    That happened until "Gee Sing,"
In "fifty-two" I left my home –
    I bid farewell to "Hong Kong"–
I started with Cup Gee to roam
    To the land where they use the "long tom."

CHORUS: O ching hi ku tong mo ching ching,
          O ching hi ku tong *chi do,*
          Cup Gee hi ku tong mo ching ching,
          Then what could Gee or I do?

2

In forty days I reached the Bay,
    And nearly starved I was sir,
I cooked and ate a dog one day,
    I didn't know the laws sir.
But soon I found my dainty meal
    Was 'gainst the city order,
The penalty I had to feel –
    Confound the old Recorder.

3

By paying up my cost and fines
    They freed me from the locker,
And then I started for the mines –
    I got a pick and rocker.

I went to work in an untouched place,
    I'm sure I meant no blame sir,
But a white man struck me in the face
    And told me to leave his claim sir.

4

'Twas then I packed my tools away
    And set up in a new place,
But there they would not let me stay –
    They didn't like the cue race.
And then I knew not what to do,
    I could not get employ,
The Know Nothings would bid me go –
    'Twas *tu nah mug ahoy.*

5

I started then for Weaverville
    Where Chinamen were thriving,
But found our China agents there
    In ancient feuds were driving.
So I pitched into politics,
    But with the weaker party;
The Canton's with their clubs and bricks
    Did drub us out "right hearty."

6

I started for Yreka then;
    I thought that I would stay there,
But found for even Chinamen
    The "diggings" wouldn't pay there.
So I set up a washing shop,
    But how extremely funny,
The miners all had dirty clothes,
    But not a cent of money.

7

I met a big stout Indian once,
    He stopped me in the trail, sir,
He drew an awful scalping knife,
    And I trembled for my tail, sir.
He caught me by the hair, it's true,
    In a manner quite uncivil,

But when he saw my awful cue,
    He thought I was the devil.

8

Oh, now my friends I'm going away
    From this infernal place, sir;
The balance of my days I'll stay
    With the Celestial race, sir.
I'll go to raising rice and tea;
    I'll be a heathen ever,
For Christians all have treated me
    As men should be used never.

[Taylor, 1856.]

John Chinaman

1

John Chinaman, John Chinaman,
    But five short years ago,
I welcomed you from Canton, John –
    But wish I hadn't though;

2

For then I thought you honest, John,
    Not dreaming but you'd make
A citizen as useful, John,
    As any in the State.

3

I thought you'd open wide your ports,
    And let our merchants in,
To barter for their crapes and teas,
    Their wares of wood and tin.

4

I thought you'd cut your queue off, John
    And don a Yankee coat,
And a collar high you'd raise, John,
    Around your dusky throat.

5

I imagined that the truth, John,
  You'd speak when under oath,
But I find you'll lie and steal too –
  Yes, John, you're up to both.

6

I thought of rats and puppies, John,
  You'd eaten your last fill,
But on such slimy pot-pies, John,
  I'm told you dinner still.

7

Oh, John, I've been deceived in you,
  And in all your thieving clan,
For our gold is all you're after, John,
  To get it as you can.

[Appleton, 1855.]

Report ot the President on the Japanese in San Francisco, 1906

[From Senate Document No. 147, 59th Congress, Second Session; read on December 18, 1906: entitled Message from the President of the United States transmitting the final report of Secretary Metcalf on the situation affecting the Japanese in the city of San Francisco, California.]

To the Senate and House of Representatives:

I enclose herewith for your information the final report made to me personally by Secretary Metcalf on the situation affecting the Japanese in San Francisco. The report deals with three matters of controversy—first, the exclusion of the Japanese children from the San Francisco schools; second, the boycotting of Japanese restaurants, and third, acts of violence committed against the Japanese.

As to the first matter, I call your especial attention to the very small number of Japanese children who attend school, to the testimony as to the brightness, cleanliness, and good behavior of these Japanese children in the schools, and to the fact that, owing to their being scattered throughout the city, the requirement for them all to go to one special school is impossible of fulfilment and means that they can not have school facilities. Let me point out further that there would be no objection whatever to excluding from the schools any Japanese on the score of age. It is obviously not desirable that young men should go to school with children. The only point is the exclusion of the children themselves. The number of Japanese children attending the public schools in San Francisco was very small. The Government has already directed that suit be brought to test the constitutionality of the act in question; but my very earnest hope is that such suit will not be necessary, and that as a matter of comity the citizens of San Francisco will refuse to deprive these young Japanese children of education and will permit them to go to the schools.

The question as to the violence against the Japanese is most admirably put by Secretary Metcalf, and I have nothing to add to his statement. I am entirely confident that, as Secretary Metcalf says, the overwhelming sentiment of the State of California is for law and order and for the protection of the Japanese in their persons and property. Both the chief of police and the acting mayor of San Francisco assured Secretary Metcalf that everything possible would be done to protect the Japanese in the city. I authorized and directed Secretary Metcalf to state that if there was failure to protect persons and property, the entire power of the Federal Government within the limits of the Constitution would be used promptly and vigorously to enforce the observance of our treaty, the Supreme law of the land, which treaty guaranteed to Japanese residents everywhere in the Union full and perfect protection for their persons and property; and to this end everything in my power would be done, and all the forces of the United States, both civil and military, which I could lawfully employ, would be employed. I call especial attention to the concluding sentence of Secretary Metcalf's report of November 26, 1906.

THEODORE ROOSEVELT
The White House
December 18, 1906

[Secretary Metcalf in the appendix to President Theodore Roosevelt's message to the Senate lists case histories of violence done to Japanese persons in San Francisco as the legacy which they inherited. Three of a much larger number given are provided here:]

T. Kadono, 121 Haight Street. I am a student and a member of the Japanese Y.M.C.A. On the 5th day of August, 1906, on Laguna Street, between Haight and Page Streets, at 10:40 A.M. on my way to church, I was attacked by about 30 people, men ranging from 15 to 25 years of age. They followed me down the street and beat me over the head and face with their fists. I tried to resist them, but they were too strong for me. They made my nose bleed. I went to St. Thomas Hospital for medical treatment. I complained to the superintendent of the Japanese Presbyterian Mission and was advised by him not to make any complaint to the police. I was laid up for a week on account of this attack. I have a blood-stained shirt which I can produce if necessary.

I. Ikeda, 1608 Geary Street. I have a fruit store—about a month ago—October 5, 1906—some bad boys came to my store and stole fruit and threw stones into the store. On September 2, 1906, down in the wholesale district

(I do not know the name of the street), as I was driving my wagon some men started to throw fruit at me, then pieces of brick hitting my back. The reins of the rig got loose, and I was obliged to stop and get down to fix them. I had no sooner gotten down than somebody came up and hit me in the face, and gave me a black eye. I made complaint about this to the Japanese Association. I could identify the man who hit me.

H. Akagi, 115 Church Street. I have a furniture store. On October 20, 1906, at 7 o'clock P.M. on Page Street, between Steiner and Pierce Streets, as I was delivering goods to my customers, two young men, about 17 or 18 years of age, knocked the merchandise out of my hands and slapped my face. I took no action, and did not report this case to the police. On October 30, I applied to Werdenthal and Goslinger Electrical Workers, 151 Church, to make electrical connections at my store. On November 3, the manager of the establishment flatly refused, saying that he was a member of the Japanese and Korean Exclusion League and could not work in a Japanese establishment; otherwise he said he would be fined $50 by the League. On this account my store is still without electrical connections.

Executive Order of President Roosevelt, March 14, 1907

Whereas by the act entitled "An act to regulate the immigration of aliens into the United States," approved February 20, 1907, whenever the President is satisfied that passports issued by any foreign government to its citizens to go to any country other than the United States or to any insular possession of the United States or to the Canal Zone, are being used for the purpose of enabling the holders to come to the continental territory of the United States to the detriment of labor conditions therein, it is made the duty of the President to refuse to permit such citizens of the country issuing such passports to enter the continental territory of the United States from such country or from such insular possession or from the Canal Zone.

And whereas upon sufficient evidence produced before me by the Department of Commerce and Labor, I am satisfied that passports issued by the Government of Japan to citizens of that country or Korea and who are laborers, skilled or unskilled, to go to Mexico, to Canada and to Hawaii, are being used for the purpose of enabling the holders thereof to come to the continental territory of the United States to the detriment of labor conditions therein:

I hereby order that such citizens of Japan or Korea, to wit: Japanese or Korean laborers, skilled or unskilled, who have received passports to go to Mexico, Canada or Hawaii, and come therefrom, be refused permission to enter the continental territory of the United States.

It is further ordered that the Secretary of Commerce and Labor be, and he hereby is, directed to take thru the Bureau of Immigration and Naturalization, such measures and to make and enforce such rules and regulations as may be necessary to carry this order into effect.

Mr. A. Sbarboro to the Asiatic Exclusion League, 1908

In 1860 I followed General Winn, a founder of the patriotic Order of the Native Sons of the Golden West, from door to door for the purpose of organizing "Anti-Chinese Clubs." This was the first strong movement taken in the matter in California, and I assure you that it was up-hill work. Meetings were held, speeches were made, strong resolutions were adopted, but for many years without success. After a time, however, conventions were held and strong petitions were sent to Washington, praying that California be saved from the threatening inundation of the Chinese coolies.

Our Eastern brethren paid little attention to us. The few Chinamen they saw in their midst were quite a curiosity to them. They did not understand our danger. On the change of every President of the United States new efforts were made by California for relief, and finally the movement became so strong and unanimous that after twenty-five or thirty years of fervent work Congress saw the necessity of passing a Chinese Exclusion Bill. This made the people of California happy—meetings of congratulation were held and salutes were fired; but lo, and behold! the bill which gave so much happiness to the people of California was vetoed by President Hayes.

California is composed of people who do not surrender by defeat. Additional meetings were held, new efforts were made, until finally another Congress again passed the Chinese Exclusion Bill, and this time, fortunately, it was signed by the President of the United States.

Although the bill did not exclude, as is proven by the fact that to-day we have nearly as many Chinese in California as we had twenty years ago, still the number of the undesirable race has not been increased.

But now a new danger is threatening us. A race far more dangerous than the Chinese is gradually occupying our fair State. The Japanese who are living in their overcrowded islands find California a paradise, and unless some measure be speedily taken they will come by thousands and tens of thousands to our shores.

Whilst the Chinaman is an undesirable person because he never changes his habits or garments, the Japanese, although he does change his garments, is a far more dangerous acquisition to our State.

Contracts made with Chinamen are generally observed, whilst it is a well-known fact that the Japanese are entirely unreliable with their agreements. Many farmers know this to their sorrow.

Some few years ago the crop of the vineyard of the Italian-Swiss Colony at Madera was so large that extra pickers had to be found. White people could not be had, so Mr. P. C. Rossi, president of the Colony, hired a company of Japanese to pick grapes, at the high price of $1.50 per ton. They worked for a few days, when they suddenly quit, without notice, and left for another place where, we were informed afterwards, they obtained a little more. This naturally occasioned a great loss to our Colony, as we expected that the Japanese would finish the picking of the grapes, and consequently had made no other provision for the work.

It is a well-known fact that the Japanese, neither as a farmer or as a servant, is reliable. He will as soon leave his mistress on the eve of a dinner which she has prepared for a large number of guests, as he will leave the farmer during harvest time. The Japanese is, however, enterprising, and a great adept in imitating.

The Manufacturers' and Producers' Association of California some time ago received astonishing information from a traveler in Japan. He stated that a manufacturer of dental instruments in London had sent a traveling agent to Japan to sell some of his instruments at $50 per set, which cost $40 to make in England. The salesman, on offering them to a Japanese artisan, was shown by the Japanese an identical set of instruments with the London maker's own name, which the Japanese were selling in Japan for $14 per set.

Several Japanese firms have already engaged in fruit raising in California. It is useless to say that they can not only compete but drive away every one of our fruit-growers out of the State, if they are permitted to embark in large numbers in this industry. They will also learn to manufacture everything that we can make, and will soon drive our manufacturers and mechanics out of business by their unprecedented facilities of cheap living and long, patient working.

I do verily believe that if the Japanese should be permitted to come to this country in unlimited numbers, they would in a few years, by their thrift, enterprise and frugality of living, transform California into a Japanese colony.

It will, therefore, be seen what a great necessity there is for our Government to take prompt action in closing the doors to these undesirable people. If we allow them to gain a strong foothold here, it will be a very difficult matter to get rid of them.

The Japanese are not as peaceable or inoffensive as the Chinese. They have shown that they make as good soldiers as any in the world, and if our Government should disagree with the Mikado it might not take long for him to land half a million Japanese in Manila, and with their formidable navy and torpedo boats, manned by their life-despising and reckless men, give a hard tussle to our own navy at a long distance from home. Before an occasion for this unpleasant situation arises, let us by all means make a treaty with Japan excluding the Japanese laborers from coming to our shores.

The sparsely settled, broad acres of California, and the Western States do require immigration, but that immigration must be of the right kind, composed of the Caucasian race which soon assimilate with us. We can welcome the German, the French, the Italian, the Swiss, the English, the Slavs, and even the Turks, for although on their arrival they are generally uncouth and sometimes unclean, they in a few years pick up the American ideas and adopt American customs. Their children born in this country soon forget their ancestors' mother language and become some of the best citizens, always ready to serve their country with their lives when in need.

It is this kind of immigration which has in one hundred years transformed the deserts of America into the most prosperous, energetic and richest country on the face of the earth. These people must we continue to welcome with open arms, but if we want happiness and prosperity to be maintained in this fair country and handed down to our posterity, we must keep out of it the people of the Mongolian race.

The reading of Mr. Sbarboro's address was heartily received.

[Proceedings of the Asiatic Exclusion League, September 1908, pp. 15–16.]

Bibliography

Abella, R. "Letter to Sola, January 29, 1817," *Archbishopric Archives* 3 (1817): 125. Bancroft Library, University of California, Berkeley.

Allen, J. M. *We-ne-ma*. New York: Vantage Press, 1956.

Allen, Steve. *The Ground is Our Table*. New York: Doubleday, 1966.

Anonymous. "Our First Families," *Hutchings' Illustrated California Magazine* 5 (1861):435–436.

Bailey, H. C. *Indian Slaves*. Unpublished manuscript of 5 pages, in authors' possession, which bears the note "Arranged and Copyrighted by F. F. Latta (1930)."

Baker, C. C. "Mexican Land Grants in California." *Historical Society of Southern California Publications* 9 (1914):236–244.

Bancroft, H. H. *The Native Races of the Pacific States of North America*. Vol. 1, *Wild Tribes* (1874). Vol. 5, *Primitive History* (1876). New York: D. Appleton and Co.

———. *History of California*. Vols. 1–7. San Francisco: The History Co., 1884–1890.

———. *Popular Tribunals*. Vols. 31, 32. *History of the Pacific States of North America*. San Francisco: The History Co., 1887.

———. *California inter pocula*. Vol. 35. *The Works of Hubert Howe Bancroft*. San Francisco: The History Co., 1888.

———. *Essays and Miscellany*. Vol. 38. *The Works of Hubert Howe Bancroft*. San Francisco: The History Co., 1890.

Banton, M. P. *Race Relations*. London: Tavistock Publications, 1967.

Barth, G. *Bitter Strength: A History of the Chinese in the United States, 1850–1870*. Cambridge: Harvard University Press, 1964.

Beasley, D. L. *The Negro Trail Blazers of California*. Los Angeles: Times Mirror Printing and Binding House, 1919.

Beechey, F. W. *Narrative of a Voyage to the Pacific and Beering's Strait*. London: H. Colburn and R. Bentley, 1831.

Bernard, W. S. "The Law, the Mores and the Oriental." *Rocky Mountain Law Review* 10 (1933):105–116, 163–177.

Berthold, V. M. *The Pioneer Steamer, California: 1848–1849*. Boston and New York: Houghton Mifflin Co., 1932.

Bolton, H. E. "The Mission as a Frontier Institution in the Spanish American Colonies." *American Historical Review* 23 (1917):42–61.

Boscana, A. R. "Chinigchinich: a Historical Account of the Origin, Customs, and

Traditions of the Indians at the Missionary Establishment of St. Juan Capistrano, Alta California." In Alfred Robinson, *Life in California*, pp. 227–341. New York: Wiley and Putnam, 1846.

Bosworth, A. R. *America's Concentration Camps.* New York: Norton, 1967.

Bowman, J. N. "The Resident Neophytes (Existentes) of the California Missions." *Historical Society of Southern California Quarterly* 40 (1958):138–148.

Bowman, J. N., and R. F. Heizer. "Anza and the Northwest Frontier of New Spain." *Southwest Museum Papers*, No. 20. Los Angeles: Southwest Museum, 1967.

Boyle, W. H. *Personal Observations on the Conduct of the Modoc War.* Los Angeles: Westernlore Press, 1959.

Brady, C. T. *Northwestern Fights and Fighters.* Part II, *Modoc War*, pp. 229–325. New York: McClure Co., 1907.

Brewer, W. H. *Up and Down California in 1860–1864.* Berkeley and Los Angeles: University of California Press, 1949.

Brooks, B. S. *Brief of the Legislation and Adjudication Touching the Chinese Question Referred to the Joint Commission of Both Houses of Congress.* San Francisco: Women's Co-operative Printing Union, 1877.

Brooks, J. T. *Four Months among the Gold-Finders in California.* London: D. Bogue, 1849.

Brown, W. S. *California Northeast, the Bloody Ground.* Oakland: Biobooks, 1951.

Browne, J. Ross. *California Constitutional Convention, 1849. Report of the Debates in the Convention of California, on the Formation of the State Constitution in September and October, 1849.* Washington: J. T. Towers, 1850.

———. "The Coast Rangers, II: The Indian Reservations." *Harpers Magazine* 23 (1861):306–316.

———. *Crusoe's Island: A Ramble in the Footsteps of Alexander Selkirk, with Sketches of Adventure in California and Washoe.* New York: Harper and Bros., 1867.

———. *The Indians of California.* San Francisco: The Colt Press, 1944. (A reprint of *Crusoe's Island.*)

Bruff, J. G. *Gold Rush: The Journals, Drawings and Other Papers of J. Goldsborough Bruff.* G. W. Read and R. Gaines, eds. New York: Columbia University Press, 1949.

Buck, F. A. *A Yankee Trader in the Gold Rush.* Boston and New York: Houghton Mifflin Co., 1930.

Buell, R. L. "The History of Japanese Agitation in the United States." *Political Science Quarterly* 37 (1922):605–638.

———. *Japanese Immigration.* Boston: World Peace Foundation, 1924.

Buffum, E. G. *Six Months in the Gold Mines.* London: Richard Bentley, 1850.

California Development Association. *Survey of the Mexican Labor Problem in California.* San Francisco, 1928.

California Historical Society. *California Gold Discovery: Centennial Papers on the Time, the Site and Artifacts.* Special Publications, No. 21. 1947.

California Legislature. *Majority and Minority Reports of the Special Joint Committee on the Mendocino War.* C. T. Botts, State Printer, 1860. 75pp.

California Legislature, Special Committee on Chinese Immigration. *Chinese Immigration, its Social, Moral and Political Effect.* Report to the California State Senate by F. P. Thompson, Supt. Sacramento: State Printing Office, 1878.

California State Board of Control. *California and the Oriental.* Report of the State Board of Control of California to Gov. Wm. D. Stephens, June 19, 1920. Sacramento: State Printing Office, 1920.

California State Fair Employment Practice Commission. *Negro Californian Population, Employment, Income, Education.* San Francisco: San Francisco Fair Employment Practice Commission, Division of Fair Employment, 1963.

Carr, J. *Pioneer Days in California.* Eureka, Calif.: Times Publishing Co., 1891.

Caughey, J. W. *The Indians of Southern California in 1852: The B. D. Wilson Report and a Selection of Contemporary Comment.* San Marino: Huntington Library, 1952.

Chu, D., and S. Chu. *Passage to the Golden Gate: A History of the Chinese in America to 1910.* Garden City, New York: Doubleday, 1967.

Clappe, L. A. K. S. (Dame Shirley). *The Shirley Letters from the California Mines, 1851–1852.* New York: A. Knopf, 1949.

Clark, M. M. *Health in the Mexican American Culture: A Community Study.* Berkeley and Los Angeles: University of California Press, 1959.

Clyman, J. "James Clyman, American Frontiersman, 1792–1881; the Adventures of a Trapper and Covered Wagon Emigrant as Told in His Own Reminiscences and Diaries." C. L. Camp, ed. California Historical Society, 1928.

Commission on International and Interracial Factors in the Problems of Mexicans in the United States. *Report of the Commission on International and Interracial Factors.* George L. Cody, D.D., chairman. 1926.

Cook, S. F. *Population Trends among the California Mission Indians.* Ibero-Americana, no. 17. Berkeley: University of California Press, 1940.

———. *The Conflict between the California Indian and White Civilization.* 3 vols. Ibero-Americana, nos. 21, 22, 23. Berkeley and Los Angeles: University of California Press, 1943.

———. "Expeditions to the Interior of California, 1820–1840." *University of California Anthropological Records* 20, no. 5 (1962).

———. "The Destruction of the California Indian." *California Monthly,* December 1968, pp. 15–19.

Coolidge, M. R. *Chinese Immigration.* New York: H. Holt and Co., 1909.

Cosgrove, G. "A Diplomatic Incident of the Little Mariposa." *California Historical Society Quarterly* 21 (1942):358–362.

Cowan, R. E., and B. Dunlap. *Bibliography of the Chinese Question in the United States.* San Francisco, 1909.

Cowan, R. G. *The Admission of the Thirty-first State by the Thirty-first Congress.* Los Angeles: Torrez Press, 1962.

Cox, O. C. *Caste, Class, and Race: A Study in Social Dynamics.* Garden City, New York: Doubleday, 1948.

Coy, O. C. "Evidences of Slavery in California." *The Grizzly Bear* 19, no. 6 (1916): 1–2.

———. *The Humboldt Bay Region, 1850–1875.* Los Angeles: California State Historical Association, 1929.

———. *In the Diggings in "Forty-Nine."* Los Angeles: California State Historical Association, 1948.

Currie, A. H. "Bidwell Rancheria." *California Historical Society Quarterly* 36 (1957):313–325.

Dakin, S. B. *A Scotch Paisano*. Berkeley: University of California Press, 1939.

Dale, E. E. *The Indians of the Southwest: A Century of Development Under the United States*. Norman: University of Oklahoma Press, 1949.

Daniels, R. *The Politics of Prejudice: The Anti-Japanese Movement in California and the Struggle for Japanese Exclusion*. Berkeley and Los Angeles: University of California Publications in History, vol. 71, 1962.

Delano, A. *Across the Plains and among the Diggings*. New York: Wilson-Erickson, Inc., 1936. (First edition, 1854.)

de Massey, E. *A Frenchman in the Gold Rush: The Journal of Ernest de Massey, Argonaut of 1849*. California Historical Society, Special Publications, No. 2. 1927.

Department of Industrial Relations. *American Indians in California*. San Francisco: State Department of Industrial Relations, Division of Fair Employment, 1965.

Derby, G. H. *The Topographical Reports of Lt. Geo. H. Derby*. F. P. Farquhar, ed. California Historical Society Special Publications, No. 11. 1932.

Eaves, L. M. *A History of California Labor Legislation*. Berkeley: University of California Publications in Economics, vol. 2, 1910.

Egenhoff, E. L. *The Elephant as They Saw It*. California State Division of Mines. Centennial Supplement to *California Journal of Mines and Geology* for October 1949.

Eliot, C. W. *Japanese Characteristics*. New York: American Association for International Conciliation, Publication No. 17. 1913.

Ellison, W. H. "The Federal Indian Policy in California, 1846–1860." *Mississippi Valley Historical Review* 9 (1922):37–67.

Engelhardt, Z. *The Missions and Missionaries of California*. Vol. 2, *Upper California*. Santa Barbara: Mission Santa Barbara, 1929 (rev. ed.). Vol. 4, *Upper California*. San Francisco: James H. Barry Co., 1915.

Farnham, T. J. *Life, Adventures, and Travels in California* ("Pictorial Edition"). New York: Nafis and Cornish, 1855.

Farwell, W. B. *The Chinese at Home and Abroad*. Together with the report of the special committee of the Board of Supervisors of San Francisco on the condition of the Chinese quarter of that city. San Francisco: A. L. Bancroft and Co., 1885.

Fey, H. E., and D. McNickle. *Indians and Other Americans*. New York: Harper and Bros., 1959.

Font, P. *Diary of the Anza Expedition, 1775–1776*. In H. E. Bolton, *Font's Complete Diary*. Berkeley: University of California Press, 1931.

Forbes, J. D. *The Indian in America's Past*. Englewood Cliffs, N.J.: Prentice-Hall, 1964.

———. *Afro-Americans in the Far West: A Handbook for Educators*. Berkeley: Far West Laboratory for Educational Research and Development, n.d. (ca. 1967).

———. "Black Pioneers: The Spanish-Speaking Afro-Americans of the Southwest." *Phylon* 27 (1966):233–246.

———. *Native Americans of California and Nevada*. Berkeley: Far West Laboratory for Educational Research and Development, 1969.

Gates, P. W. "Adjudication of Spanish-Mexican Land Claims in California." *Huntington Library Quarterly* 21 (1958):213–236.

Goodman, C. L. *The Establishment of State Government in California, 1846–1850.* New York: Macmillan, 1914.

Griffith, B. W. *American Me.* Boston: Houghton Mifflin Co., 1948.

Guinn, J. M. "The Passing of the Old Pueblo." *Historical Society of Southern California Publications* 5 (1901):113–120.

———. "The Sonoran Migration." *Historical Society of Southern California Publications* 8 (1911):31–36.

Hagan, W. T. *American Indians.* Chicago: University of Chicago Press, 1961.

Hanke, L. *The Spanish Struggle for Justice in the Conquest of America.* Philadelphia: University of Pennsylvania Press, 1959.

Hargis, D. E. "Native Californians in the Constitutional Convention of 1849." *Historical Society of Southern California Quarterly* 26 (1954):3–13.

Hawgood, J. A. "The Pattern of Yankee Infiltration in Mexican Alta California, 1821–1846." *Pacific Historical Review* 27 (1958):27–37.

Heizer, R. F. "Civil Rights in California in the 1850's—a Case History." *Kroeber Anthropological Society Papers*, No. 31 (1965):129–137.

———. *The Indians of Los Angeles County: Hugo Reid's Letters of 1852.* Los Angeles: Southwest Museum, 1968.

Heizer, R. F., and John Mills. *The Four Ages of Tsurai.* Berkeley and Los Angeles: University of California Press, 1952.

Hittell, J. S. "Mexican Land-Claims in California." *Hutchings' Illustrated California Magazine* 2 (April 1858):442–448.

Hittell, T. H. *History of California.* 4 vols. Vols. 1 and 2, San Francisco: Pacific Press Publishing House and Occidental Publishing Co., 1885; vols. 3 and 4, N. J. Stone and Co., 1897.

Holt, H. *Wanted—A Final Solution of the Japanese Problem.* New York: American Association for International Conciliation, Publ. No. 74. 1914.

Hoopes, A. W. *Indian Affairs and Their Administration with Special Reference to the Far West, 1849–1860.* Philadelphia: University of Pennsylvania Press, 1932.

Huddleston, L. E. *Origin of the American Indians: European Concepts, 1492–1729.* Austin: University of Texas Press, 1967.

Hurt, P. *The Rise and Fall of the Know-Nothings in California.* San Francisco: California Historical Society, 1930.

Hutchinson, C. A. "The Mexican Government and the Mission Indians of Upper California, 1821–1835." *The Americas* 21 (1965):335–362.

———. *Frontier Settlement in Mexican California.* Yale Western Americana Series, No. 21. New Haven: Yale University Press, 1969.

Ichihashi, Y. *The Japanese in the United States.* Palo Alto: Stanford University Press, 1932.

Imbelloni, J. *La segunda esfinge indiana.* Buenos Aires: Libreria Hachette, 1956.

Ingels, H. H. "The History of the Workingman's Party in California." Master's thesis, University of California, June 1919.

Johnson, H. B. *Discriminations Against the Japanese in California: A Review of the Real Situation.* Berkeley: Press of the Courier Publishing Co., 1907.

Johnson, T. T. *Sights in the Gold Regions, and Scenes by the War.* New York: Baker and Scribner, 1849.

Jordan, W. D. *White Over Black: American Attitudes Toward the Negro, 1550–1812.* Chapel Hill: University of North Carolina Press, 1968.

Kelly, W. *A Stroll Through the Diggings of California*. Oakland: Biobooks, 1950.

Kenny, R. W. *History and Proposed Settlement of Indian Claims in California*. Sacramento: California State Printing Office, 1944.

King, C. *Mountaineering in the Sierra Nevada*. Boston: J. R. Osgood and Co., 1872.

Kloosterberger, W. *Involuntary Labor Since the Abolition of Slavery*. Leiden: E. J. Bull, 1960.

Konvitz, M. R. *The Alien and the Asiatic in American Law*. Ithaca, N.Y.: Cornell University Press, 1946.

Kwan, K. M. "Assimilation of the Chinese in the United States: An Exploratory Study in California." Ph.D. dissertation in Sociology and Social Institutions, University of California, June 1958.

Langsdorff, G. H. von. *Langsdorff's Narrative of the Rezanov Voyage to Nueva California in 1806*. San Francisco: Press of T. C. Russell, 1927. (Original edition: *Bemerkungen Auf einer Reise um die Welt in den Jahren 1803 bis 1807*. Frankfurt am Mayn: F. Williams, 1812.)

Lapp, R. M. "The Negro in Gold Rush California." *Journal Negro History* 49, no. 2 (1964):81–98.

Lasuen, F. de. "Representacion; San Carlos Mission, Nov. 12, 1800." *Santa Barbara Mission Archives* 2 (1800):206. (Bancroft Library, University of California, Berkeley.)

Lee, M. B. *Problems of the Segregated School for Asiatics in San Francisco*. Master's thesis, University of California, December 1921.

Leonard, Z. *Adventures of Zenas Leonard, Fur Trader and Trapper, 1831–1836*. Cleveland: Burrows Bros., 1904.

Lindquist, G. E. "Indian Treaty Making." *Chronicles of Oklahoma* 26 (1948):416–448.

Linton, R., ed. *Acculturation in Seven American Indian Tribes*. New York: Appleton-Century, 1940.

Lowell, T. R. *The Biglow Papers*, first series, No. 2. New York: G. P. Putnam, 1848.

Lurie, N. O. "The Indian Claims Commission Act." *Annals of the American Academy of Political and Social Sciences* 311 (1957):56–70.

Lynch, R. N. "The Development of the Anti-Japanese Movement." *Annals of the American Academy of Political and Social Sciences* 93 (January 1921):47–50.

McCulloh, J. H. *Researches on America, Being an Attempt to Settle Some Points Relative to the Aborigines of America*. Baltimore: J. Robinson, 1817.

McKenzie, R. D. *Oriental Exclusion*. Chicago: University of Chicago Press, 1928.

MacKintosh, J. *The Discovery of America by Christopher Columbus and the Origin of the American Indians*. Toronto: W. J. Coates, 1836.

McLeod, A. *Pigtails and Gold Dust: A Panorama of Chinese Life in Early California*. Caldwell, Idaho: The Caxton Printers, Ltd., 1947.

McNickle, D'A. *They Came Here First*. Philadelphia: J. B. Lippincott, 1949.

McWilliams, C. *Brothers Under the Skin*. Boston: Little, Brown and Co., 1943.

———. *Prejudice, Japanese-Americans: Symbol of Social Intolerance*. Boston: Little, Brown and Co., 1944.

———. *North from Mexico: The Spanish Speaking People of the United States*. New York: Lippincott, 1949.

Malin, J. C. *Indian Policy and Westward Expansion*. Lawrence: University of Kansas Press, 1921.

Mauldin, H. *Notes on Lake County History.* Unpublished manuscript in hands of the authors. n.d.

Mears, E. G. *Resident Orientals on the American Pacific Coast: Their Legal and Economic Status.* Preliminary report prepared for the July 1927 Conference of the Institute of Pacific Relations in Honolulu. New York: American Group Institute of Pacific Relations, 1927.

Miller, S. C. *The Unwelcome Immigrant: The American Image of the Chinese, 1785–1882.* Berkeley and Los Angeles: University of California Press, 1969.

Mitchell, S. L. "The Original Inhabitants of America Shown to be of the Same Family and Lineage with Those of Asia." *Transactions American Antiquarian Society* 1 (1820):325–332.

Morefield, R. H. "The Mexican Adaptation in American California, 1846–1875." Master's thesis, University of California, Berkeley, 1955.

Oswalt, W. H. *This Land Was Theirs.* New York: John Wiley, 1966.

Parsons, G. F. *The Life and Adventures of James W. Marshall.* Sacramento: J. W. Marshall and W. Burke, 1870.

Paul, R. W. *The Abrogation of the Gentlemen's Agreement.* Cambridge, Mass.: Harvard University Press, 1936.

———. "The Origins of the Chinese Issue in California." *Mississippi Valley Historical Review* 25 (1938):181–196.

———. *California Gold.* University of Nebraska Press, 1966.

Payne, D. P. *Captain Jack, Modoc Renegade.* Portland, Oregon: Binfords and Mort, 1938.

Pearce, R. H. *The Savages of America: A Study of the Indians and the Idea of Civilization.* Baltimore: Johns Hopkins Press 1953 (rev. ed. 1965).

———. *Savagism and Civilization: A Study of the Indian and the American Mind.* Baltimore: Johns Hopkins Press, 1967.

Pearl, N. "Writing on the Chinese in California." Master's thesis, University of California, Berkeley, December 1938.

Pitt, L. *The Decline of the Californios: A Social History of the Spanish-speaking Californians, 1846–1890.* Berkeley and Los Angeles: University of California Press, 1966.

Powers, S. *Tribes of California. Contributions to North American Ethnology,* Vol. 3. Washington, 1877.

Provinse, J. "The American Indian in Transition." *American Anthropologist* 56 (1954):387–394.

Robinson, A. *Life in California.* New York: Wiley and Putnam, 1846.

Robinson, W. W. *Land in California.* Berkeley and Los Angeles: University of California Press, 1948.

———. *The Indians of Los Angeles: A Story of the Liquidation of a People.* Los Angeles: G. Dawson, 1952.

Rowell, C. "Chinese and Japanese Immigrants—a Comparison." *Annals of the American Academy of Political and Social Science* 34 (1909):223–230.

Royce, C. C. *Indian Land Cessions in the United States.* Bureau American Ethnology Annual Report 18, pt. 2., 1899.

Royce, J. *California, a Study of American Character.* New York and Boston: Houghton Mifflin Co., 1886. ,

Sandmeyer, A. L. *The Anti-Chinese Movement in California.* Urbana: University of Illinois Press, 1939.

Scharrenburg, P. "The Attitude of Organized Labor Toward the Japanese." *Annals of the American Academy of Political and Social Science* 93 (1921):34–38.

Schrieke, B. J. O. *Alien Americans: A Study of Race Relations.* New York: Viking Press, 1936.

Servin, M. P. "The Secularization of the California Missions: A Reappraisal." *Southern California Quarterly* 47 (1965):133–149.

Shinn, C. H. *Land Laws of Mining Districts.* Baltimore: Johns Hopkins University Studies in History and Political Science. Second series, Vol. 12, 1884.

————. *Mining Camps: A Study in Frontier Government.* New York: Alfred A. Knopf, 1948.

Simpson, G. *An Overland Journey Round the World, During the Years 1841 and 1842.* Philadelphia: Lea and Blanchard, 1847.

Simpson, G. E., and J. M. Yinger, eds. *American Indians and American Life.* Annals of the American Academy of Political and Social Science Vol. 311, May 1957.

Smith, H. N. *Virgin Land: The American West as Symbol and Myth.* Cambridge: Harvard University Press, 1950.

Snodgrass, M. P., compiler. *Economic Development of American Indians and Eskimos, 1930–1967: A Bibliography.* Washington, D.C.: U.S. Department of Interior. Bibliography Series No. 10, 1968.

Sparks, T. A. *China Gold.* Fresno: Academy Literary Guild, 1954.

Spicer, E. H. *Cycles of Conquest.* Tucson: University of Arizona Press, 1962.

Stanton, W. *The Leopard's Spots.* Chicago: University of Chicago Press, 1960.

State Advisory Commission on Indian Affairs. *Progress Report to the Governor and the Legislature by the State Advisory Commission on Indian Affairs (Senate Bull. No. 1007) on Indians in Rural and Reservation Areas.* Sacramento: State Printing Office, 1966.

Steiner, S. *The New Indians.* New York: Harper and Row, 1967.

Stewart, O. C. "Kroeber and the Indian Claims Commission Cases." *Kroeber Anthropological Society Papers*, No. 25 (1961):181–190.

Taylor, B. *Eldorado, or Adventures in the Path of Empire.* New York: A. Knopf, 1949.

tenBroek, J., E. N. Barnhart, and F. W. Matson. *Prejudice, War, and the Constitution.* Berkeley and Los Angeles: University of California Press, 1954 (3d printing, 1968).

Thomas, D. S. *The Salvage.* Berkeley and Los Angeles: University of California Press, 1952.

Thurman, S. B. *Pioneers of Negro Origin in California.* San Francisco: Acme, 1949.

Tupper, E., and G. McReynolds. *Japan in American Public Opinion.* New York: Macmillan Co., 1931.

U.S., Circuit Court (9th). *The Invalidity of the "Queue Ordinance" of the City and the County of San Francisco.* Opinion of the Circuit Court of the United States for the District of California in *Ho Ah Kow* v. *Matthew Nunarr* delivered July 7, 1879. Stephen J. Field, Circuit Judge. Printed from a revised copy. San Francisco: J. L. Rice and Co., 1879. (Bancroft Library, Chinese Immigration Pamphlets, Vol. 2).

U.S., Commission on Civil Rights. *Hearings Before the United States Commission on Civil Rights.* Hearings held in Los Angeles, Calif., January 25 and 26, 1960; San Francisco, Calif., January 27 and 28, 1960. Washington, D.C.: Government Printing Office, 1960.

U.S., Department of Interior. *Federal Indian Law*. Washington, D.C., 1958.

van Nostrand, J. *A Pictorial and Narrative History of Monterey, Adobe Capital of California, 1770–1847*. California Historical Society. Special Publications, No. 43. 1968.

Washburn, W. *The Indians and the White Man*. Garden City, New York: Doubleday, 1964.

Webb, E. B. *Indian Life at the Old Missions*. Los Angeles: W. F. Lewis Publications, 1952.

Weber, F. J. "The California Missions and Their Visitors." *The Americas* 24 (1968):319–336.

West, H. J. *The Chinese Invasion*. San Francisco: A. L. Bancroft, 1873.

Williams, M. F. *History of the San Francisco Committee of Vigilance of 1851: A Study of Social Control on the California Frontier in the Days of the Gold Rush*. Berkeley: University of California Publications in History, Vol. 12, 1921.

Wilson, B. D. *The Indians of Southern California in 1852*. J. W. Caughey, ed. San Marino, California: Huntington Library Publications, 1952.

Winsor, J. *Narrative and Critical History of America*. Boston and New York: Houghton Mifflin Co., 1889.

Wright, D. M. "The Making of Cosmopolitan California: An Analysis of Immigration, 1848–1870." *California Historical Society Quarterly* 19 (1949):323–343; 20(1941):65–79.

Young, C. C. *Mexicans in California*. Report of Gov. C. C. Young's Mexican Fact-Finding Committee. Sacramento: California State Printing Office, 1930.

Yount, G. C. *George C. Yount and His Chronicles of the West, Comprising Extracts From His "Memoirs" and From the Orange Clark "Narrative."* Denver: Old West Publishing Co., 1966.

Index